Creating Our Identities in Service-Learning and Community Engagement

Advances in Service-Learning Research

Shelley H. Billig, Series Editor

Creating Our Identities in Service-Learning and Community Engagement

edited by

Barbara E. Moely
Tulane University, New Orleans

Shelley H. Billig
RMC Research Corporation, Denver

Barbara A. Holland
University of Western Sydney, Australia

Information Age Publishing, Inc.
Charlotte, North Carolina • www.infoagepub.com

Library of Congress Cataloging-in-Publication Data

Creating our identities in service-learning and community engagement / edited by Barbara E. Moely, Shelley H. Billig, Barbara A. Holland.

    p. cm. — (Advances in service-learning research)

  Includes bibliographical references.

  ISBN 978-1-60752-288-1 (paperback) — ISBN 978-1-60752-289-8 (hardcover) — ISBN 978-1-60752-290-4 (e-book) 1. Teachers—In-service training—United States. 2. Community and college—United States. 3. Identity (Philosophical concept) I. Moely, Barbara E. II. Billig, Shelley. III. Holland, Barbara A.

  LB1731.C6946 2009

  370.11'5—dc22

                                       2009035544

Printed in the United States of America

CONTENTS

v

PART III
SERVICE-LEARNING STUDENTS' ACADEMIC, PERSONAL, INTERPERSONAL, AND CIVIC OUTCOMES

PART IV
RESEARCH PERSPECTIVES: IDENTITY, CHALLENGES, AND NEW DIRECTIONS

ACKNOWLEDGMENTS

We offer special thanks to Vincent Ilustre, executive director, and Katie Houck, assistant director of the Center for Public Service at Tulane University for their advice and support in producing this volume. We thank the researchers who submitted papers and those who graciously gave their time to review papers. We are especially grateful to the authors whose work appears here—we very much enjoyed working with them and appreciate their creative efforts, their diligence, and their cooperation throughout the process of completing this volume.

INTRODUCTION

Barbara E. Moely, Shelley H. Billig and Barbara A. Holland

This is the ninth volume in the *Advances in Service-Learning Research* series, which began in 2002 with the volume, *Service-Learning: The Essence of the Pedagogy*, edited by Andrew Furco and Shelley Billig. They remarked on the "recent groundswell of service-learning activity in K-12 and higher education" that sparked interest in gaining a better understanding of service-learning practice and its effects. But they noted that, despite this interest, the research on service-learning at that time was still limited. Considerable progress has been made since then, with increasing diversity in research topics and in the quantity of work being produced, yet issues of quality and rigor persist. The recent formalization of the International Association for Research on Service-Learning and Community Engagement (IARSLCE) organization enhances communication and collaboration among researchers, increases the visibility of outstanding work through an awards program, strengthens the process of peer review, and provides a structure for individuals from various academic disciplines, community agencies, and institutional offices to learn from each other. Further, the association's work has encouraged a broadening of intellectual focus from service-learning to the larger, more inclusive domain of campus-community engagement, which is opening the way to research on innovative practices and organizational and cultural issues.

Creating Our Identities in Service-Learning and Community Engagement
pp. ix–xiv

The chapters in this volume address questions of interest to both researchers and practitioners, presenting research findings and techniques that give a new lens for looking at campus-community collaborations and their impacts, and thereby enriching understanding of the field of service-learning and community engagement (SLCE). A theme that appears and reappears in these chapters is that of identity formation. Within the SLCE field, the concept of identity is being applied not only to individuals, but to cultural groups, organizations, and even institutions.

Identity theory has been used extensively in the years since Erik Erickson (1950) first presented the concept of identity in his elaboration of stages of human development. He saw identity formation as a challenge of the adolescent period, when the young person is concerned with self-definition. According to Erikson (1963) "this sense of identity provides the ability to experience one's self as something that has continuity and sameness and to act accordingly." (p. 42). Identity is an organizing concept around which the individual is able to integrate varied aspects of the self and aim for consistency in behavior.

Perhaps it is appropriate at this point in the building of the SLCE field to be concerned about identity. Marcia (1966) described a process through which the individual moves toward the creation of a sense of identity, including the exploration and consideration of possibilities for one's individual identity and a decision involving commitment to one or more of these possibilities. Work that has been done to build the practice of SLCE and to answer research questions reflects the first process, that of exploration and gathering of information. On the basis of what has been learned, researchers have begun to abstract and generalize so as to arrive at organizing concepts for the field. Both the practice of SLCE and the research addressing SLCE are reaching a critical point at which stakeholders are deeply considering identity, whether dealing with institutional character, campus-community partnership relationships, student conceptualizations of their engagement, or the research field itself. The chapters below are grouped into four parts, representing different areas in which research questions are concerned with identity conceptualizations.

INSTITUTIONALIZATION OF SLCE

Part I includes three papers of interest to program leaders and administrators, as well as to researchers, focused on efforts to build and sustain community engagement programs. Saltmarsh and his colleagues (chapter 1) are concerned with identity at the level of the institution. They analyze the applications submitted by institutions of higher education for consideration by the Carnegie Foundation for the Advancement of Teaching for its 2006 Elective Classification for Community Engagement. They find that a some campuses have revised promotion and tenure guidelines to reward community engaged scholarship, thus creating institutional identities defined by a policy-level commitment to community-engaged scholarship. However, the researchers also find that the number of institutions achieving an engagement identity through policy is still limited.

Jetson and Rohan, in chapter 2, identify practices underway at 25 research-extensive universities to encourage engaged scholarship, using information primarily from institutional Web sites. They organize these into six categories that contribute to the planning, implementation, management, and evaluation of engaged scholarship. Grouping practices according to estimates of cost, Jetson and Rohan summarize a wide range of activities that can be adopted by institutions aiming to increase their community engagement efforts.

An essential step in building engagement is positive involvement of faculty in service-learning and engaged scholarship. In spite of the extensive efforts that have been made over the years to prepare faculty to offer service-learning courses, there is still relatively little research on the outcomes of such efforts. McGuire and her colleagues (chapter 3) organize faculty development around the DEAL model of critical reflection, focusing on learning by both the faculty member and his/her students. In their chapter, they describe a faculty learning community that began with a focus on assessment of students' reflection, but grew over time to include a deliberate consideration of faculty gains in pedagogical effectiveness and understanding as a result of employing the DEAL, thus creating a model of the connections between student learning and faculty change.

CAMPUS-COMMUNITY PARTNERSHIPS

In Part II, the emphasis moves outside the institution into the community, with the focus on building strong, mutual, effective working relationships between members of the campus and community partners. Both papers in this section emphasize the importance of creating mutual understanding in order for effective collaboration to take place. Janke (chapter 4) uses theory and research on social and organizational identity to describe partnership relationships. Consistent with this volume's theme of creating identities, Janke suggests that partners must develop a sense of themselves as members of a unified group, creating a partnership identity, in order to collaborate effectively and maintain their efforts over time. Through intensive study of five partnerships, she characterizes collaborations that do or do not achieve mutual identity and identifies key characteristics of a partnership identity.

Phillips and Ward, in chapter 5, conceptualize campus-community partnerships in terms of two dimensions: type of partnership: moving from transactional arrangements based on convenience and regular practice through two intermediate stages to a transformative stage (in which there is true mutuality of effort and reward for campus and community in educational, service and research efforts); and the extent of transformation shown in partnerships, focusing on the degree to which partnerships have developed joint communal identities, moving from individual relationships between a few campus and community members through two intermediate stages to a communal identity stage (in which partnerships have transformed the identities of both the institutions and the community organizations). Partnerships that have achieved the highest levels on these two dimensions would be characterized by what Saltmarsh and colleagues (chapter 1) called an institutional identity in support of community engagement. However, partnerships can be effective at transactional levels, as well, if relationships are intentionally crafted and aligned with the shared intentions for the partnership.

STUDENT OUTCOMES

Part III features reports of empirical research on students engaged in service-learning. In chapter 6, Billig shows the importance of high-quality service-learning for K-12 students' academic achievement and school-related behaviors. Her work validates the standards for K-12 service-learning that have been formalized on the basis of relevant research findings. Students who participated in high quality service-learning, as defined by the standards, showed consistently more positive outcomes for achievement measures and indices of appropriate school behavior than did students who were not involved in service-learning.

Harwood and Radoff (chapter 7) describe programs created by a middle school-university partnership, in which university students mentored middle school youth as they developed community action projects. Unique aspects of the research were the concern for outcomes of both the mentors and the youth, and the use of interviews with both youth and mentors in gaining a picture of youth gains. The middle-school students showed social and emotional development (including social self awareness, self-esteem, and self-efficacy), increased community understanding, and improved academic attitudes, according to both self-reports and the reports of their mentors. The college students, who were enrolled in Education courses as they carried out the year-long programs, gained skills relevant to teaching, as well as knowledge of youth and community.

Simons and her colleagues (chapter 8) describes the impact on college students of service-learning experiences that emphasize diversity and the appreciation of cultural differences, using racial identity theory as a basis for understanding changes in students' attitudes. Students engaged in cultural-based service-learning viewed films that emphasized diversity or more neutral films and created reflection papers relating film content to their service-learning experiences. On several quantitative measures, service-learners showed increased awareness of racial issues, and increases on scales measuring ethnic identity and interpersonal problem-solving skills. Those in the high diversity condition also showed higher endorsement of social justice attitudes and greater academic engagement at the end of their service-learning course. Journals written at the beginning, during, and at the end of the service experience were analyzed using concepts from racial identity theory to describe movement from less to more mature perspectives on race issues.

PERSPECTIVES ON SLCE RESEARCH

Part IV is concerned with past, current, and future research in SLCE. Smith and her colleagues (chapter 9) focus on the nature of research in the field of service-learning, offering an opportunity to reflect upon the identity of this research field. In 2003, Billig and Eyler discussed the status of service-learning as a field, making the case that this pedagogy does exhibit a distinct identity, with standard practices, a knowledge base, and supportive structures of various kinds. Smith and her colleagues use a library and information science research method, citation analysis, to characterize research recently published in two major outlets for work in service-learning. They find that scholars publishing in service-learning represent a wide variety of disciplines, thus showing a high degree of interdisciplinarity. This interdisciplinarity poses particular challenges to researchers, who must find ways to access and master a complex research literature, to communicate with scholars from different backgrounds, and to build the case in their institutions for the value of their work. At the same time, interdisciplinarity may provide unique opportunities for growth.

In her paper, presented as a plenary at the conference, Vogelgesang (chapter 10) reflects upon what can be learned from research to date on service-learning and community engagement and offers suggestions for future directions, especially emphasizing the importance of longitudinal work to determine the long-term significance community engagement during K-12 or college years. Vogelgesang emphasizes the importance of collaborative research efforts and suggests possible roles for IARSCLE in supporting future research.

The plenary panel organized by Gelmon (chapter 11) offers international perspectives on service-learning and community engagement, including current issues and likely future directions in each of four different national settings: Australia, Mexico, South Africa, and the United States. Opportunities for and barriers to research in the field are discussed within each cultural context, and suggestions offered for future research.

Finally, in a concluding chapter (chapter 12), the editors of this volume suggest next steps in building the field, through the application of research to practice and the further support of research efforts. Following up on Billig's research supporting the K-12 service-learning standards (chapter 6), the authors propose a process similar to that used with K-12 to create standards for service-learning in higher education. The authors also offer suggestions about activities that the IARSLCE can initiate to support high-quality and useful research in SLCE.

REFERENCES

Billig, S. H., & Eyler, J. (Eds.). (2003). *Deconstructing service-learning: Research exploring context, participation, and impacts*. Greenwich, CT: Information Age.

Erikson, E. H. (1950). *Childhood and society*. New York: Norton.

Furco, A., & Billig, S. H. (Eds.). (2002). *Service-learning: The essence of the pedagogy*. Greenwich, CT: Information Age.

Marcia, J. E. (1966). Development and validation of ego identity status. *Journal of Personality and Social Psychology, 3,* 551-558.

PART I

BUILDING INSTITUTIONAL IDENTITIES IN SUPPORT OF SERVICE-LEARNING AND COMMUNITY ENGAGEMENT

CHAPTER 1

COMMUNITY ENGAGEMENT AND INSTITUTIONAL CULTURE IN HIGHER EDUCATION

An Investigation of Faculty Reward Policies at Engaged Campuses

John Saltmarsh, Dwight E. Giles, Jr., KerryAnn O'Meara, Lorilee Sandmann, Elaine Ward, and Suzanne M. Buglione

ABSTRACT

Through an examination of the 2006 applications for the Elective Classification for Community Engagement from the Carnegie Foundation for the Advancement of Teaching, this study explores the ways in which promotion and tenure policies reward community-engaged scholarship. Evidence from the applications and from campus documents reveals examples of significant shifts in policy that reflect cultural changes. At the same time, there is evidence of persistent and deep-seated resistance to change that values and

Creating Our Identities in Service-Learning and Community Engagement
pp. 3–29
Copyright © 2009 by Information Age Publishing

legitimizes community-engaged scholarship. Campuses that have revised their promotion and tenure guidelines to incorporate community engagement across the faculty roles seem to have institutional identities defined by commitments to the stewardship of local communities.

INTRODUCTION

The last 20 years mark a period of pressures from multiple sources to change promotion and tenure systems in higher education. In the late 1980s and early 1990s, tenure was attacked by the popular press, state legislators, and trustees for being biased against women and minorities, protecting unproductive faculty, and overly valuing faculty research, while woefully neglecting undergraduate education and outreach (O'Meara & Rice, 2005; O'Meara, Terosky, & Neumann, 2008).

Promotion and tenure remains one of the foremost ways an institution articulates its values; it is how institutions and their leaders value the individuals who work there and what they do (O'Meara, 2002). As such, it is a pivotal lever for change and the area in which we are likely to see the deepest struggles over legitimate forms of research and how research should be assessed and rewarded. Faculty unions argued the case for the advantages of tenure in terms of recruiting and retaining talented faculty, ensuring quality and rigor, and protecting academic freedom, but even so, the tenure system changed by the end of the 1990s in three primary ways: First, fiscal realities sped up replacement of tenure lines with non-tenure track, full-time and part-time appointments, making the tenure system still the most coveted positions but available to fewer and fewer entrants to the academy (Schuster & Finkelstein, 2006). Second, several workplace reforms were instituted—among them posttenure review to increase accountability for faculty—and stop-the-clock and parental-leave policies for academics who are parents. Third, scholarship was redefined and reassessed in promotion and tenure processes (Boyer, 1990; Glassick, Huber, & Maeroff, 1994; O'Meara, et al., 2008).

Hundreds of campuses have attempted to revise their promotion and tenure guidelines to acknowledge a broader definition of scholarship, and particularly to define the scholarship of teaching and the scholarship of community engagement as legitimate scholarly work and then reward it accordingly (Braxton, Luckey, & Helland, 2002; O'Meara & Rice, 2005). Among campuses that are potentially inclined to reward community-engaged scholarship are 76 institutions that received the 2006 Carnegie Classification for Community Engagement. These campuses completed a campus assessment that included items evaluating institutional reward policies. As Rhoades (2009) points out, the community engagement classification represents an effort on the part of the Carnegie Foundation "to inscribe in academic structures and in the consciousness of faculty" an emphasis on "the value of the local" (p. 12). The value of the local is associated closely with an epistemological struggle over the value of community-based practitioner knowledge: What is "legitimate" knowledge in higher education, and is there a place for forms of scholarship that value community-based knowledge?

In this chapter, we describe the application process for the Elective Carnegie Classification for Community Engagement. We then discuss the conceptual framework for the study and our research questions. Our review of the literature is constructed around an "integrated model" for understanding faculty engagement developed by Sandmann, Saltmarsh, and O'Meara (2008) as part of larger research team,[1] that contextualizes why and how promotion and tenure is key in moving campuses toward institutionalization of community engagement. The integrated model helped us to bring together evidence and understandings from the work done around the institutionalization of engagement (Holland, 2001; Holland & Gelmon, 1998; Hollander, Saltmarsh, & Zlotkowski, 2001) and research on change in institutional culture (Eckel, Hill, & Green, 1998; Guskin, 1996; Hearn, 1996; Kezar & Eckel, 2002a, 2002b). Finally, the findings reported here are part of a larger study of faulty rewards at community engaged campuses (Giles, Saltmarsh, Ward, & Buglione, 2008; Saltmarsh, Giles, Ward, & Buglione, in press) and draws implications from findings on the current state of promotion and tenure in the most engaged of institutions as well as overall efforts to reform faculty roles and rewards.

The Elective Carnegie Community Engagement Classification

The 2006 Elective Community Engagement Classification offered by the Carnegie Foundation for the Advancement of Teaching defines community engagement as the collaboration between higher education institutions and their larger communities (local, regional/state, national, global) for the mutually beneficial exchange of knowledge and resources in a context of partnership and reciprocity. The foundation provided campuses with a framework for documenting community engagement activity. This framework has four sections: (1) institutional commitment, (2) institutional identity and culture, (3) curricular engagement, and (4) outreach and partnerships. The first two sections constitute what the foundation describes as "foundational indicators." The application process is such that campuses must be able to document all of the foundational indicators, and only after doing so are they able to complete the application process by addressing the "curricular engagement indicators," the "outreach and partnership indicators," or both (Driscoll, 2008). For the purpose of this study, campuses provided documentation related to institutional reward policies within these foundational indicators of institutional commitment, identity, and culture.

Within the foundational indicators, the framework contains an "optional questions" subsection. Here, documentation can be provided about institutional reward policies. The optional questions, not to be confused with our research questions, include a primary question and two subquestions:

- Question: Do the institutional policies for promotion and tenure reward the scholarship of community engagement?
- Subquestion A: If yes, how does the institution categorize the community engagement scholarship? (Service, Scholarship of Application, other)
- Subquestion B: If no, is there work in progress to revise the promotion and tenure guidelines to reward the scholarship of community engagement?

The application questions are aimed at three aspects of rewarding community-engaged scholarship: (1) current policy, (2) faculty roles rewarded for community engagement, and (3) potential or existing initiatives to revise the current guidelines, assuming that changes in promotion and tenure guidelines to reward community-engaged scholarship have not been implemented.

Conceptual Framework

The foundational indicators that comprise the first section of the Foundation's community engagement framework focus on institutional identity, culture, and commitment. These indicators also reflect an understanding that community engagement is an element of transformative institutional change and that institutional transformation is characterized by changes in institutional culture. Campuses that receive the Carnegie Community Engagement classification demonstrate that they have implemented changes in the core work of the institution.

In their 1998 study of transformational change in higher education, Eckel, Hill, and Green defined transformational change as that which "(1) alters the culture of the institution by changing select underlying assumptions and institutional behaviors, processes, and products; (2) is deep and pervasive, affecting the whole institution; (3) is intentional; and (4) occurs over time" (p. 3). Changes that "alter the culture of the institution" (p. 3) require "major shifts in an institution's culture—the common set of beliefs and values that creates a shared interpretation and understanding of events and actions" (p. 3). Attention to deep and pervasive change focuses on "institution-wide patterns of perceiving, thinking, and feeling; shared understandings; collective assumptions; and common interpretive frameworks"—the "ingredients of this 'invisible glue' called institutional culture" (p. 3). It is precisely these elements of institutional culture that constitute the foundational indicators of the community engagement framework.

Transformational change occurs when shifts in the institution's culture have developed to the point where they are both pervasive across the institution and deeply embedded in practices throughout the institution (see Exhibit 1.1). Eckel et al. (1998) describe adjustment (Quadrant 1) as

> a change or series of changes that are modifications to an area. One might call this "tinkering."... changes of this nature are revising or revitalizing, and they occur when current designs or procedures are improved or extended. An adjustment may improve the process or quality of the service, or it might be something new; nevertheless, it does not drastically alter much. (p. 5)

The change has little depth and is not pervasive across the institution. Isolated change (Quadrant 2) is "deep but limited to one unit or a particular area: it is not pervasive." Campuses in the third quadrant achieved far-reaching change that "is pervasive but does not affect the organization very deeply." Quadrant four represents deep and pervasive change that transforms the institutional culture. Eckel et al. call this change in "the innermost core of a culture … our underlying assumptions; these deeply ingrained beliefs" that "are rarely questioned and are usually taken for granted." Transformational change, they write, "involves altering the underlying assumptions so that they are congruent with the desired changes" (1998, p. 3-5). Examining the Carnegie Foundation's Framework for the Community Engagement Classification in light of Eckel et al.'s work suggests that campuses that achieve the classification have undergone shifts in institutional culture that have led to change such that community engagement is both deep and pervasive.

A proposition that emerges from this conceptual framework, and from the literature on both community engagement in higher education and institutional change, is that campuses that received the Elective Carnegie Classification for Community Engagement provided sufficient evidence to be located in the fourth quadrant, demonstrating transformational

Depth		
	Low	**High**
Low	Adjustment (1)	Isolated Change (2)
High	Far-Reaching Change (3)	Transformational Change (4)

Pervasiveness (vertical label, left side)

Source: Adapted from Eckel et al. (1980).

Exhibit 1.1.   Two dimensions of transformational change.

change reflected in institutional reward policies that are artifacts of an academic culture that values community engagement.

Research Questions

The central research question for this study is: To what extent have engaged colleges and universities reshaped institutional reward policies to provide incentives for faculty to undertake community-engaged scholarship? Secondary questions include: How do institutional policies for promotion and tenure reward the scholarship of community engagement? What area(s) of the faculty role (i.e., scholarship, teaching, and/or service) do institutional promotion and tenure guidelines define as the area of faculty work in which engagement is rewarded? Is the revision of promotion and tenure guidelines part of the response associated with establishing an institutional identity of community engagement?

Literature Review

In "An Integrated Model for Advancing the Scholarship of Engagement: Creating Academic Homes for the Engaged Scholar," Sandmann et al. (2008) observed that the creation of a supportive environment for faculty engagement includes changes in the institutional culture of colleges and universities and is associated with the qualities and characteristics of change located in the fourth quadrant of the Eckel et al.'s (1998) model for institutional change. From this perspective, efforts to redefine scholarship must be reflected in academic norms and institutional reward policies that shape the cultures of the academy. Engagement needs to be seamlessly woven into what Schön calls "the formal and informal rules and norms that govern such processes as the screening of candidates for promotion and tenure" (1995, p. 32). Sandmann et al. argue that in order to gain a deeper understanding of the institutionalization of faculty engagement, researchers must ask a key question: What institutional factors contribute to a supportive environment for faculty to practice community engagement?

As an approach for investigating this question and others, the authors proposed an integrated model that incorporates the following four elements: (1) preparing future faculty, (2) the scholarship of engagement, (3) promising practices of institutional engagement, and (4) institutional change models in higher education. These four elements are aligned along two axes, the horizontal axis representing faculty socialization, and the vertical axis representing institutionalization. This framework is designed to address the complexity of institutional change , the need for transformational change to address significant cultural shifts in faculty work, and the kind of transformational change necessary for engaged scholarship to become a core value of higher education. The aim of transformation "assumes that college and university administrators and faculty will alter the way in which they think about and perform their basic functions of teaching, research, and service, but they will do so in ways that allow them to remain true to the values and historic aims of the academy" (Eckel et al., 1998, p. 3). The model suggests that it is at the intersections of faculty socialization and institutional change that deep, pervasive, sustained transformation that fosters the scholarship of engagement will occur (see Exhibit 1.2).

Exhibit 1.2 depicts four main "homes" for engaged scholarship, each of which is located at the intersection of the socialization and institutionalization axis. The bottom right quadrant marks institutions as the intersection of faculty practice of the scholarship of engagement and the kind of institutional structures, administration, and culture necessary to sup-

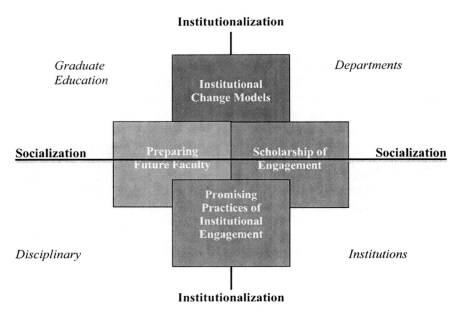

Exhibit 1.2.   An integrated model.

port and sustain faculty engagement. The model reflects assessments conducted by researchers on the importance of institutional attention to promotion and tenure processes for valuing and legitimizing engagement as a core function of the institution (Driscoll & Lynton, 1999; Driscoll & Sandmann, 2001; Rice, 1996). The institutionalization axis is grounded in an approach to institutional transformation through which systemic change is implemented effectively when multiple components of an institution are addressed simultaneously and change processes are guided by an intentional change strategy. Though we will consider of all the quadrants of the model in the discussion section at the end of this chapter, the focus of this study is on the bottom right quadrant, which represents the institutional home for engagement.

The foundation of creating an institutional culture supportive of community engagement and community engaged scholarship is the process of reciprocal relationships with community partners. The 2006 Elective Community Engagement Classification interprets community engagement through the lens of reciprocity: "the *collaboration* between higher education institutions and their larger communities (local, regional/state, national, global) for the *mutually beneficial exchange* of knowledge and resources in a context of partnership and *reciprocity*" (emphasis added).

The framework establishes a core value of reciprocity that contrasts community engagement that is done "to" or "in" the community with engagement that is collaborative, mutually beneficial, and multidirectional. Reciprocity specifically signals a shift in campus-community partnerships toward relationships that are defined by a multidirectional flow of knowledge and expertise in collaborative efforts to address community-based issues. Reciprocity in community relationships has an explicit and intentional democratic dimension framed as inclusive, collaborative, and problem-oriented work, in which academics share knowledge-generating tasks with the public and involve community partners as participants in public problem solving.

Reciprocity is grounded in sharing what were once perceived as exclusively academic tasks with non-academics and encouraging the participation of non-academics in ways that enhance scholarly inquiry. The term further implies scholarly work that is conducted with shared authority and power with those in the community at all stages of the research process, from defining the research problem, choosing theoretical and methodological approaches, conducting the research, developing the final products, and participating in peer evaluation. Reciprocity operates to facilitate the involvement of individuals in the community not just as consumers of knowledge and services but also as participants in the larger public culture of democracy (Dzur, 2008).

One characteristic of the scholarship of engagement, according to Boyer (1996), is that it "means creating a special climate in which the academic and civic cultures communicate more continuously and more creatively with each other ... enriching the quality of life for us all" (p. 20). That special climate is explicitly and intentionally reciprocal. The scholarship of engagement O'Meara and Rice (2005) note, is based on reciprocity and "calls on faculty to move beyond 'outreach,'... What it emphasizes is genuine *collaboration*: that the learning and teaching be multidirectional and the expertise shared. It represents a basic reconceptualization of faculty involvement in community-based work" (p. 28). The framework that the Carnegie Foundation provides for community engagement is shaped by this reconceptualization and views community engagement as grounded in faculty teaching, research, and service that are defined by reciprocity.

Reciprocity also implies that community-engaged scholarship is assessed differently than more traditional forms of scholarship. Glassick et al. (1997) in *Scholarship Assessed,* observe that new forms of scholarship are "not always a peer-reviewed article or book" (p. 38). Community-engaged scholarship redefines what constitutes a "publication" and redefines who is a "peer" in the peer review process. For example, community-engaged work that leads to a report to a school committee—

theoretically-based, systematically studied and analyzed, thoughtfully communicated and shared, and critically reflected upon—may not look the same as a journal article in a top-tier research journal and may be best evaluated by a member of the school committee. Engaged scholarship as legitimate academic knowledge generation and dissemination has to be evaluated through a process that accounts for the unique nature of the research.

Understanding the extent to which engaged colleges and universities have reshaped institutional policies to reward community engaged scholarship requires an examination of the artifacts of institutional culture (is it articulated in the promotion and tenure guidelines?) to explore the espoused values the culture expresses for community engaged scholarship (is it in the criteria for evaluating engaged scholarly work?) as well as to understand the underlying assumptions about the relationship of academic knowledge to community-based knowledge (is reciprocity expressed through the criteria?).

METHOD

Of the 76 campuses awarded the Carnegie Foundation's Community Engagement Classification in 2006, five received the classification for Curricular Engagement only, nine received the classification for Outreach and Partnerships only, and 62 received the classification for both Curricular Engagement and Outreach and Partnerships. For the purposes of this study, the authors focused on these latter 62 campuses, which emerged as the most engaged. These are the campuses that have institutionalized engagement through the curriculum and through community outreach. We surmised that these campuses would be more likely to have community engagement articulated in the institutional reward policies. The questions related to institutional reward policies appear in a section of the framework that included five optional questions; campuses were instructed that they were to answer two of these five questions. Campuses could respond to the questions with "yes" followed by documentation, "no" followed by an explanation, or could choose not to address a particular question.

We were unable to gain permission to use the application for five campuses for this study. Of the 57 campuses we studied, 33 elected to answer yes to the question on institutional reward policies and provided documentation to support their answer.[2] None of the campuses answered no. Twenty-four campuses chose not to address the question. Instead, they answered two of the other optional questions that did not focus on faculty roles and rewards. Our assumption is that a campus that chose not to answer the question on promotion and tenure policies did not have such policies in place, nor were they in the process of revising them.

Before analyzing the applications, we disaggregated the data to examine the context of the campuses that chose to answer the question on institutional reward policies and those that did not. We considered, for instance, whether the campus was public or private, 4-year or 2-year, its size and setting, and its Basic Carnegie Classification. This analysis yielded rich information for understanding the institutional context (Lee, 1999; Maxwell, 2005).

Using a qualitative approach (Denzin & Lincoln, 2000), our analyses consisted of a textual analysis of the applications followed by an analysis of the official promotion and tenure guidelines from the applicants' campuses.[3] Using both the application documentation and the official policy documents, we used a process of concept mapping to code the documents and identify emergent concepts, themes, and patterns (Creswell, 1997; Trochim, 1989). Finally, after coding the applications using the four themes that emerged, we used a modified axial coding process (Creswell, 1997) that mined each campus's data for evidence (or lack thereof) supporting the themes we had identified in the application. This allowed us to contextualize the occurrence of the themes and to more readily identify incongruities between application narratives and available promotion and tenure guidelines.

One limitation of our approach is that we used the promotion and tenure guidelines at the institutional level even though on many of the campuses, promotion and tenure criteria are defined at the college or departmental level. Additionally, while the promotion and tenure guidelines were often contained in one document such as a faculty handbook, in some cases references to faculty community engagement activity appeared in multiple places. One campus, for instance, noted in its application, "Community engagement scholarship is categorized differently in different documents." Further, the sample size for this study is small. Only 76 campuses received the classification for both curricular engagement and outreach and partnerships, and less than half of those campuses chose to answer the question of promotion and tenure guidelines that include community engaged scholarship. Further study can build upon the current research to include the 125 campuses that received the classification in 2008. Additionally, for the 2008 applications, the questions related to rewarding community engaged scholarship are no longer optional, thus more campuses have provided data on promotion and tenure policies.

RESULTS

Of the campuses that answered the application questions regarding promotion and tenure policies, 18 were 4-year public institutions, 13 were private colleges or universities, and one was a 2-year public college. Additionally, six of those campuses were land-grant institutions, 19 were research institutions, and 18 were residential campuses. In coding the data for strong and consistent patterns, four key findings emerged. These findings did not correspond in any meaningful way with the disaggregated institutional demographic data (i.e., public or private, 4-year or 2-year, size and setting, and Basic Carnegie Classification).

In 2006, 107 campuses began the application process, and 89 of those campuses submitted a completed application. While there is no evidence why 18 campuses did not ultimately submit their applications, the conceptual model suggests that campuses that are in quadrant one and quadrant two of the model—adjustment or isolated change—could not provide the documentation for the Foundational Indicators and, thus, could not complete the process. Arguably, community engagement work had not yet been institutionalized on those campuses. The model also suggests that the 89 campuses that did submit their applications had achieved some level of institutionalization such that community engagement was associated with far-reaching or transformational change on campus. The evaluation by the Carnegie Foundation of the applications from 13 of the 89 campuses (those that applied but did not receive the classification) indicates that the depth and pervasiveness of campus change did not warrant a claim of institutionalization of community engagement or, therefore, classification from the Carnegie Foundation. Thus, of the original 107 campuses, 76 received the classification.

Finding 1: Campuses are broadening categories of research in ways that provide legitimacy for community-engaged scholarship.

Sixteen of the 33 campuses that responded that they had community-engaged scholarship either (1) had revised their policies to incorporate community-engaged scholarship, (2) had revised their guidelines to incorporate broader notions of scholarship using Boyer's categories, opening the possibility of rewarding community-engaged scholarship, or (3) were in the process of revising their policies in ways that made room for community-engaged scholarship. There were almost three times as many campuses in the process of revising promotion and tenure guidelines that specifically incorporated community engagement as a form of research than campuses that had reached the point in the revision process of implementing new policies for community-engaged scholarship. Of the

Exhibit 1.3.   Applications and Institutional Reward Policies

Campus Applications	Number of Campuses N = 62 (Applicants that received the classification for both curricular engagement and outreach and partnerships) N = 57 (Applications available)
Campuses that responded to the question in the application on promotion and tenure guidelines	33
Campuses that are revising or have revised their guidelines to include community-engaged scholarship	16
Campuses that have Boyerized guidelines	9
Campuses that have guidelines that specifically include community-engaged scholarship (research)	7

17 campuses that did not indicate involvement in revision, those applications either did not address community-engaged scholarship or research as part of their application or specifically identified community engagement as part of the service role of faculty (see Exhibit 1.3).

Of the 16 campuses involved with policy revisions, nine had addressed revision of guidelines through a process of broadening notions of scholarship by adopting Boyer's categories (1990). Only seven of the 16 campuses, which included four of the campuses with Boyerized guidelines, had explicit criteria articulating the legitimacy of engaged scholarship—that is, community engagement defined a legitimate form of research.

Four of the 16 campuses that expressed involvement in a process of revising faculty rewards issued responses similar to the following:

All departments have been asked to review tenure and promotion guidelines to ensure that engagement of students with community is part of the expectation for faculty ... we are currently moving to revise the faculty handbook tenure and promotion guidelines to reflect the importance of community engagement as scholarly activity.

What is not known from this statement is how long the process has been going on or if it will result in revised policies. In the case of one of these four campuses, the application identified revisions proposed by an advisory committee (the "publication of research ... connected with ... public service should be considered creative work insofar as they present new ideas or incorporate the candidate's scholarly research") but the adopted guidelines that appear in the faculty handbook do not reflect the suggested changes.

Nine of the 16 campuses have made changes to faculty roles and rewards through Boyer's broadened notion of scholarship, with six campuses noting that "community engagement scholarship fits logically as scholarship of integration, application or teaching." Yet this broadening of the definition of scholarship did not, for the most part, specifically recognize and reward community engagement as faculty scholarship. These six campuses employ Boyer's categories in ways that include a broader view of scholarly activity that is inclusive of community engagement, but maintain a traditional evaluation process through academic peer-reviewed publications, as in the following example:

> Scholarship of Application: This involves applying disciplinary expertise to the exploration or solution of individual, social, or institutional problems; it involves activities that are tied directly to one's special field of knowledge and it demands the same level of rigor and accountability as is traditionally associated with research activities.

This conception of research not only fails to make a distinction between application and engagement, but it also does not broaden notions of what counts as publication and who is considered a peer in the peer-review process. Further, while a campus application claims that community engagement can be rewarded under the scholarship of application, it was not unusual to find policy statements that did not specifically articulate community engagement as an element of "application." For instance, one Boyerized set of guidelines states,

> Application involves asking how state-of-the-art knowledge can be responsibly applied to significant problems. Application primarily concerns assessing the efficacy of knowledge or creative activities within a particular context, refining its implications, assessing its generalizability, and using it to implement changes.

Of the nine campuses that adopted Boyer's categories, three of them specifically articulated a shift in terminology from application to engagement. As one Boyerized policy document articulated, scholarship of engagement entails "community-based research, technical assistance, demonstration projects, impact assessment, and policy analysis," as well as "scholarly work relating to the study or promotion of public engagement."

Finding 2: Promotion and tenure material revealed a persistent struggle over language, definition, and discourse.

Exhibit 1.4.   Frequency of Terminology Used: Number of Applications Mentioning Each Term

Terminology Reflected in Applications	Frequency of Use
Service to the community/public	10
Service-learning	8
Community engagement	7
Application—from Boyer	6
Outreach/engagement (extension)	5
Engaged scholarship	2
Civic engagement	2
Scholarship of community engagement	2
Scholarship related to public engagement mission	2
Community-Based research	1
Scholarly civic engagement	1
Service-related publications	1
Scholarship which enhances public good	1
Civic engagement scholarship	1
Public scholarship	1

One of the most striking observations about this data set is the variation in discourse both in terms of terminology and definitions used. This is not surprising in general since new or emerging phenomena go through a period of definition and coalescence of meanings. In fact, the Carnegie optional questions use both the terms "scholarship of community engagement" and "community engagement scholarship" interchangeably. Exhibit 1.4 provides a list of 15 terms mentioned in either the application or the campus promotion and tenure materials.

Exhibit 1.4 illustrates that community engagement is most frequently categorized as service provided by the faculty member, often with the emphasis on the faculty member's expertise, or what Ernest Lynton originally called "faculty professional service" (Lynton, 1995). This formulation of the faculty's service role is exemplified in the following application response: "community service consists of activities that require the faculty member's expertise, either the specialized expertise in the faculty member's field or the general skills possessed by all members of the faculty, and that contribute to the public welfare outside the institution."

Service-learning was the second most frequently used term in describing community engagement for faculty. In three of the applications and their associated campus policies, an engaged form of teaching was linked to faculty scholarship. For example, one campus's faculty handbook states, "one should recognize that research, teaching, and community outreach often overlap." Thus the two most frequently cited uses of the term "engagement" were in reference to the faculty's teaching or service roles, not to scholarship or research.

In Exhibit 1.4, there is a total of eight of all terms combined that use the word "scholarship" or "scholarly," illustrating the diversity of terms applied in this emerging shift of how scholarship is viewed. The lack of consistency and clarity associated with community engagement is reminiscent of a 2002 report from the American Association of State Colleges and Universities, which points out that while engagement has become

> Shorthand for describing a new era of two-way partnerships between America's colleges and universities and the publics they serve ... it also presents the risk that the term can say everything and nothing at the same time.... The lack of clear definition can leave some campuses and their leaders with the impression that they are "doing engagement," when in fact they are not. (p. 8)

We did find a few examples where campuses were trying to clarify and reconcile varying or conflicting terminology or definitions. The quote below, excerpted from an application, is exemplary in that it acknowledges widespread disparities that few campuses seemed to be addressing:

> It is interesting to note that during the past year the campus homepage made a change from "civic engagement" to "community engagement" on the front page. External affairs and marketing recognizes that community engagement is a broader category and is likely to be better understood from an external perspective. Civic engagement activities are listed under this community engagement link on the Web site. CSL is currently distinguishing between (a) community engagement, which is defined solely by the location of the activity (e.g., teaching, research, and service in the community), and (b) civic engagement, which is defined as teaching, research, and service that is both in and *with* the community.

As this example illustrates, there is great variation in the discourse within campuses as well as among them in the terms used to define community engagement. Where there is lack of clarity around what community engagement means, it becomes difficult, if not impossible, to establish criteria for evaluating it.

> ***Finding 3: While promotion and tenure policies emphasize community engagement as a faculty service role, community engagement also is associated in some cases with an integrated faculty role across teaching, research, and service.***

Exhibit 1.5.   How the Applications Rewarded Community Engagement: Number of Applications Mentioning Each Category

Teaching Only	Research Only	Service Only	Teaching and Research	Teaching and Service	Research and Service	Teaching, Research, & Service	NA*
1	0	11	0	2	4	8	7

Note: *For example, guidelines that claimed to value public scholarship but did not specify criteria for how it would be evaluated.

Overall, there is variable evidence that community-engaged scholarship is part of clearly articulated and accepted criteria for promotion and tenure. There is great variation in the policy documents (typically the campus faculty handbook) in how community engagement is "counted"—that is, as teaching, research, or service. Exhibit 1.5 indicates both the variation and the tendency to include community engagement as a faculty service activity.

Analysis of the applications and campus policies indicates that faculty engagement with community, regardless of its relationship to teaching or scholarship, is placed in the traditional category of service. Yet the applications also reveal examples of community engagement across the faculty roles, especially when there is conceptual clarity and when community engagement is clearly defined and delineated as scholarly work. One campus's policies state that

> the university's strong commitment to public engagement may be reflected in any or all of these categories [teaching, research, and service]. Public engagement is defined as discipline-related collaborations between faculty members and communities, agencies, organizations, businesses, governments, or the general public that contribute significantly to the external constituency by sharing the University's intellectual and cultural assets.

The way community engagement is defined determines its place in the work of faculty.

There seems to be some evidence that community engagement shapes policy formation toward integration. For one campus, the promotion and tenure guidelines state that

> one should recognize that research, teaching, and community outreach often overlap. For example, a service-learning project may reflect both teaching and community outreach. Some research projects may involve both research and community outreach. Pedagogical research may involve both research and teaching.

At another campus

> a faculty member's community engagement activities may be defined and
> recognized by [the] college's faculty committee ... in any of the three cate-
> gories of expected and assessed performance for tenure-track and tenured
> faculty: (1) research/scholarship, (2) teaching, and/or (3) service. The com-
> mittee ... is likely to recognize a faculty member's community engagement
> work as scholarship when it is part of his/her record of research and publica-
> tion, as teaching when it involves [theory-practice] courses or community
> engagement or is part of a partnership or community project that enhances
> the college's service profile.

These examples convey not only the seamlessness and integration
across faculty roles but also a clear articulation of how community engagement is explicitly rewarded across all areas of faculty work.

Finding 4: Promotion and tenure materials revealed little evidence that reciprocity is valued, assessed, or even authentically understood.

Of the 33 campuses that answered the questions related to promotion
and tenure policies, only seven articulated a framework of reciprocity in
their relationship with community partners. The discourse indicative of
non-reciprocal relationship uses terminology such as "service to" or
"application to" the community. For example, a number of applications
defined service as "service to the community" and scholarship that
includes "the application of knowledge in responsible ways to ... the
larger community." The discourse around community engagement that is
done "to" or "in" the community is contrasted with applications that
expressed collaborative, multidirectional relationships that indicate reciprocity. For example, one campus defined community-engaged scholarship as "the partnership of university knowledge and resources with those
of the public and private sectors." For another campus, reciprocity is
found in policy documents specifying that "accomplishments in extension
and engagement represent *an ongoing two-way interchange of knowledge,
information, understanding, and services* between the university and the
state, nation, and world" (emphasis in application).

Most of the campuses that employ Boyer's categories to revise policies
are doing so in ways that express application and not engagement, as in
the following example: "The Scholarship of Application—seeking and
gaining success in the application and implementation of knowledge."
Only two applications made an explicit distinction between the scholarship of application and the scholarship of engagement—along with a distinction between partnership and reciprocity. One campus's promotion
and tenure policy states that

Engaged scholarship now subsumes the scholarship of application. It adds to existing knowledge in the process of applying intellectual expertise to collaborative problem-solving with urban, regional, state, national and/or global communities and results in a written work shared with others in the discipline or field of study. Engaged scholarship conceptualizes "community groups" as all those outside of academe and requires shared authority at all stages of the research process from defining the research problem, choosing theoretical and methodological approaches, conducting the research, developing the final product(s), to participating in peer evaluation.

This conceptualization of engagement and reciprocity also implies that community-engaged scholarship is assessed differently than traditional scholarship, reinforcing the point that new forms of scholarship are "not always a peer-reviewed article or book" (Glassick et al., 1997, p. 38). In one application, criteria for publications include "reports, including technical reports, reports prepared for a community partner or to be submitted by a community partner." In another, evidence of high quality scholarship could be demonstrated through "letters from external colleagues, external agencies, or organizations attesting to the quality and value of the work."

DISCUSSION

The Problem of Reciprocity

One of the most significant shortcomings that emerged from our analysis of the 2006 applications is in the area of establishing reciprocal campus-community relationships. Our findings are consistent with what Driscoll (2008) reported of the classified campuses, that "most institutions could only describe in vague generalities how they had achieved genuine reciprocity with their communities" (p. 41). This is significant because at its core, authentic engagement depends on—and is in fact defined by— reciprocity; without reciprocity in community relationships, there cannot be engagement.

Reciprocity as a core value provides the grounding for changes in institutional practices, which in turn can compel significant changes in institutional culture. The seven campuses with characteristics locating them in the fourth quadrant of the Eckel et al. model also were the campuses that used a discourse consistent with a culture that supports reciprocity in community partnerships along with the implications of reciprocity for a wide range of campus practices. They are the campuses that have undergone change in the innermost core of the academic culture.

Resistance to Change

Considering that only 33 campus applications addressed the question on how community engagement was included in promotion and tenure guidelines, we surmised that nonresponse to the questions indicates resistance to the kind of cultural change involved with authentic reciprocity and implied by a revision of promotion and tenure policies. It may be that the resistance to community engagement has deep roots in the research university culture of higher education and the way research is defined. The dominant culture of higher education defines the faculty role in a hierarchical way, valuing research above teaching and service. It also operates under a research hierarchy in which basic research is valued above other forms of research and in which the dominant epistemology is often identified as technocratic, scientific, or positivist, grounded in an institutional epistemology of expert knowledge housed in the university and applied externally (Stokes, 1997; Sullivan, 2000). Further, in the research culture, positivist ways of knowing—of generating knowledge—are what determine legitimate knowledge in the academy. In this cultural scheme, other forms of knowledge are not valued—including community-based practitioner knowledge.

Fundamentally, the question of knowledge generation is an epistemological question where

> there exists an affinity of positivist understandings of research for "applying" knowledge to the social world on the model of the way engineers "apply" expert understanding to the problems of structures.... This epistemology is firmly entrenched as the operating system of much of the American university. (Sullivan, 2000, p. 29)

Yet, as O'Meara and Rice (2005) point out, "the expert model ... often gets in the way of constructive university-community collaboration" because it does not "move beyond 'outreach,'" or "go beyond 'service,'" (p. 28). The process involved in moving beyond application to engagement involves sharing previously academic tasks with nonacademics and encouraging collaboration in the generation of new knowledge. Reciprocity signals an epistemological shift that values not only expert knowledge that is rational, analytic, and positivist but also a different kind of rationality that is more relational, localized, and contextual and favors mutual deference between laypersons and academics. With reciprocity, knowledge generation is a process of cocreation, which involves "the design of problem-solving actions through collaborative knowledge construction with the legitimate stakeholders in the problem" (Greenwood, 2008, p. 327).

The research university culture has a pervasive influence across higher education regardless of institutional type or mission—and a particular epistemology determines the foundations of the dominant research culture:

> All of us who live in research universities are bound up in technical rationality, regardless of our personal attitudes toward it, *because it is built into the institutional arrangements—the formal and informal rules and norms—that govern such processes as the screening of candidates for tenure and promotion.* Even liberal arts colleges, community colleges, and other institutions of higher education appear to be subject to the influence of technical rationality by a kind of echo effect or by imitation. Hence, introducing the new scholarship into institutions of higher education means becoming involved in an epistemological battle. It is a battle of snails, proceeding so slowly that you have to look very carefully in order to see it going on. But it is happening nonetheless. (Schön, 1995, p. 32; emphasis added)

That it is happening is evident in the Carnegie applications and campus policies. The evidence of resistance, however, is also apparent. In a culture that privileges certain forms of research, other forms of research are not valued or rewarded. Research universities largely operate under narrow definitions of basic and applied research and do not regard engaged research as legitimate. In the logic of a prestige hierarchy dominated by research universities, engaged research is neither basic nor applied research and therefore cannot be counted as research at all. According to this logic, engaged scholarship can be counted as service, but not as research. Thus, our findings confirm what Driscoll (2008) observed of the 2006 applicants, that "most institutions continue to place community engagement and its scholarship in the traditional category of service and require other forms of scholarship for promotion and tenure" (p. 41).

The Prestige Culture and Community Engagement

The dominance of the culture of the research university reflects the pervasive culture of striving in higher education, asserting the desire to strive toward becoming a top-tier research university (O'Meara, 2007) to move up the hierarchy, to increase competitive market advantage, and to gain prestige. We suggest that the evidence indicates that the broader culture of striving in higher education and the implications of that culture on institutionalizing community engagement is significant. Over the first two application cycles (2006 and 2008), 215 campuses have received the elective classification for Community Engagement from the Carnegie Foundation for the Advancement of Teaching. That number accounts for just 6% of the more than 3,500 higher education institutions in the United States. As Rhoades, Kiyama, McCormick, and Quiroz (2008) have written, in the dominant culture of striving to become highly ranked research universities,

> national institutions are of a higher quality than local ones, which are defined as "parochial."... To be parochial is to be narrow-minded—constrained by local, particularistic commitments that undermine the pursuit of excellence according to universalistic, meritocratic standards. Quality is defined by and equated with mobility in a national marketplace of and competition for the best, cosmopolitan faculty. (p. 214).

In what they describe as the "nationally oriented system of research universities," a striving toward cosmopolitan norms leads to "devaluing institutions that are oriented and recruit locally.... And they help us understand the distance between research universities and their local communities" (Rhoades et al., p. 211). The culture of striving shaped by nationally oriented research universities serves as a powerful counterweight to local engagement.

Institutional Culture and Community Engagement

In Phase 3 of our study, we are focusing on the seven campuses that have revised promotion and tenure guidelines to specifically value and reward community engagement not only in the service role but in the faculty roles of teaching and research. In examining these campuses, it appears that size, whether they are public or private, or institutional profile does not seem to be a predictor of policy change. The campuses range in size from just over 4,700 to over 44,000. Five are public and two are private institutions. In terms of their Carnegie Basic Classification, one is RU/H: Research Very High, two are RU/H: Research High, two are DRU: Doctoral Research Universities, one is Master's L (larger programs), and one is Master's S (smaller programs).

In trying to understand commonalities among these campuses, it is apparent that more than half are members of the American Association of State Colleges and Universities (AASCU). AASCU campuses are made up of 430 public colleges and universities with institutional identities defined in part by the characteristic of being "stewards of place." These are campuses that "engage faculty, staff and students with the communities and regions we serve—helping to advance public education, economic development and the quality of life for all with whom we live and who support our work" (AASCU Web site). Applying the lens of "stewards of place," we went back to the data set and found that of the 62 campuses that received the elective classification for curricular engagement and outreach and partnerships, 19 were AASCU campuses.

The evidence suggests that these campuses, with identities defined by stewardship of place, are perhaps countering the culture of striving defined by research universities. The AASCU campuses, and arguably the seven campuses in the third phase of the study as well as others that received the classification, all have seemingly redefined what it is that they are striving to become—an institutional model of excellence that privileges the local. Thus, for an institution to be a "steward of place" means that even as "the demands of the economy and society have forced institutions to be nationally and globally aware, the fact remains that state colleges and universities are inextricably linked with the communities and regions in which they are located" (AASCU, 2002, p. 9). Exercising "stewardship of place" does "not mean limiting the institution's worldview; rather, it means pursuing that worldview in a way that has meaning to the institution's neighbors, who can be its most consistent and reliable advocates" (AASCU, 2002, p. 9).

We consider it highly plausible that this institutional ethos of being a "steward of place" is what links the campuses in our study that have revised their promotion and tenure guidelines. These institutions seem to have counterbalanced the local with the national and international and in the process have redefined their place in the dominant culture of academia's prestige hierarchy typified by major research universities and the striving that defines much of the hierarchy, competitiveness, and meritocracy of higher education. Perhaps there is a different kind of striving being exercised—for a new model of excellence that counterbalances the local with the cosmopolitan and in which teaching, research, and service effectiveness is measured against a standard of stewardship of place.

Community Engagement and Institutional Change

Our proposition—that the campus recipients of the Carnegie Classification for Community Engagement demonstrated transformational change reflected in institutional reward policies that are artifacts of an academic culture that values community engagement—is not supported by the evidence. As we noted above, only seven of the 33 campuses could be identified, based on available data, as having made deep and pervasive changes in their promotion and tenure policies that would place them in the fourth quadrant of the matrix. A revised proposition, grounded in the data, is that campuses that received the Carnegie Classification for Community Engagement provided sufficient evidence to be located in the *third or fourth* quadrant of the model, with a number of campuses demonstrating movement from the third to the fourth quadrant reflected in institutional reward policies under review as an indication of an academic culture that is changing in ways that could support community engagement.

This revised proposition is consistent with the literature on the strength of faculty culture and values in higher education and the difficulty of implementing meaningful institutional change through a process that requires intentionality over time. It is also consistent with an understanding that change in institutional reward policies that contributes toward creating a supportive environment for engaged faculty is only a part of what is needed for change that affects the scholar's "academic home" at the intersection of change in the disciplines, departments, graduate education, and the institution. While the current study only considered institutional-level policies, it nonetheless suggests that even the most engaged institutions are accommodating community-engaged faculty work to traditional norms of faculty roles. They are still struggling to get engagement into the sacred grove of legitimate scholarship.

While our findings suggest that there cannot be institutional homes for engaged scholars until promotion and tenure policies and processes change to provide a supportive environment for engaged faculty, at the same time, the Integrated Model reinforces the understanding that campuses will struggle to achieve transformational change unless there is complementary support in the other academic homes—graduate programs, disciplines, and departments—all of which are affected by and implicated in the striving and prestige hierarchy of higher education. While a great deal of change is emerging in disciplinary associations and in departmental cultures, doctoral programs predominantly emphasize very traditional forms of research, as do disciplinary associations, journals, and academic presses. Part of what the Integrated Model points to is the need for disciplinary associations, departments, and graduate education to support community-engaged scholarship in the ways that the most supportive campuses have through institutional reward policies. Only with this alignment of the academic homes will campuses be able to fully institutionalize community engagement and a new model of institutional excellence will emerge defined by a commitment to the local and an ethos of stewardship of place.

NOTES

1. The research team consists of the authors as well as R. Eugene Rice, senior scholar at the Association of American Colleges and Universities, and Amy

Driscoll, Senior Scholar at the Carnegie Foundation for the Advancement of Teaching. Sandmann, Saltmarsh, O'Meara and Giles presented the "integrated model" at the 2008 International Research Conference on Service-Learning and Community Engagement as a way to get feedback from researchers and practitioners on the utility of the model and ways to refine it. Each of the authors continue work as part of the research team and are exploring research on different parts of the model as well as opportunities to create programs based on the model.

2.   In 2005, the Carnegie Foundation conducted a pilot of the Framework with 14 campuses. Those 14 campuses supplied documentation and then were invited to supply supplemental documentation in 2006. For the purposes of our selection, we included all of the Pilot campuses in the group of campuses that answered "Yes" to the institutional reward policy question regardless of whether we were able to obtain their application. In some cases we were able to obtain their application consisting of either the 2005 documentation or the 2006 application, or both. In the cases where the 2006 application was available and the campus chose not to answer the optional question about promotion and tenure guidelines, we did not count them in the "Yes" group even though they were a Pilot campus. Eight pilot campuses are included in the final sample. It should be noted that of the 33 campuses that answered "Yes" to the question about whether the institution has policies that reward the scholarship of engagement, two of the institutions are non-tenure granting.

3.   The process of obtaining official documents related to promotion and tenure guidelines consisted of web-based searches on the campus Web site. For three of the 33 campuses in the sample, no tenure and reward polices were publicly available. It should also be noted that document retrieval took place in early 2008; this means that in some cases the official polices may reflect revisions that took place after the application was submitted on September 1, 2006.

REFERENCES

American Association of State Colleges and Universities. (2002). *Stepping forward as stewards of place: A guide for leading public engagement at state colleges and universities*. Washington, DC: Author.

Boyer, E. (1990). *Scholarship reconsidered: Priorities of the professoriate*. Princeton, NJ: Carnegie Foundation for the Advancement of Teaching.

Boyer, E. (1996). The scholarship of engagement, *Journal of Public Service and Outreach, 1*(1), 11-20.

Braxton, J. M, Luckey, W., & Helland, P. (2002). Institutionalizing a broader view of scholarship through Boyer's four domains. *ASHE-ERIC Higher Education Report, 29*(2), 1-20.

Creswell, J. W. (1997). *Qualitative inquiry and research design: Choosing among five traditions*. Thousand Oaks, CA: SAGE.

Denzin, N. K., & Lincoln, Y. S. (2000). *Handbook of qualitative research* (2nd ed.). Thousand Oaks, CA: SAGE.

Driscoll, A. (2008, January-February). Carnegie's Community-Engagement Classification: Intentions and insights. *Change, 40*(1), 39-41.

Driscoll, A., & E. Lynton. (1999). *Making outreach visible: A guide to documenting professional service and outreach.* Washington, DC: American Association for Higher Education.

Driscoll, A., & Sandmann, L. R. (2001). From maverick to mainstream: The scholarship of engagement. *Journal of Higher Education Outreach and Engagement, 6*(2), 9–19.

Dzur, A. W. (2008). *Democratic professionalism: Citizen participation and the reconstruction of professional ethics, identity, and practice.* University Park: The Pennsylvania State University Press.

Eckel, P. B., Hill, B., & Green, M. (1998). *On change: En route to transformation* (Occasional Paper No. 1). Washington, DC: American Council on Education.

Giles, D. E., Jr., Saltmarsh, J., Ward, E., & Buglione, S.M. (2008, November). *An analysis of faculty reward policies for engaged scholarship at Carnegie classified community engaged institution.* Paper presented at the meeting of the Association for the Study of Higher Education, Jacksonville, FL.

Glassick, C. E., Huber, M. T., & Maeroff, G. (1997). *Scholarship assessed: Evaluation of the professoriate.* San Francisco: Jossey-Bass.

Greenwood, D. J. (2008). Theoretical research, applied research, and action research: The deinstitutionalization of activist research. In C. R. Hale (Ed.), *Engaging contradictions: Theory, politics, and methods of activist scholarship* (pp. 319-340). Berkeley: University of California Press.

Guskin, A. E. (1996). Facing the future: The change process in restructuring universities. *Change, 28*(4), 27–37.

Hearn, J. C. (1996). Transforming U.S. higher education: An organizational perspective. *Innovative Higher Education, 21*, 41–51.

Holland, B. (2001, November). *Measuring the role of civic engagement in campus missions: Key concepts and challenges.* Paper presented at the ASHE Symposium: Broadening the Carnegie Classifications Attention to Mission: Incorporating Public Service, Richmond, VA.

Holland, B. A., & Gelmon, S. B. (1998). The state of the "engaged campus." *AAHE Bulletin, 51*, 3–6.

Hollander, E., Saltmarsh, J., & Zlotkowski, E. (2001). Indicators of engagement. In L. A. Simon, M. Kenny, K. Brabeck, & R. M. Lerner (Eds.). *Learning to serve: Promoting civil society through service-learning* (pp. 31-49). Norwell, MA: Kluwer Academic.

Kezar, A., & Eckel, P. (2002a). Examining the institutional transformation process: The importance of sensemaking and inter-related strategies. *Research in Higher Education, 43*(3), 295-328.

Kezar, A., & Eckel, P. (2002b). The effect of institutional culture on change strategies in higher education universal principles or culturally responsive concepts? *Journal of Higher Education, 73*(4), 435-461.

Lee, T. W. (1999). *Using qualitative methods in organizational research.* Thousand Oaks, CA: SAGE.

Maxwell, J. (2005). *Qualitative research design: An interactive approach*. Thousand Oaks, CA: SAGE.

O'Meara, K. A. (2002). Uncovering the values in faculty evaluation of service as scholarship. *Review of Higher Education, 26*(1), 57–80.

O'Meara, K. A. (2007). Striving for what? Exploring the pursuit of prestige. In J. C. Smart (Ed.). *Higher education: Handbook of theory and research* (Vol. 22, pp. 121-179). New York: Elsevier.

O'Meara, K. A., & Rice, R. E. (Eds.). (2005). *Faculty priorities reconsidered: Encouraging multiple forms of scholarship*. San Francisco: Jossey-Bass.

O'Meara, K., Terosky, A. L., & Neumann, A. (2008). *Faculty careers and work lives: A professional growth perspective: ASHE Higher Education Report, 34*(3). San Francisco: Jossey-Bass.

Rhoades, G. (2009, January-February). Carnegie, Dupont Circle and the AAUP: (Re)Shaping a cosmopolitan, locally engaged professoriate. *Change, 41*(1), 8-13.

Rhoades, G., Kiyama, J. M., McCormick, R., & Quiroz, M. (2008). Local cosmopolitans and cosmopolitan locals: New models of professionals in the academy. *The Review of Higher Education, 31*(2), 209-235.

Rice, R. E. (1996). *Making a place for the new American scholar*. Washington, DC: American Association for Higher Education. Forum on Faculty Roles and Rewards.

Saltmarsh, J., Giles, D. E., Jr., Ward, E., & Buglione, S.M. (in press). Rewarding community-engaged scholarship. In L. R. Sandmann, C. H. Thornton, & A. J. Jaeger (Eds.), *Institutionalizing community engagement in higher education: The first wave of Carnegie classified institutions. New Directions for Higher Education*. Indianapolis, IN: Jossey-Bass/Wiley.

Sandmann, L., Saltmarsh, J., & O'Meara, K. (2008). An integrated model for advancing the scholarship of engagement: Creating academic homes for the engaged scholar. *Journal of Higher Education Outreach and Engagement, 12*(1), 47-64.

Schön, D. A. (1995, November/December). Knowing-in-action: The new scholarship requires a new epistemology. *Change, 27*(2), 27-34.

Schuster, J. H., & Finkelstein, M. J. (2006). *The American faculty: The restructuring of academic work and careers*. Baltimore: Johns Hopkins University Press.

Stokes, D. E. (1997). *Pasteur's Quadrant: Basic science and technological innovation*. Washington, DC: Brookings Institution Press.

Sullivan, W. M. (2000). Institutional identity and social responsibility in higher Education. In T. Ehrlich (Ed.), *Civic responsibility and higher education*. Phoenix, AZ: Oryx Press.

Trochim, W. M. (1989). An introduction to concept mapping for planning and evaluation. *Evaluation and Program Planning, 12*, 1-16.

CHAPTER 2

MAKING ENGAGEMENT COUNT

Toward a Model System of Institutional Support for Engaged Scholarship at Research-Extensive Universities

Judith A. Jetson and Rohan Jeremiah

ABSTRACT

In this implementation research project, we document practices that promote engaged scholarship at 25 research-extensive universities and offer a model of a system of supports for engaged scholarship. Using Web-based research and qualitative methods, we employed a thematic analysis to place practices into a matrix and provide current examples of support for engagement activities. Future research, including a larger number of campuses and more varied data sources, is recommended to describe growth in the support of engaged scholarship at research-extensive universities. Finally, we call for creation of a national clearinghouse of best practices in supportive policies, programs, and activities.

Creating Our Identities in Service-Learning and Community Engagement
pp. 31–52

BACKGROUND

There is a new energy, enthusiasm and commitment to community engagement at research universities as we move into the early years of the twenty-first century. When the land-grant system emerged in the United States during the last years of the nineteenth century, it ushered in a new type of university committed to outreach, and, according to the land-grant movement's author, Vermont legislator Justin S. Morrill, aiming to "have learning more widely disseminated." Nearly 125 years later, thanks to the influence of the Kellogg Commission and Ernest Boyer in the 1990s and the leadership of several key national organizations—Carnegie Foundation for the Advancement of Teaching, Campus-Community Partnerships for Health, and Campus Compact—the movement has re-emerged and is growing exponentially. Leadership is coming from the top as well as from enthusiastic new and experienced faculty, from student scholars as well as activists, and from both our elected leaders and grass-roots organizations.

In 2006, this new movement was energized by the first formal classification system for community engagement, established by the Carnegie Foundation for the Advancement of Teaching. A diverse group of 76 public and private U.S. colleges and universities were identified by Carnegie through a self-study and nomination process as involved in "the collaboration between institutions of higher education and their larger communities for the mutually beneficial exchange of knowledge and resources in a context of partnership and reciprocity." At a research university, it is important to make clear the distinction between engaged *partnerships for research* and other types of engagement achieved through outreach, volunteer activities, or service-learning classes. According to the Carnegie Web site, "[The] *Partnerships* [category] focuses on collaborative interactions with community and related scholarship for the mutually beneficial exchange, exploration, and application of knowledge, information, and resources (research, capacity building, economic development, etc.)." It is important to make a distinction between community-engaged scholarly work, which can be documented and measured for promotion and tenure purposes, and the more traditional service or outreach activities typical of extension programs at land-grant universities or service at community colleges. A total of 147 academic institutions completed applications for Carnegie elective classification in 2008, with 120 of them achieving classification. Many report that the process of documenting their engagement activities has resulted in bringing increased recognition and viability to academic programs that support and reward engagement.

Chief among the engaged scholarship practices currently recognized and considered effective in increasing student learning and retention is service-learning. This is due in large part to supportive efforts by national organizations (such as Campus Compact) and federal grants (Learn and Serve America), and the research on its effectiveness stimulated by the *Michigan Journal of Community Service Learning*, the *Advances in Service-Learning Research* volumes, and the International Association for Research on Service-learning and Community Engagement. Another popular method of engaged scholarship is community-based participatory action research (CBPAR), which has been advocated by such organizations as Campus-Community Partnerships for Health and supported by federal grants from NIH and other agencies. While the techniques of service-learning and CBPAR and their impact on students and community are now regularly addressed at conferences and through professional development offerings on many campuses, as well as in scholarly publications, little has been done to document activities of research universities that support and facilitate the growth of research productivity in engaged scholarship.

DEFINING ENGAGED SCHOLARSHIP

Engaged scholarship is a relatively recent paradigm among American colleges and universities, challenging the long-standing status quo of traditional discipline-driven research. When Ernest Boyer (1990) broadened the traditional definition of scholarship to include four dimensions—discovery, integration, application, and teaching—he began to shape the scholarship of engagement. According to Cox (2006, p. 125), research "becomes the scholarship of engagement through its active and interactive connection with people and places outside of the university in the activities of scholarship, setting goals, selecting means and methods, applying means and methods, reflecting on results, and dissemination of the results." Van de Ven (2006, p. 9), considers the scholarship of engagement to be a way to address the gap between theory and practice and defines it as "a participative form of research for obtaining the different perspectives of key stakeholders in studying complex problems." The Wingspread recommendation (2004) that teaching, research and service be reframed to *engaged teaching and learning* and *engaged research and discovery* blends the active, collaborative language of engaged scholarship with traditional university reward system verbiage, providing further guidance.

The special case of engaged scholarship and its institutionalization at research universities lies in the need for faculty scholars to extend the community-based experience beyond a single service-learning course or project, in order to develop a program of research that can be presented at professional conferences, be published, attract external funding and receive credit in the most rigorous promotion and tenure systems. In order to achieve recognition as engaged scholarship, the research findings must also be shared with the community—a very different audience with a different set of standards. Thus, engaged scholarship requires a unique set of skills and supports for research faculty.

Drawing upon these definitions and activities, our proposition is that engaged scholarship at research universities includes a continuum of scholarly activities—among them, needs assessments, evaluations, service-learning classes, demonstration projects, community-led research and creative work, and multiple avenues of dissemination—which follow established principles of community engagement, meet student and community needs, and lead directly to outcomes that are valued in the established academic reward system (i.e., engaged faculty publish their research in top-tier refereed journals and bring in significant external grants to support their future research and that of their graduate students). Optimally, these activities will be carried out with leadership from the President, Provost and Board of Trustees, but can easily emerge as individual choices among faculty or groups of faculty interested in extending their scholarship. Teaching, research and service are all part of the academic evaluation system, but since research is most heavily emphasized in promotion and tenure decisions at research-extensive universities, engaged faculty must deliberately plan their scholarship to produce results valued by their institutional reward system, as well as by the community. Campus Community Partnerships for Health (Campus Community Partnerships for Health, 2009) created a model Promotion and Tenure package in 2007 and also has provided a Community-Engaged Scholarship Toolkit, with guidelines on how engaged scholarship can be planned and carried out in order to lead to promotion and tenure, but more is needed with regard to how institutions can encourage and support this scholarship.

THE PRESENT STUDY: MODELS OF ENGAGEMENT AT SELECTED U.S. RESEARCH UNIVERSITIES

We undertook the present study of engaged scholarship at research extensive universities in order to identify strategies likely to increase the quality, impact and sustainability of engaged scholarship in a time of budget constraints. We documented existing practices that advance engaged research among urban, research-extensive universities, focusing on programs, activities and support to faculty, researchers and students pursuing engaged research and discovery as well as engaged teaching and learning.

We identified institutional and financial support committed to program creation and promotion, and initiatives and activities that seemed most sustainable, especially in terms of efficiency and cost. Our study also sought to identify the models that research-extensive universities currently follow to organize and integrate their engaged scholarship efforts and used that information to derive an overall model for a system of engaged scholarship.

This project produced a database that provides information on ways to implement engaged scholarship practices at research-oriented universities at a time when funds are scarce. While recognizing the importance of finding money to award seed money grants for engaged research and teaching, this study also looked at ways in which "business as usual" practices, such as communication, dissemination, faculty development and progress indicators, might be revised to assure permeation of engaged scholarship throughout all parts of the university.

METHOD

We chose geographically diverse universities from among the membership of the Association of American Universities (AAU) and those ranked as engaged by Carnegie, in order to create a list of 24 schools that varied by region, size and age of the university (See Exhibit 2.1). They also varied in length of time involved with and diffusion of engagement practices.

For this report, the primary data source was an online review of university Web sites and community engaged research centers. We used a thematic analysis to describe tools and activities of engagement. At the same time, we used content analysis to look specifically at how these tools and activities were operationalized in order to maximize their results. Then, the results were inserted into a matrix in order to identify the tools most frequently and efficiently used at several institutions and a model was created.

RESULTS/DISCUSSION

Themes of Engaged Scholarship: Change, Connections, Leadership

Despite their unique strategies and approaches, all of the models we studied were geared towards relatively similar goals and outcome measures, centered on the promotion of responsible research activities that sustain community and university collaboration and thus, strengthen

Exhibit 2.1. Research Universities Included in the Sample

University	Department	Web Site
Arizona State University	Office of Academic Community Engagement Services	http://uc.asu.edu/asep/
California State University	Monterey Bay- Service-Learning Institute	http://service.csumb.edu/site/x3561.xml
Indiana University-Purdue University Indianapolis	Center for Service and Learning	http://csl.iupui.edu/
Loyola University, Chicago	Center for Experiential Learning	http://www.luc.edu/experiential/engaged_scholars.shtml
Michigan State University	Office of University Outreach and Engagement	http://outreach.msu.edu/
	Office of University-Community Partnerships	http://outreach.msu.edu/ucp/default.asp
	National Center for the Study of University Engagement	http://ncsue.msu.edu/esss/default.aspx
Northeastern University	Center of Community Service	http://www.northeastern.edu/servicelearning/
Ohio State University	Office of Outreach and Engagement	http://outreach.osu.edu/
Portland State University	Center for Academic Excellence/ Community-University Partnerships	http://www.pdx.edu/cae/partnership-initiative
Stanford University	John W. Gardner Center for Youth and Their Communities	http://jgc.stanford.edu/
	Hass Center	http://haas.stanford.edu
Syracuse University	Office of Engagement Initiatives	http://connectivecorridor.syr.edu/
Tufts University	Tisch College of Citizenship and Public Service	http://activecitizen.tufts.edu/
Tulane University	Center for Public Service	http://tulane.edu/cps/
University of Alabama at Birmingham	Office for Service-Learning	http://main.uab.edu/Sites/undergraduate-programs/academic-engagement/service-learning/
University of California Berkeley	Office of Educational Development	http://teaching.berkeley.edu/civic.html
University of California San Francisco	Clinical and Translational Science	http://ctsi.ucsf.edu/research/community-pubs

University of Cincinnati	Center for Community Engagement	http://www.uc.edu/sas/cce/
	Academic Health Center	http://www.uc.edu/health/
	Community Design Center	http://www.uc.edu/cdc/home.html
University of Denver	Center for Community Engagement and Service Learning	http://www.du.edu/engage/index.htm
University of Georgia	Office of Public Service and Outreach	http://outreach.uga.edu/
University of Illinois at Urbana-Champaign	Office of Public Engagement	http://engagement.illinois.edu/
University of Maryland-College Park	Coalition for Civic Engagement and Leadership	http://www.terpimpact.umd.edu/
University of Michigan	Ginsberg Center	http://ginsberg.umich.edu/resources/for_faculty.html
	Michigan Journal of Community Service Learning	http://www.umich.edu/~mjcsl/
University of North Carolina at Chapel Hill	Carolina Center for Public Service	http://www.unc.edu/cps/index.php
University of Pittsburgh	Community Outreach Partnership Center	http://www.pitt.edu/~copc/
University of San Francisco	Center for Public Service and the Common Good	http://www.usfca.edu/mccarthycenter/research/overview.html
University of South Florida	Collaborative for Children, Families and Communities	http://www.usfcollab.usf.edu
	Center for Leadership & Civic Engagement	http://volunteer.usf.edu/default.asp

engaged scholarship. Among all the models and approaches we have reviewed, three themes emerged: *change*, *connection* and *leadership*.

One of the shared fundamentals is the idea of engaged scholarship promoting change, especially change in university and community relationships. For example, Michigan State University's Outcome-Asset Impact model (Michigan State University O-AIM Model, 2009) has three core concepts that facilitate iterative methodologies for thinking and organizing programs that will have an impact through change strategies. The University of Denver has adopted the Asset-Based Community Development (ABCD) model first conceptualized by John Kretzmann and John McKnight with Northwestern University's Asset-Based Community Development Institute (University of Denver Center for Community Engagement and Service Learning, 2006). It stresses achievable outcomes among the principles of recognition, strengths, gifts, talents and assets, which are all crucial to and lead to the process of community change. Portland State University, one of the prominent leaders among urban engaged campuses, sees its role as providing learning space for the community beyond its campus, to create and transit meaningful knowledge for its engaged scholarship partners to be central participants in changing the global society (Portland State University, 2009).

To ensure that change is achievable, most models encourage partnerships that are linked to practice, making connections between classroom-based learning and real world experience. This linkage ensures that engaged scholars' work is applicable and accessible to all invested parties. One way that is shown is with a service-learning prism such as that developed by California State University Monterey Bay (California State University Monterey Bay, 2009), illustrating that learning is a transformative, engaged process for meaningful service and reflection. Michigan State University's leadership implements this linkage within and through its Office of Outreach Partnerships, which spearheads all campus engaged scholarship activities and provides support to faculty, students and the community. One of the boldest moves was made by Arizona State University when it transformed its campus into a location of Social Embeddedness (Arizona State University, n.d.). ASU is poised to have a huge impact because it is the largest public research university with a goal of creating an environment of interactive and mutually supportive partnerships with communities of Arizona.

Making connections between partners and practice has the greatest chance of creating change when it is supported by the leadership of a central office or administration that has the commitment to engagement and the capacity to provide support to key players. In the cases studied, university administrators provided strong support for engaged scholarship, including a clear mandate and resources. Strong support was backed with strategic moves, such as establishing the Center for Service and Learning at IUPUI and the Office of Outreach Partnership Office at Michigan State University. At Portland State University, the university's success as leader in urban campus engagement was spearheaded by the formation of a top-tier position, associate vice provost for engagement and director for community-university partnerships, who leads the mandate with human and financial resources to support faculty scholarship and student programs linkages to the communities. Other examples include University of Denver's Center for Community Engagement and Service Learning, which has clear objectives, goals and resources that closely articulate with the university's goals for engaged scholarship, and the Office of the Vice Chancellor for Public Service and Engagement and The Carolina Center for Public Service at the University of North Carolina at Chapel Hill.

We are cognizant that each model has been adapted to the dynamics of its university's environment and commitments for engaged scholarship. For example, the O-AIM model has proven to be suitable for land-grant institutions such as Michigan State, allowing engaged scholarship activities to draw upon the university's extension programs throughout the state of Michigan. Arizona State University's Social Embeddedness model is suited to an urban, publicly funded research university, and its challenge will be to ensure that its engaged scholarship measures are implemented throughout the state of Arizona. California State University—Monterey Bay and the University of Denver, as regional universities, have emphasized different but equally important approaches that focus on service-learning and social justice, establishing the classroom as the place to create necessary connections for community change, and leading ultimately to an expansion of student and faculty participation in engaged scholarship.

These engaged scholarship models have been established with specific goals for each university, appropriate to the strengths and needs of the campus and communities involved. They do not provide a discrete road-map for others to follow, but rather suggest a process or journey that each university may undertake. It takes many years to implement a model, even with strong commitments from many key players. Further study of their progress over time will help determine which approaches have particular value in building and sustaining engaged scholarship endeavors.

Toward a Model of Institutional Support for Engaged Scholarship

The process of developing our model involved gathering and synthesizing a great deal of information, and an iterative process of discussion, presentation and refinement with the help of a committed and experience group of faculty, administrators, staff and students. We also sought the advice of experts with a national perspective: Tim Stanton, Stanford University (personal communication, March 2008), and Amy Driscoll at the Carnegie Foundation for the Advancement of Teaching (personal communication, February 2009).

After reviewing approaches at a number of institutions, and considering how the themes of change, connections and leadership inter-relate, we created a model of institutional support for engaged scholarship. Based on traditional constructs of management (Drucker, 1954), the model emphasizes the cyclical nature of planning, management and evaluation. The model also incorporated implementation as an area of special

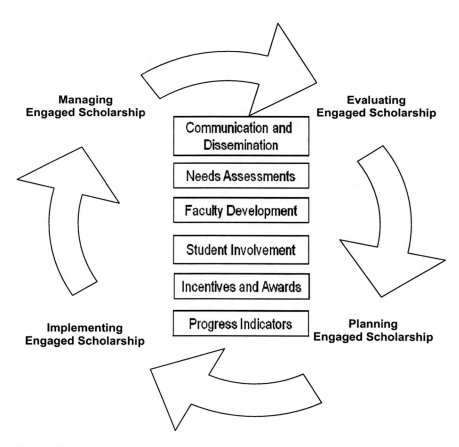

Exhibit 2.2.   Model system of institutional support for engaged scholarship: Making and managing connections between all participants.

importance (as suggested by Van de Ven, 2007) serving as the fourth element in the dynamic portion of the model (see Exhibit 2.2).

This model incorporates the guiding principles of engagement identified by Ersing, Jetson, Jones and Keller (2007) in their study of university-community engagement in an urban neighborhood: Establishing reciprocal relationships, taking a strength-based approach, seeking sustainability from the onset, taking slow incremental steps, matching effort with strategic plans, being enterprising, making sure results are disseminated at the university and in the community, and finding creative solutions as problems arise. These principles helped us to select the categories of engagement practice shown at the center of the model, which we used to classify the tools of engagement identified in our study of research universities. Several new dimensions emerged, as well, as we considered the skills, knowledge, abilities, and support that faculty and students need to be successful in engaged scholarship.

After reviewing the three themes identified earlier (change, connections and leadership) we determined the process of making and managing connections is where institutional support can be most effective. Therefore, for the second aspect of the model, we identified categories of practices that facilitate making and sustaining connections in engaged scholarship: communication and dissemination; needs assessment; faculty development; student involvement; incentives and awards; and progress indicators.

Communication and Dissemination

Each service-learning project typically has at least five groups of participants with distinct interests: University administration, community members, staff, faculty, and students. From the beginning of participation in engagement efforts, knowledge generated must be collected and made available in ways that are meaningful to participants, both within the university and in the communities involved.

Needs Assessments

Determination of the needs of all participants is essential for planning and evaluation of progress. In engaged scholarship, needs assessments are often a natural way to create a list from which priorities for future research and service-learning classes can emerge. They create a shared vocabulary, thus increasing trust and understanding between university and community partners.

Faculty Development

Training and mentoring efforts have been shown to be effective in supporting new faculty members' involvement in engaged scholarship, as well as helping more senior faculty retool their skills to the different demands of engaged scholarship and partnerships (e.g., McGuire, Strong, Lay, Ardemagni, Wittberg, & Clayton, this volume).

Student Involvement

Practices in this category address the roles students play through their participation in community-engaged learning, research, and scholarship.

Incentives and Awards

Practices here include programs or activities that foster and promote substantive partnerships in engaged teaching and learning, as well as engaged research and discovery.

Progress Indicators

It is important that we have metrics to document milestones in the growth of the institution's engaged scholarship that are meaningful to all parties, and to characterize the benefits, as well as shortcomings requiring improvement.

Practices at Research Universities Supporting the Scholarship of Engagement

We searched through hundreds of pages of Web sites and reports, in order to synthesize current practices of universities to encourage engaged scholarship, which are shown in Exhibit 2.3. Some of the discoveries we made are not captured there, as documentation of activities varied greatly based on local conditions and institutional history. The reader is advised to consult the references and resources section for Web-based sources. In some areas—particularly progress indicators—metrics are still in development, so examples are scarce. Examples of faculty development programs are plentiful, while more work needs to be done to capture all of the Needs Assessment approaches that are currently used in the field but not readily found on Web sites.

Exhibit 2.3 provides examples of a wide range of engagement activities. For example, there are high profile, well-funded programs that have strong support of their university presidents, with major funding to establish centers of engaged research and service-learning on their campuses (i.e., University of Wisconsin-Milwaukee, Tulane University). Midlevel programs usually support faculty who develop engaged research programs, engaged departments and a rich variety of engaged learning opportunities for students; some also evidenced one-on-one consultations, seed grants to collect pilot data for NIH or NSF submissions, and

Exhibit 2.3.   Current University Practices Supporting Engaged Scholarship

Tool of Engaged Scholarship	*Cost Categories (Low: $0–$30,000; Medium: $30,001–$75,000; High: $75,001–*

Communication and dissemination	**Low Cost**
	• University of Michigan Provost sponsors a yearly "John Dewey lecture" through the university's Ginsberg Center
	  http://ginsberg.umich.edu/resources/for_faculty.html#dewey
	• University and community electronic newsletter:
	  University of South Florida's Collaborative for Children, Families and Communities
	  http://usfcollab.fmhi.usf.edu/
	• University of South Florida's College of Education sponsors a community engagement resource Web site:
	  http://www.coedu.usf.edu/main/CommunityEngagement/communityengagement.html
	
	Medium Cost
	• University of California, San Francisco's Clinical and Translational Science Institute has a Web site with electronic copies of articles and reports on community engagement:
	  http://ctsi.ucsf.edu/research/community-pubs
	• Portland State University maintains a map of university-community partnerships around the world on their Web site:
	  http://partner.pdx.edu/world
	
	High Cost
	• University of Michigan's Ginsburg Center publishes the *Michigan Journal of Community Service Learning*
	  http://www.umich.edu/~mjcsl/
	• Tufts University has developed research guides to raise awareness among Tufts University campus and surrounding communities with a particular emphasis on local partner communities.
	  http://activecitizen.tufts.edu/?pid=8

Needs assessment	**Low Cost** • University of South Florida's Collaborative for Children, Families and Communities sponsored a university community summit that brought together university officials and faculty, community members and agencies to create a list of major needs affecting youth residing in Hillsborough County. *http://usfcollab.fmhi.usf.edu/*

(Table continues on next page)

Exhibit 2.3. (Continued)

Tool of Engaged Scholarship	Cost Categories (Low: $0–$30,000; Medium: $30,001–$75,000; High: $75,001–)
	Medium Cost • The University of North Carolina-Chapel Hill sponsors a Tar Heel bus tour to help faculty gain a better understanding of North Carolina. The tour highlights the university's public service commitment by promoting scholarship and service that are responsive to the concerns of the state and contribute to the common good. *http://www.unc.edu/bustour/* • Ohio State University's Office of University Outreach and Engagement assists departments and colleges assess their current outreach and engagement programs and identify models for outreach and engagement: *http://outreach.osu.edu/resources.php*
Faculty development	**Low Cost** • Indiana University Purdue University Indianapolis (IUPUI) Office of Service Learning provides numerous workshops on creating and assessing service learning courses. *http://csl.iupui.edu/osl/* • The University of Michigan's Ginsburg Center provides introductory workshop on the fundamentals of service-learning and is available to faculty, departments, schools and colleges. *http://ginsberg.umich.edu/resources/for_faculty.html* • Portland State University offers one-on-one faculty support to design new curriculum, syllabi and develop instructional strategies. *http://www.pdx.edu/cae/cbl-faculty-resources* • Ohio State University offers outreach and engagement workshops. *http://service-learning.osu.edu/* • Indiana University Purdue University Indianapolis (IUPUI) Center for Service and Learning developed Boyer Scholars and the Faculty Fellow in Service Learning programs offering a $5,000 stipend to faculty who teach service learning classes. It also offers $750–$1,500 to fund service learning assistant positions. *http://csl.iupui.edu/OSL/2c.asp*
	Medium Cost • Indiana University Purdue University Indianapolis (IUPUI) Office of Service Learning consults with faculty members interested incorporating service learning into their courses. *http://csl.iupui.edu/osl/2c4.asp* • Tulane University created a Junior Faculty Mentorship Program which links senior faculty members to junior faculty as part of a service engaged scholarly development program. Senior faculty members receive $2,500 and junior faculty receive $1,500 each plus a stipend to attend a 10-week seminar on service-learning pedagogy and course instruction. *http://tulane.edu/cps/faculty/faculty-seminar.cfm* • Ohio State University's Roads Scholars Programs sponsors a tour of the state to meet faculty members at other schools who work with community partners and university students. *http://outreach.osu.edu/roads_scholar.php*

Student involvement and advocacy	**Low Cost** • University of South Florida (USF) Center for Leadership & Civic Engagement has a student leadership program, recruiting experienced students to lead service-learning and volunteer activities. *http://volunteer.usf.edu/leadership.html* **Medium Cost** • The University of Maryland-College Park sponsors undergraduate teaching assistants up to 10 hours per week to support the design, transformation and management of service-learning components in current course offerings. *http://www.csl.umd.edu/resources/uta.htm* • Indiana University Purdue University Indianapolis (IUPUI) Center for Service and Learning reimburses tuition fees of students who help faculty members develop a service learning class, project or research endeavor. *http://csl.iupui.edu/csl/osl/2b3.asp* • Tulane University's Center for Public Service recruits, trains, and supervises student leaders who assist faculty with coordination of service-learning projects. *http://tulane.edu/cps/programs/fellows-index.cfm*
Program, incentives, and awards	**Low Cost** • The University of Michigan offers small development grants—up to $500 each year—to faculty for costs associated with teaching a service-learning course. *http://ginsberg.umich.edu/resources/for_faculty.html#grants* • The University of North Carolina-Chapel Hill issues Public Service Awards to honor individual students, faculty, staff and university units and organizations for extraordinary and exemplary public service. *http://www.unc.edu/cps/public-service-awards-index.php* • Tulane University offers course development grants (up to $5,000) to faculty members and their departments, to be used to develop a department's capstone public service course. *http://tulane.edu/cps/faculty/upload/PS-Capstone-Grant.pdf* • University of Michigan sponsors Arts of Citizenship—faculty grants for public scholarship in arts, humanities and design (up to $20,000) that can be used to hire project staff, purchase research materials, pay travel and event cost, and award summer supplemental pay and release time for faculty. *http://www.artsofcitizenship.umich.edu/about/program.html*

(Table continues on next page)

Exhibit 2.3. (Continued)

Tool of Engaged Scholarship	Cost Categories (Low: $0–$30,000; Medium: $30,001–$75,000; High: $75,001–

Medium Cost

- The University of Michigan's Ginsburg Center Faculty Initiative Grants (up to $10,000) are available for teaching innovations and new research initiatives in new course projects.
  http://ginsberg.umich.edu/resources/for_faculty.html#grants

- Ohio State University: OSU CARES Seed Grants are available (up to $10,000) to support development of interdisciplinary teams of university personnel who do outreach and engagement.
  http://osucares.osu.edu/grantsprogram.htm

- The University of North Carolina—Chapel Hill sponsors a Faculty Engaged Scholars Program to advance faculty involvement in the scholarship of engagement. Each recipient gets a stipend of up to $7,500 per year, for each of the 2 years (maximum $15,000).
  http://www.unc.edu/cps/faculty-engaged-scholars-index.php

- Ohio State University Extension has Personnel Support Grants (Up to $25,000 per grantee) to support OSU employees' efforts in outreach and engagement, in collaboration with OSU Extension.
  http://osucares.osu.edu/grantsprogram.htm

- Ohio State University has Service-Learning Initiative Grants, $3,000 for development of service-learning courses and $350 for course enhancement.
  http://service-learning.osu.edu/rfp.php

- Tulane University has offered Public Service Planning Grants (up to $35,000 for academic departments) for planning and institutionalizing new or continuing public service offerings.
  http://cps.tulane.edu/programs.cfm

High Cost

- Ohio State University's Office of University Outreach and Engagement sponsors Excellence in Engagement Grants that support interdisciplinary teams of faculty members in building their research in scholarly outreach and engaged initiatives. Up to $100,000 is available to each team receiving support.
  http://outreach.osu.edu/funding.php

Progress indicators

Medium Cost

• Several universities employ a process for service-learning course designation, which allows for regular reporting of both the number of community-engaged courses and the number of students enrolled.

Northeastern University:

http://www.northeastern.edu/servicelearning/faculty/designation.html

University of Alabama at Birmingham:

http://main.uab.edu/Sites/undergraduate-programs/academic-engagement/service-learning/32481/

University of San Francisco:

http://serve.usfca.edu/OSL/about/service_learning.html

High Cost

• Michigan State's Outreach and Engagement Measurement Instrument (OEMI) gathers numerical data along seven dimensions: time spent, issue, design, forms, locations, partners, and funding.

http://ncsue.msu.edu/measure.aspx

sponsor graduate research assistants (i.e., IUPUI, UNC-Chapel Hill). Some low-cost examples create databases of existing engaged teaching and research programs, or facilitate discussions with community organizations that lead to collaboration on community projects (i.e., Portland State, University of Maryland). Exhibit 2.3 represents a synthesis of promising practices that we identified through literature reviews and internet searches.

CONCLUSIONS, LIMITATIONS, AND RECOMMENDATIONS

This report provides a multi-faceted model for understanding the process by which universities can support and promote engaged research. A second contribution it makes is to provide information about those engagement strategies that currently support the research mission of colleges and universities, which can in turn be used to improve their engagement portfolio. The report documents existing programs and activities that have been used to support engaged scholarship, and is significant because it is the first project to systematically collect and highlight best practices in engagement at a wide range of research-extensive universities.

The limitation of this study is that it included only 25 colleges and universities and the research consisted of a review of documents and materials already published on Web sites and available electronically. A more detailed analysis is recommended for future research, which would include on-campus interviews with administrators and champions of engaged scholarship, at a larger number of institutions.

Since this study was completed, we have learned of other model-building efforts that could help to refine this model. For example, an "integrated model for advancing the scholarship of engagement" is being developed by John Saltmarsh, Lorilee Sandmann, KerryAnn O'Meara, and Dwight Giles, and was presented in 2008 at the 8th Annual International Research Conference on Service-Learning and Community Engagement. A Web-based survey of promising practices in engagement is being undertaken by Jeri Childers, Mary Grant, Alice Warren, Lisa Braverman, the UCEA Outreach and Engagement Community of Practice (COP), Association for Continuing Higher Education, Canadian Association for University Continuing Education and Higher Education Network for Community Engagement (UCEA Outreach and Engagement COP et al., 2008) and is yielding intriguing results. All of this bodes well for the emergence of a system of support for engaged scholarship at research universities, moving engagement from the margins to front and center on a sustaining basis.

We hope this report serves to stimulate a comprehensive, national effort to collect, maintain and share information about community engaged scholarship programs, activities and policies in an effort to grow the field of practice. Further, this report can provide advocates of engaged scholarship a ready list of mechanisms they can put in place at their own institution, such as improved resources for field placements and student internships, increased access to grants and contracts for engaged scholarship, greater encouragement of faculty efforts in engaged scholarship, and creation of community-friendly and easily-accessed systems for sharing information about engaged scholarship activities.

ACKNOWLEDGMENTS

This study was made possible by a grant from Florida Campus Compact, and benefitted from the advice, input and discussions with engaged faculty and administrators attending the 2008 annual meeting of the International Association for Research on Service-Learning and Community Engagement, and the 2009 Gulf-South Summit.

REFERENCES AND RESOURCES

Allee, V. (2002). *A value network approach for modeling and measuring intangibles.* Retrieved March 15, 2008 from www.value-networks.com/howToGuides/A_ValueNetwork_Approach.pdf

Boyer, E. L. (1990). *Scholarship reconsidered: priorities of professorate.* Menlo Park, CA: Jossey-Bass.

Boyer, E.L. (1996). The scholarship of engagement. *Journal of Public Outreach.* *1*(1), 11-20.

Bringle, R. G., Games, R., & Malloy, E. A. (Eds.). (1996). Colleges and universities as citizens: Issues and perspectives. In *Colleges and universities as citizens* (pp. 1-16). Needham Heights, MA: Allyn & Bacon.

Bringle, R. G., & Hatcher, J. A. (1995). A service-learning curriculum for faculty. *Michigan Journal of Community Service Learning, 2,* 112-122.

Bringle, R. G., & Hatcher, J. A. (1996). Implementing service learning in higher education. *Journal of Higher Education, 67,* 221-239.

Bringle, R. G., Hatcher, J. A, & Holland, B. (2007). Conceptualizing civic engagement: Orchestrating change at a metropolitan university. *Metropolitan Universities, 18*(3), 57-74.

Brukardt, M. J., Holland, B., Percy, S. L., & Zimpher, N. (2006). The path ahead: What's next for university engagement? In S. L. Percy, N. L. Zimpher, & M. J. Brukardt (Eds.), *Creating a new kind of university: Institutionalizing community-university engagement* (pp. 242-259). Boston: Anker.

Calleson, D. C., Jordan, C., & Seifer, S. D. (2005). The scholarship of community engagement: Is faculty work in communities a true academic enterprise? *Academic Medicine, 80*(4), 317-321.

Campus Community Partnerships for Health. (2009). *Community campus partnerships for health.* Retrieved May 11, 2009, from Community—Campus Partnerships for Health Web site: http://www.ccph.info/

Campus Compact. (2002). *Indicators of Engagement Project.* Retrieved February 12, 2008, from http://www.compact.org

Carnegie Foundation for the Advancement of Teaching. (2009). *Community engagement elective classification.* Retrieved from http://www.carnegiefoundation.org/classifications/index.asp?key=1213

Carolina Center for Public Service, (2000). *Mission, Carolina Center for Public Service, University of North Carolina-Chapel Hill.* Retrieved May 23, 2008, from http://www.unc.edu/cps/our-office-about.php

Community Outreach Partnership Center. (2000). *Mission & goals, Community Outreach Partnership Center, University of Pittsburgh.* Retrieved May 23, 2008, from http://www.pitt.edu/~copc/index_mission.html

Cox, D. (2006). The how and why of the scholarship of engagement. In S. L. Percy, L. Zimpher, & M. J. Brukardt (Eds.). *Creating a new kind of university: Institutionalizing community-university engagement* (pp. 122-135). Bolton, MA: Anker.

Diamond, R. M. (2004). *Preparing for promotion, tenure and annual review: A faculty guide.* Bolton, MA: Anker.

Diamond, R. M., & Bronwyn, A. E. (1993). *Recognizing faculty work: Reward systems for the year 2000.* San Franscisco: Jossey-Bass.

Drucker, P. (1954) *The practice of management.* New York: Harper.

El Ansari, W. (1999). *A study of the characteristics, participant perceptions and predictors of effectiveness in community partnerships in health personnel education: The case of South Africa.* Unpublished doctoral thesis, University of Wales College, Newport, United Kingdom.

Ersing, R. L., Jetson, J., Jones, R., & Keller, H. (2007). Community engagement's role in creating institutional change within the academy: A case study of East Tampa and the University of South Florida. In S. B. Gelmon & S. H. Billig (Eds.), *Service-learning: From passion to objectivity* (pp. 177-195). Charlotte, NC: Information Age.

Gibson, C. (2006). *Citizens at the center: A new approach to civic engagement.* Retrieved May 11, 2009 from http://www.casefoundation.org/sites/default/files/citizens-at-the-center.pdf

Green, L., & Glasgow, R. (2006). Evaluating the relevance, generalization, and applicability of research: Issues in external validation and translation methodology. *Evaluation and the Health Professions, 29*(1), 126-153.

Hashagen, S. (2002). *Models of community engagement.* Retrieved May 7, 2009, from http://lead.scdc.org.uk/uploads/modelsofcommunityengagement.pdf

Imagining America—Tenure Team Initiative. (n.d.). *The tenure team initiative on public scholarship.* Retrieved May 11, 2009, from http://www.imaginingamerica.org/TTI/TTI.html

Indiana University-Purdue University Indiana. (2006). *Mission and vision.* Retrieved May 23, 2008, from http://www.iupui.edu/about/vision.html

International Association for Research on Service-learning and Civic Engagement. (2009). *Conferences and awards.* Retrieved May 11, 2009 from http://www.researchslce.org/index.html

Jordan, C. (Ed.). (2007). *Community-engaged scholarship review, promotion & tenure package.* Peer Review Workgroup, Community-Engaged Scholarship for Health Collaborative, Community-Campus Partnerships for Health. Retrieved February 10, 2008, from http://www.ccph.info

Kecskes, K. (2006) *Engaging departments: Moving faculty culture from private to public individual to collective focus for the common good.* Bolton, MA: Anker.

Kellogg Commission on the Future of State and Land-Grant Universities. (2000). *Returning to our roots.* Washington, DC: National Association of State Universities and Land Grant Colleges.

Kretzmann, J., & McKnight, J. (1993) *Building communities from the inside out: A path toward finding and mobilizing a community's assets.* Chicago: ACTA Publications.

National Review Board for the Scholarship of Engagement. (n.d.). *The scholarship of engagement online.* Retrieved May 11, 2009, from http://schoe.coe.uga.edu/index.html

Nyden, P. (2003). Academic incentives for faculty participation in community-based participatory research. *Journal of Internal Medicine, 18,* 576-585.

Oats, K. K., & Leavitt, L. H. (2003). *Service-learning and learning communities: Tools for integration and assessment.* Washington, DC: Association of American Colleges and Universities.

Pasque, P. A., Smerek, R. E., Dwyer, B., Bowman, N., & Mallory, B. L. (Eds.). (2005). *Higher education collaboratives for community engagement and improvement.* Ann Arbor, MI: National Forum on Higher Education for the Public Good.

Ramanos, M., Edelman, D., & Arefi, M. (2006). *UC/Community interactions and collaborations: A study of peer institutions main report.* Cincinnati, OH: University of Cincinnati School of Planning.

Reed, C. S., & Brown, R.E. (2001) Outcome-Asset impact model: Linking outcomes and assets. *Evaluation and Program Planning, 24*(3), 287-95.

Seifer, S. D., Shore, N., & Holmes, S. L. (2003). *Developing and sustaining community-university partnerships for health research: Infrastructure requirements.* Report to the NIH Office of Behavioral and Social Sciences Research. Retrieved May 12, 2008, from www.ccph.info

Shapiro, E. D., & Coleman, D. L. (2000). The scholarship of application. *Academic Medicine, 75*(9), 895-8.

Small, S., & Uttal, L. (2005). Action-oriented research: Strategies for engaged scholarship. *Journal of Marriage and Family, 67,* 936-948.

Sullivan, M., Kone, A., Chrisman, N., Ciske, S., & Krieger, J. (2001). Researcher and researched-community perspectives: Toward bridging the gap. *Health Education and Behavior, 28*(2), 130-149.

University of Cincinnati. (2008). *Mission, University of Cincinnati.* Retrieved May 23, 2008, from http://www.uc.edu/about/mission.html

University of Pittsburgh. (1995). *Mission & vision, University of Pittsburgh.* Retrieved May 23, 2008, from http://www.ir.pitt.edu/factbook/fbweb05/general/MISSION.PDF

Van de Ven, A. (2007). *Engaged scholarship: A guide for organizational and social research*. New York: Oxford University Press.

University Continuing Education Association. (2008). *A survey of promising practices in engagement*. Retrieved May 12, 2008 from http://www2.opd.outreach.vt.edu:8080/outreach/controller/welcome

Zlotkowski, E. (1999). Pedagogy and engagement. In R. G. Bringle, R. Games, & E. A. Malloy (Eds.), *College and universities as citizens* (pp. 96-120). Boston: Allyn & Bacon.

CHAPTER 3

A CASE STUDY
OF FACULTY LEARNING
AROUND REFLECTION

A Collaborative Faculty Development Project

**Lisa McGuire, David Strong, Kathy Lay,
Enrica J. Ardemagni, Patricia Wittberg, and Patti Clayton**

ABSTRACT

This chapter presents data generated from a faculty development initiative grounded in the DEAL Model of Critical Reflection for service-learning (Ash & Clayton, 2004; Ash, Clayton, & Atkinson, 2005; Ash, Clayton, & Moses, 2008). This faculty learning community involved assessment of student learning resulting from reflection on service experiences and assessment of faculty changes in pedagogy in the implementation of the DEAL Model. Using case study methodology, both written student products and faculty syllabi and assignments were analyzed, and a focus group was convened to explore the benefits and challenges of learning this reflective pedagogy. A model of the connections between student learning and faculty change is presented, and implications are discussed for future research related to the relationship between student and faculty learning.

Creating Our Identities in Service-Learning and Community Engagement
pp. 53–72

INTRODUCTION

Faculty development focused on building capacity for effective teaching has among its most important goals improved student learning. However, recent critics of the scholarship of teaching and learning highlight its overemphasis on classroom *teaching*, with *learning* in a secondary position (Boshier & Huang, 2008). Service-learning pedagogy utilizes organized community service and documentation of learning through reflection (Bringle & Hatcher, 1999). Yet it is clear that faculty, who may be more comfortable with traditional ways of teaching, require new knowledge, skills, support, and motivation in order to move toward such innovative pedagogies as service-learning (Ash & Clayton, 2004; Bok, 1990). Scholars have called for a more systematic study of faculty needs, challenges, and rewards in implementing service-learning pedagogy (Hatcher & Bringle, 1997; Holland, 1999), a research agenda that is consistent with Boyer's (1990) call for the development of a scholarship of teaching in higher education. This article shares the results of investigation into student learning and faculty change associated with a faculty development initiative focused on critical reflection in service-learning.

For several years, our university provided an institutional context of strong support for service-learning pedagogy. This includes a well-established Center for Service and Learning with multiple funding sources to support faculty development around service-learning pedagogy. As part of these efforts, a consultant provided faculty development on the DEAL Model for integrating critical reflection and assessment in service-learning (Ash & Clayton, 2004; Ash, Clayton, & Atkinson, 2005; Ash, Clayton, & Moses, 2008). This model was created by students and faculty at North Carolina State University in an explicit effort to harness the power of assessment integrated with teaching and service-learning It posits three important, sequential steps in the process of critical reflection: *Description* of experiences in an objective and detailed manner; *Examination* of those experiences in light of explicit learning objectives in the categories of academic enhancement, civic learning, and personal growth; and *Articulation of the Learning* that results in such a way as to encourage and support improvements in learning and in service.

The DEAL Model includes associated tools and rubrics grounded in Paul and Elder's (2005) intellectual standards for critical thinking and in Bloom's (1956) Taxonomy. Students are challenged to support their claims with evidence, to clarify the meaning of the terms they use, to consider alternative perspectives, to reason logically, to represent others' ideas with fairness (Paul & Elder) across developmentally-appropriate levels of reasoning—from identification, description, and application at the more basic level to analysis, synthesis, and evaluation in settings designed to promote higher order reasoning (Bloom).

Faculty in this study participated in a series of professional development workshops on the DEAL Model, exploring its implementation both within and beyond service-learning. A subset of the participants of the original workshops decided to continue working together as a community of learners (Brown & Campion, 1992; Shulman & Shulman, 2004); additional members joined after a subsequent round of workshops on the DEAL Model. These faculty members, from the disciplines of Spanish, Sociology and Social Work, used the model in their own undergraduate and graduate teaching and investigated resultant student learning. They also examined their own learning processes of professional development and scholarship, noting evidence of changes in their understanding and in their practice. This case study was designed to generate questions and hypotheses for future inter-institutional research. The case study methodology was used to explore the relationship between faculty development and student/faculty change as manifested in three discrete but inter-connected Scholarship of Teaching and Learning (SoTL) projects. Results presented include: (a) an evaluation of student learning from DEAL-based assignments, (b) an evaluation of faculty learning through the examination of changes in faculty communication with students and (c) an evaluation of faculty learning through a focus group examination of the overall process. Discussion includes analysis of the faculty learning community utilizing Guskey and Yoon's (2009) synthesis of factors for effective faculty development as well as presentation of a model to conceptualize the interactive process between student learning and faculty development.

LITERATURE REVIEW

The role of faculty and the need for faculty development have been identified as vital to service-learning as pedagogy in higher education (Bringle & Hatcher, 1999). "Faculty development is the cornerstone for the implementation of academic service-learning in colleges and universities" (Rice & Stacey, 1997, p. 64). Faculty are motivated toward service-learning for various reasons (Holland, 1999) but also must have the support of the institution in order to advance these initiatives (Bringle, Hatcher, Jones, & Plater, 2006). Service-leaning is a central pedagogical strategy for universities to strive toward a comprehensive and sustainable civic engagement agenda.

The need for higher education to study multiple pedagogies has been a professional challenge since Boyer (1990) articulated the scholarship of teaching during his tenure as the director of the Carnegie Foundation for the Advancement of Teaching. This area of research on teaching development and practice in higher education was stimulated by the Carnegie Foundation, which has over 100 years of experience researching and advocating for the support of professional teaching in American higher education (Shulman, 2005). One promising form of professional development to enhance teaching is the community of learners approach (Brown & Campion, 1996; Shulman & Shulman, 2004). Shulman & Shulman (2004) articulated a model to capture the essence of the teacher learning community process that identified features for accomplished teacher development, including vision, motivation, understanding, practice, reflection, and community.

More recently, Guskey and Yoon (2009) report on an American Institutes for Research study that reviewed evidence of the impact of professional development on student achievement among K-12 students: Factors such as workshops, outside experts, time for follow-up, activities, and content were identified as important to successful impact on student achievement. The fact that only 9 studies of more than 1,300 reviewed addressed the relationship between faculty development and student achievement indicates the widespread challenges of evaluating the processes of faculty learning and student learning in a holistic manner (Guskey & Yoon, 2009). These challenges have emerged in the initial efforts to study faculty development in service-learning that will be discussed below.

Building upon early Campus Compact efforts to move from professional development for individual faculty to department level efforts to change culture and rework curricula, Rice and Stacey (1997) highlight both the cognitive and affective nature of faculty development around service-learning, positing a group collaborative effort through a Faculty Fellows program as a model structure to facilitate the process. Other scholars researching faculty development around service-learning have identified the challenges to implementing the pedagogy and the impact of service-learning on faculty, while calling for additional research (Driscoll, 2000; Harwood et al., 2005; Pribbenow, 2005).

The authors of this study conducted a meta-analysis of five studies, all of which involved empirical evidence from faculty learning around the pedagogy of service-learning, and identified the following four themes:

- Satisfaction and support for teaching (Driscoll, 2000; Harwood et al., 2005; Pribbenow, 2005; Rice & Stacey, 1997);
- Diverse motivations for involvement in service-learning including involvement in scholarship of teaching and learning (Driscoll, 2000; Harwood et al., 2005; Rice & Stacey, 1997);
- Obstacles to implementing and maintaining service-learning (Driscoll, 2000; Harwood et al., 2005; Pribbenow, 2005); and

- Emphasis on student learning processes and outcomes (Harwood et al., 2005; Pribbenow, 2005).

Pribbenow (2005) begins to move understanding of faculty development beyond logistical preparation for implementing service-learning to an emphasis on the experiential nature of the faculty learning process: "faculty development must be developmental, accepting them with the skills, knowledge, and perspectives they bring and allowing them to grow in the directions they choose" (p. 35). It is interesting to note that only the most recent articles highlight student learning processes and outcomes specifically as an emphasis for faculty development around service-learning. Although there is recent emphasis on faculty development to address student learning processes and outcomes, none of the studies identified a structure or process to provide a means to integrate student learning and faculty learning as related or interdependent processes.

Another important area for literature review is on the DEAL Model of structured critical reflection, around which this faculty development initiative was organized. The DEAL Model was developed in order to "generate, deepen, and document learning" (Ash & Clayton, 2004), in relation to reflection on service-learning activities. Additionally, Ash and Clayton developed grading rubrics that incorporated Bloom's Taxonomy (1956) and Paul and Elder's (2006) standards of critical thinking. As a part of the scholarship on the DEAL Model, Ash et al. (2005) examined changes in students' critical thinking and higher order reasoning abilities across drafts of a single reflection product and over the course of a semester; they also examined variation in critical thinking and higher order reasoning across the learning goal categories of academic enhancement, civic engagement, and personal growth. The investigators found that although scores on written products for both the learning objective and critical thinking rubrics did improve over the course of the semester; students showed more improvement on the latter and struggled more in the academic enhancement category.

METHOD/RESULTS

This article utilizes a case study design, one of the most common forms of qualitative research, which is designated by its *selection* of a single unit for a specific purpose, rather than a specific method of analysis (Stake, 2005). This faculty learning community was selected based upon the participants' awareness of changes in their own understanding and practice. The changes were supported by evidence from a series of scholarship projects that initially focused on student assessment, but grew to include assessment of faculty learning through the process of professional development and scholarship. These projects triangulate the evidence of growth among members of the faculty learning community and provide support for the model developed that conceptualizes the relationship between student and faculty learning. Specific methodologies and results from the three scholarship projects undertaken by the faculty learning community are presented in sub-sections below on student learning and faculty learning. As the faculty learning community developed over time, the participants utilized a participatory approach where "primary voice manifests through aware self-reflective action" (Guba & Lincoln, 2005, p. 196).

Description of the Faculty Learning Community

This case study examines the development and implementation of a community of learners framework for faculty development that seeks to integrate both student and faculty learning as well as maximize the opportunity for the scholarship of teaching and learning around service-learning pedagogy. Conceptualized by the participants as a faculty learning community, a group of three service-learning faculty self-selected to participate in this effort after attending a series of workshops on the DEAL Model of Critical Reflection. This cohort became known as "DEAL I." In 2005, the workshop series was offered again and the participants formed a second cohort ("DEAL II"). Two members from the second cohort joined the three DEAL I members and these five members created the current faculty learning community. Over the next 3 years, this faculty learning community continued to explore the use of reflection in service-learning and increasingly began to develop an interest in examining the interdependence of the processes of student learning and faculty development. Exhibit 3.1 illustrates the positioning of the DEAL-based faculty learning community that provided the context for this process, as the interface between faculty development and service-learning. Exhibit 3.2 expands on the niche of the faculty learning community, highlighting the deepening process of learning activities and reflection that eventually led to the development of scholarship activities through the undertaking of multiple SoTL projects. This faculty learning community was not only collaborative and reflective but also became focused deliberately on scholarship.

Results From SoTL Projects

Assessment of Student Learning

The three faculty members engaged in the DEAL I initiative focused on applying the DEAL Model's critical thinking (CT) rubrics to reflections that were produced as assignments in three classes (two of which were

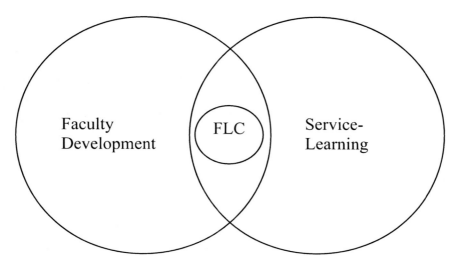

Note: FLC = faculty learning community.

Exhibit 3.1.   Scholarship of teaching and learning in service-learning (part 1).

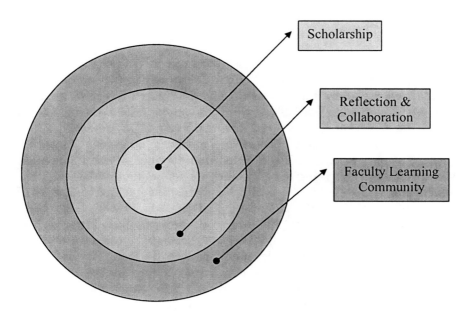

Exhibit 3.2.   Faculty learning community (expanded).

service-learning and one which was not) over the course of one semester. The purpose of this project was to determine if using the DEAL Model improved critical thinking skills of students during one semester of coursework. After participating in workshops to learn the basic mechanics of the DEAL Model, a select group of faculty was energized to continue learning about reflection assignments. This group decided to focus upon the prospect of enhancing student critical thinking in reflections about service-learning experiences. Faculty members were looking for an opportunity to apply their knowledge of what constitutes critical thinking at a deeper level, through reading and analyzing several samples of reflections that were scored using the CT rubrics.

Faculty members agreed to analyze multiple reflective writing assignments which integrated students' service-learning activities or life experiences with the academic content of the course. Students were instructed on critical thinking, which they were expected to demonstrate in their reflections. The reflections were evaluated across one semester to assess the change in the students' critical thinking skills. Although the faculty members had been trained to use the Critical Thinking (CT) rubrics developed by Ash and Clayton, they determined that it was important to calibrate scores on the first set of reflections written by the students, not only to standardize the scores across disciplinary writing but more importantly, to increase inter-rater reliability. The three faculty involved in the DEAL I project represent the disciplines of Sociology, Social Work, and Spanish, and calibration developed the rater's reliability.

Method.   The three faculty members selected six anonymous samples from their students' reflection products from early in the semester of a specific course and a time series design (T0, T1,T2) was implemented. Each faculty member identified two of the sample reflections as low, two as medium and two as high level, based on that faculty member's score from the DEAL CT rubrics. There were interventions between T0 and T1 as well as T1 and T2, which included presentations of the CT rubrics, feedback on papers using the CT standards, an online tutorial, and class discussion of the CT rubrics. Faculty led their students through a series of instructions on critical thinking using the DEAL Model so students themselves would understand the importance of the writing projects as well as what constitutes deep thinking. The same students selected for study at T0 submitted subsequent reflection papers at T1 and T2, and these reflections were also rated by each of the three instructors and the consultant. A total of three writing samples from each of the six students, one at T0, T1, and T2, were rated by each of the three instructors as well as the consultant ($n = 18$).

The faculty learning community met together on multiple occasions to calibrate their scores using the DEAL CT rubrics. During the initial calibration meeting, the three faculty members and the consultant read each of the 18 products without knowing how the faculty had categorized their initial six samples into low, medium and high categories. Detailed discussions resulted in a consensus score on all 18 reflections. This was repeated at each point in the time series and final scores were agreed upon for each sample. Only after a score had been assigned did the other faculty members and consultant know the original faculty's individual score and categorization of low, medium or high on a reflection. The calibration provided a collaborative process in which the raters learned to apply the rubrics to reflection assignments uniformly, allowing a consensus about the score of each paper.

Results. The data are summarized in Exhibit 3.3, demonstrating that while a minimal increase occurred in those students who were scored as low by their individual instructors at T0, there was a high increase in those students who were initially ranked as high. In this figure, the first bar represents the increase in CT scores from T0 to T1 and the second bar is the increase T0 to T2. Half of the students (8 of 16) or 50% increased their CT scores from T0 to T2. While encouraging, these results demonstrated the challenges for student learning around critical thinking, particularly over the one-semester time period.

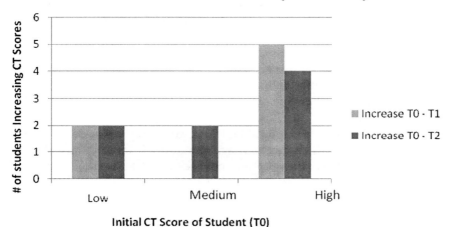

Exhibit 3.3.   Results from DEAL I investigation of critical thinking skills in reflections.

The participants involved in the DEAL I project felt that a reciprocity of learning occurred both by students and faculty involved in this scholarship project. Students who had already demonstrated a higher level of critical thinking skills improved at twice the level as those students who needed enhanced work to improve their critical thinking skills. Faculty members were particularly encouraged that they learned (1) how to apply the critical thinking standards, and, (2) to provide evaluative feedback in the usage of those standards in student products. In other words, faculty linked improvements in their skills in identifying both positive and negative utilization of the critical thinking skills with their ability to give feedback to students to improvements in student reasoning. This knowledge has the potential to improve constructive feedback provided to students, hopefully increasing their critical thinking skills. Faculty believed that without their involvement in the scholarship project, they would have been unlikely to develop the requisite skills to maximize the impact of the DEAL Model. At this point in the faculty learning initiative, the focus broadened from evaluating student reflection products to analyzing the faculty development process that shaped student learning.

Assessment of Faculty Learning— Communication With Students

As the DEAL I faculty were completing the analysis of student reflection products, DEAL II faculty decided to undertake a SoTL project to analyze faculty products that demonstrated their developing ability to successfully implement critical reflection. Faculty anecdotally agreed that using this structured style of reflection improved teaching and enhanced student learning. The DEAL Model served as an effective tool to help meet longstanding pedagogical goals that may not have been communicated successfully to students. This improved communication with students, both in terms of specific assignments and broader learning goals, such as critical thinking, multiculturalism and diversity, and understanding basic disciplinary perspectives, appeared to be a significant benefit of the DEAL Model.

Structured reflection through the DEAL Model was conceptualized as a language through which faculty may communicate more effectively with students. For students, the question often is, "What do you want us to do?" For faculty, the question is, "What do we want students to learn?" Structured reflection has served as an effective bridge between these two perspectives, by allowing students to have and share their own experiences, but in a clear and ordered way that meets course learning objectives. DEAL II faculty decided to document changes in their pedagogy, as a result of participation in this initiative.

Method/Results.   In order to analyze changes in faculty learning resulting from learning about the DEAL Model, faculty members compared and contrasted four primary forms of communication between faculty and students: course syllabi, written assignments, feedback on student work, and verbal exchanges. In all four of these areas, faculty compared communications with students before and after their involvement with the DEAL workshops and the faculty learning community. In each area, faculty documented a greater level of detail and specificity in communication with students—and perhaps most importantly a greater linking of both expectations and feedback to students with the learning objectives of the course. Not only were communications longer and more specific, they provided a practical roadmap for students to make sense of their own experiences in the context of course objectives. The results of this analysis are included in Exhibit 3.4.

Using a service-learning assignment from an Introduction to Sociology course taught by one of the participating faculty as an example, the changes in the assignment before and after involvement with the faculty development community on the DEAL Model were very clear. The assignment's purpose, pre- and post-DEAL, was for students to reflect on their service-learning experiences in the context of what they had learned over a semester in the classroom. The pre-DEAL assignment was one paragraph in length and did not go much beyond instructing students to "relate details from their service- learning projects to the relevant course concepts," as stated in the pre-DEAL course syllabus.

The papers received were predictable, as even well-written papers from strong students typically did not go beyond DEAL's "describe" level. The instructor was frustrated. While he knew students were learning something from their service experience, it seemed that learning was being

Exhibit 3.4.   Comparison of Faculty Communication with Students Pre-/Post-DEAL

Form of Communication With Student	Pre-DEAL	Post-DEAL
Syllabi	Listing service-learning as an assignment	Connecting service-learning with broader course learning objective
Assignments	Brief, vague directions	Specific, transparent objectives prompting students to move beyond description
Feedback	General words, such as "good," "unclear," and "expand"	Directed feedback using CT skills as a language both faculty and students understand

limited, and was not demonstrated in the students' written work. The students were even more frustrated, and communicated with the instructor (both verbally and via course evaluations) that while they often enjoyed the service project, they were not clear on what they were supposed to be getting out of it. Clearly, a learning opportunity was being missed.

Post-DEAL, the service-learning project itself and the learning objectives of the course remained the same. The paper assignment, however, had grown into a significantly more detailed, two-page student guide. This included a version of the DEAL Model, used to break the paper into three corresponding sections of description, examination, and articulated learning. The examination section included prompts and suggestions on how to critically analyze the service experience using sociological concepts presented in the class. Rather than straight jacketing students into "one right answer," these prompts structured student reflection and analysis in a meaningful way that meets pedagogical goals, while conveying those goals to students in a clear way. Pre-DEAL, even the stronger students struggled with making connections between course content and their service experiences. After DEAL, even students struggling with other aspects of the class benefitted from a clear structure to follow in reflecting on their service experiences. These findings are consistent with existing literature on the development of syllabi for service-learning coursework that stresses clear and prominent display of expectations for the reflection component as well as their connection to course goals (Heffernan, 2001).

Pre- and post-DEAL written feedback to students was also examined. One faculty learning participant reported that pre-DEAL, the four most commonly-used comments to students were: "interesting," "good," "expand," and "unclear." Along with providing only limited guidance to students, this type of feedback is not directly tied to the achievement of student learning objectives. Post-DEAL, faculty moved away from using these vague words, communicating to students with the intellectual standards of critical thinking that were made transparent to students when explaining the DEAL Model.

Evaluation by definition is in part subjective, to the inherent frustration of both students and faculty; this is especially evident in assignments and projects such as reflection on service-learning. The DEAL Model has provided an effective balance between student concerns about what instructors want from them, and instructor concerns about what students are learning. While still offering flexibility, the DEAL Model encourages faculty to communicate with and evaluate students along a more clear and transparent set of criteria. These changes in faculty communication with students at the beginning of a semester through the structuring of assignments as well as the more specific feedback given to students utilizing the critical thinking standards associated with the DEAL Model are strong evidence of faculty learning developed through the faculty learning community.

Assessment of Faculty Learning—Focus Group

Through participation in the DEAL-based faculty learning community and work on the SoTL projects described above, faculty realized that parallel learning was occurring. In an effort to generate, deepen, and document learning for students, faculty believed that their overall pedagogy was transformed. Faculty began to discuss the collective experiences as a faculty learning community in an informal way. In order to capture these reflections on faculty experiences with the faculty development process in utilizing the DEAL Model, a focus group was planned and conducted.

Method.   The primary question posed to focus group participants was: "What is the faculty experience of using the DEAL Model of structured critical reflection?" Members of the faculty learning community were invited to participate in the focus group. Building upon the reflective and participatory nature of the process that had been established, all five members, three from DEAL I and two from DEAL II participated in the focus group. Two doctoral students co-conducted the focus group, one posing the question and follow-up clarifying questions while the other took notes to assist in analyses. The focus group was recorded and transcribed for analyses. The doctoral students conducted a content analysis of the transcript, which included the initial coding and identification of emerging themes. They presented their analyses to the participants and the final themes were conceptualized in collaboration with the focus group participants.

Results.   Six themes which emerged from the collaboration: (1) the role of institutional support; (2) the rationale for using reflective writing; (3) structuring assignments; (4) facilitating feedback to students; (5) evidence of effectiveness; and (6) challenges for faculty. Participants acknowledged that because of institutional support each were able to commit time to the DEAL community. Three faculty members were from departments that had received "Engaged Department" grants from the university's Center for Service and Learning (3-year university grants to integrate civic engagement throughout a department's curriculum) and were planning to expand their involvement with service-learning. This was strong motivation for their initial willingness to become involved. In addition, four of the faculty respondents had been named Boyer Scholars, a university program to develop and support faculty research on service-learning. These programs supported their participation in the DEAL workshops and were clearly factors in faculty involvement in this ongoing faculty development initiative.

In addition, ongoing commitment was also strongly supported by the perceived benefits to the participants' pedagogy. Faculty participants were seeking reflection tools to connect experience with academic content in a meaningful way. They also wanted to deepen their student's intellectual engagement with the content of the course as evidenced in their reflections, by improving their critical thinking skills to both challenge and capture their learning. This focus on pedagogy is a direct link to an emphasis on the outcomes of student learning discussed below.

It was also noted that as a result of the DEAL process, faculty participants were now structuring reflection assignments utilizing the course objectives and learning goals for the experiences. This structuring allowed more specific feedback on these reflection assignments and, in turn, enabled focused attention to critical thinking. Some participants had reviewed course objectives and fine-tuned assignments accordingly. Utilizing the intellectual standards of critical thinking (Paul & Elder, 2006) influenced the review and reconstruction of a variety of assignments, beyond reflection assignments in service-learning.

Further, as students developed their ability to engage in critical thinking, faculty also developed skills at utilizing the intellectual standards to provide written feedback to students. The process of providing feedback became a dialogue between student and instructor from one assignment to the next. The rubrics associated with the DEAL Model were identified as a support to doing this in a meaningful manner.

As discussed above, initial evidence of effectiveness of structured critical reflection had been demonstrated, at least in a preliminary manner, in the research conducted by DEAL I. In the focus group, faculty participants noted improvement in student outcomes more broadly, evidencing changes in the learning process for faculty. In multiple situations, faculty were able to compare students who had learned the DEAL Model with those who had not, and the perception seemed to be that the students using DEAL were utilizing the reflection process to consider their learning and apply critical thinking.

Finally, faculty identified challenges associated with their new learning. The implementation of structured reflection assignments takes considerable time and commitment, especially in the initial implementation. Faculty participants were challenged by the learning required to fully understand Paul and Elder's (2006) intellectual standards for critical thinking in order to be able to give effective feedback. There were also challenges in providing class time to teach the model and the intellectual standards, at the same time needing to cover the requisite course content. However, once this process became established, faculty reported that student learning was impacted and the benefits transferred to subsequent classes. The intellectual standards became customary language for feedback, which students came to accept and expect. Each faculty member acknowledged that the benefits outweigh the challenges for SL as well as non-SL courses which is also evidenced by their continued participation in the faculty learning community.

DISCUSSION

The members of the DEAL faculty development initiative acknowledged that their participation in the faculty learning community improved their implementation of service-learning pedagogy, by increasing their understanding of and skills in implementing the DEAL Model (Ash & Clayton, 2004) to structure the reflection process and build critical thinking skills. Utilizing Guskey & Yoon's (2009) synthesis of successful professional development efforts, the faculty learning community described in this case study clearly demonstrated aspects of each factor. It was based upon a series of workshops, which were conducted by one of the developers of the DEAL Model. The faculty development initiative has lasted over four years, a significant amount of *time* which was defined by a series of follow-up meetings, where the members undertook a range of activities, in the form of the SoTL projects and presentations focused upon the content of a specific pedagogical practice.

As the participants in this initiative continued to discuss the findings of all of the SoTL projects and prepared to disseminate this learning to colleagues through presentations, a preliminary model for conceptualizing the interaction between student learning and faculty development emerged (see Exhibit 3.5.). This model mirrors Kolb's (1984) experiential learning model that has been previously identified as essential to the concept of reflection in the service-learning process. Exhibit 3.5 integrates and summarizes the learning gleaned from the overall faculty development process.

The model describes a circular process involving both student and faculty learning. As faculty begin to implement a model of structured critical reflection such as the DEAL Model, the first step in maximizing the impact of assignments begins with improving communication regarding the expectations for the reflections which are clearly linked to course objectives. The DEAL Model provides a structure that delineates between the description of experiences (the first step of the DEAL Model) and the

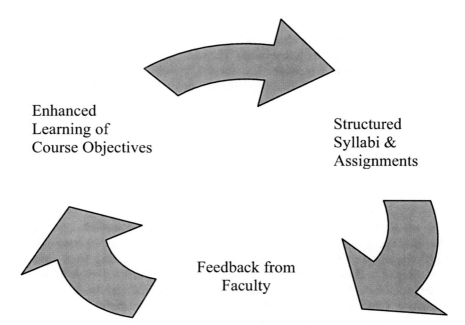

Enhanced
Learning of
Course Objectives

Structured
Syllabi &
Assignments

Feedback from
Faculty

Exhibit 3.5.   Faculty development model for implementing critical reflection pedagogy.

subsequent processes of deeper examination of these experiences in light of course content, civic engagement, and/or personal growth. The Articulated Learning pushes students to clearly identify the learning gleaned from reflection on the experience. This structuring of the assignment requires students to structure their thinking process, leading to improved learning outcomes. Assessment and feedback using Paul and Elder's (2005) intellectual standards for critical thinking facilitates student thinking about their own thinking.

Continuing the learning loop, as faculty members evaluate initial student products, they use their developing understanding of the critical thinking standards to provide specific feedback to students, which, in turn, allows students to revise and improve their reflection products to incorporate a deeper utilization of the standards in their thinking and their writing. This learning cycle creates a dynamic process in which improved faculty learning leads to improved student learning in the specific context of faculty development on service-learning. The cycle continues beyond the specific course studied and has transformed faculty members' ongoing teaching in all courses.

LIMITATIONS AND FUTURE DIRECTIONS

It must be noted that this is a qualitative case study using a participatory approach, which is not generalizable to other contexts, particularly those institutions that lack the institutional support identified here and in other literature as being vital to the process. However, this study does reflect the features identified in Guskey and Yoon's (2009) evaluation of successful teacher development efforts and pushed the participants to focus on student learning, which are clearly important to any faculty development initiative.

The model conceptualized through this faculty learning community, which integrates faculty and student learning processes, is being utilized to structure a faculty development program and a new research agenda at NC State University. Building on this foundation, subsequent phases of this research will focus more precisely on the relationship between student and faculty learning. Participating faculty will use the DEAL Model themselves to reflect on their reflection assignments and to generate ideas for enhancing learning; they will produce DEAL reflection assignments at multiple points in the faculty development process, so that investigators may track changes in their understanding of reflection as well as in their demonstrated critical thinking abilities. Syllabi, assignments, reflection prompts, grading schemes, and feedback will be collected at multiple points during the process.

Faculty will undergo one of several forms of faculty development interventions, consisting of readings, workshops, faculty learning community interactions, and participation in scholarship of teaching and learning projects. Student products will be collected for assessment throughout the semester of implementation, as will any further changes to the prompts and all faculty feedback. Rubrics will be developed to measure changes in faculty feedback, in expression of learning objectives, and so on and these rubrics will be applied to the demonstrations of faculty learning just as the current DEAL rubrics will be applied to demonstrations of student learning.

The next phase of this research will begin with in-depth qualitative investigation of a single faculty member's learning. This case study approach will generate hypotheses for investigation via a quasi-empirical, inter-institutional, multi-year study that will position faculty members from a variety of disciplines—along with their students—as subjects. As the field's understanding of the dynamics whereby faculty learning affects student learning is increased, faculty development will be strengthened.

CONCLUSION

The faculty members of this community of learners are convinced that their involvement with the DEAL Model and subsequent scholarship around teaching and learning has produced many benefits to their overall pedagogy, which continue to accrue over time. This conviction is apparent in multiple anecdotal stories from their teaching; these have been supplemented by the findings of the SoTL projects undertaken in the learning community. Through working to enhance student learning by structuring assignments and implementing evaluation rubrics focusing upon critical thinking skills, faculty were able to see improvement in focus on reflection assignments - students were "going deeper" and making stronger connections to course content in more meaningful ways. As their assignments became more focused, faculty members were then able to utilize their enhanced understanding of the critical thinking skills to give feedback that deepened student reflection in subsequent assignments. This conceptualization builds on the concept that reflective learning is often counter-normative and thus requires guided practice and capacity building (Clayton & Ash, 2004).

The link between student and faculty learning has been a powerful dynamic in supporting the efforts that are necessary to implement any new pedagogy such as service-learning. To fully understand the complexity of service-learning, and the requisite reflection processes, it is essential to investigate the mutual relationship between faculty learning and student learning. Additional research is certainly warranted to further explicate the relationship between faculty and student learning. However, the experience of this faculty development initiative provides support for a learning community approach as a viable means to view the interaction of faculty and student learning in service-learning pedagogy.

REFERENCES

Ash, S. L., & Clayton, P. H. (2004). The articulated learning: An approach to reflection and assessment. *Innovative Higher Education, 29*(2), 137-154.

Ash, S. L., Clayton, P. H., & Atkinson, M. P. (2005). Integrating reflection and assessment to improve and capture student learning. *Michigan Journal of Community Service Learning, 11*(1), 49-59.

Ash, S. L., Clayton, P. H., & Moses, M. G. (2008). *Learning through critical reflection: A tutorial for service-learning students.* Raleigh: Center for Excellence in Curricular Engagement, North Carolina State University.

Bloom, B. S. (Ed.). (1956). *Taxonomy of educational objectives. Vol. 1: Cognitive domain.* New York: McKay.

Bok, D. C. (1990). *Universities and the future of America*. Durham, NC: Duke University Press.

Boshier, R., & Huang, Y. (2008). In the house of Scholarship of Teaching and Learning (SoTL), teaching lives upstairs and learning in the basement. *Teaching in Higher Education, 13*(6), 645-656.

Boyer, E. (1990). *Scholarship reconsidered: Priorities of the professorate*. San Francisco: Jossey-Bass.

Bringle, R. G., & Hatcher, J. A. (1999). Reflection in service-learning: Making meaning of experience. *Educational Horizons, 77*(4), 179-185.

Bringle, R., Hatcher, J., Jones, S., & Plater, W. (2006). Sustaining civic engagement: Faculty development, roles, and rewards. *Metropolitan Universities, 17*(1), 62-74.

Brown, A., & Campione, J. (1996). Psychological theory and the design of innovative learning environments. In L. Schnauble & R. Glaser (Eds.), *Innovations in learning: New environments for education* (pp. 75-93). Mahwah, NJ: Erlbaum.

Clayton, P. H., & Ash, S. L. (2004). Shifts in perspective: Capitalizing on the counter-normative nature of service-learning. *Michigan Journal of Community Service Learning, 11*, 59-70.

Clayton, P. H., & Moses, M. G. (2006, October). *Course design for integrated service-learning*. Project SHINE Annual Meeting. Portland, OR.

Driscoll, A. (2000). Studying faculty and service-learning: Directions for inquiry and development. *Michigan Journal of Community Service Learning, 7*, 35-41.

Guba, E., & Lincoln, Y. (2005). Paradigmatic controversies, contradictions, and emerging confluences. In N. Denzin & Y. Lincoln (Eds). *Handbook of qualitative research* (6th ed., pp. 191-216). Thousand Oaks, CA: SAGE.

Guskey, T., & Yoon, K. (2009). What works in professional development? *Phi Delta Kappan, 90* (7), 495-500.

Harwood, A., Ochs, L., Currier, D., Duke, S., Hammond, J., Moulds, L., et al. (2005). Communities for growth: Cultivating and sustaining service-learning teaching and scholarship in a faculty fellows program. *Michigan Journal of Community Service Learning, 12*, 41-51.

Hatcher, J. A., & Bringle, R. G. (1997). Reflection: Bridging the gap between service and learning. *College Teaching, 45*(4), 153-158.

Heffernan, K. (2001). *Fundamentals of service-learning course construction*. Providence, RI: Campus Compact.

Holland, B. (1999). Factors and strategies that influence faculty involvement in public service. *Journal of Public Service and Outreach, 4*(1), 37-43.

Kolb, D. (1984). *Experiential learning: Experience as the source of learning and development*. New York: Prentice Hall.

Paul, R., & Elder, L. (2005). *The miniature guide to critical thinking: Concepts and tools*. Dillon Beach, CA: The Foundation for Critical Thinking.

Paul, R., & Elder, L. (2006). *Critical thinking: Tools for taking charge of your learning and your life* (2nd ed.) Saddle River, NJ: Prentice Hall.

Pribbenow, D. (2005). The impact of service-learning pedagogy on faculty teaching and learning. *Michigan Journal of Community Service Learning, 12*, 25-38.

Rice, D., & Stacey, K. (1997). Small group dynamics as a catalyst for change: A faculty development model for academic service-learning. *Michigan Journal of Community Service Learning, 4,* 64-71.

Shulman, L., & Shulman, J. (2004). How and what teachers learn: A shifting perspective. *Journal of Curriculum Studies, 36*(2), 257-271.

Shulman, L. (2005, September/October). To dignify the profession of the teacher. *Change, 37*(5), 22-29.

Stake, R. (2005). Qualitative case studies. In N. Denzin & Y. Lincoln (Eds). *Handbook of qualitative research: Third edition* (pp.443-466). Thousand Oaks, CA: SAGE.

PART II

DEVELOPING CHARACTERISTICS OF PARTNERSHIP IDENTITY IN FACULTY-COMMUNITY PARTNERSHIPS

CHAPTER 4

DEFINING CHARACTERISTICS OF PARTNERSHIP IDENTITY IN FACULTY-COMMUNITY PARTNERSHIPS

Emily M. Janke

ABSTRACT

In this chapter, 5 faculty-community partnerships are explored through an organizational identity framework to understand whether service-learning partners developed a Partnership Identity—a shared understanding of "who we are" as a partnership entity. Findings suggest that some partnerships may develop a Partnership Identity, while others may not, as defined by 4 characteristics: unified missions, feelings of membership in a distinctive entity, organizational structures, and expectations to endure changes in resources and membership. The development of nurturing norms and the implications for Partnership Identity on partnership effectiveness are also discussed

Creating Our Identities in Service-Learning and Community Engagement
pp. 75–101

INTRODUCTION

The development of sustained partnerships is a key element of effective college or university engagement with the community, because such partnerships provide opportunities for students, faculty, and community members to solve real-world problems (Harkavy, 2003). Yet, in a study by Abes, Jackson, and Jones (2002) of factors that motivate or deter faculty use of service-learning, many faculty members decided not to collaborate with community partners because they were anxious about coordinating the projects with partners. In addition, service-learning partnerships are time and effort intensive, may not be recognized as part of faculty's scholarly work by colleagues or promotion and tenure committees (O'Meara, 2002), and have the potential, if mismanaged, to damage wider community-campus relations.

Those faculty members who do begin partnerships often find they are difficult to maintain. Changes in leadership at colleges and universities, funding and enrollment, as well as academic schedules that follow semester terms, are inherent factors of campus life that present challenges to managing community-campus partnerships (Carriere, 2006). The difference in core work functions and structures between higher education institutions and their community partners may further prevent successful collaboration (Sebring, 1977). Failure rates are high even for profit-seeking partnerships such as mergers, joint ventures, and strategic alliances (Park & Ungson, 1997). Different types of organizations, such as public and private, may have "distinctive cultures that lead them to exhibit different values, concerns, and accountabilities, pursue different objectives, and place emphasis on different aspects of risks and benefits" (Noble & Jones, 2006, pp. 900-901). These differences can lead to difficulties in collaboration. One explanation for failures may be that partners simply never develop a shared understanding of "who we are together." Instead of beginning work on the substantive pieces of their projects, individuals struggle over who is in charge and what vision should guide the group's work (Clark, Gioia, Ketchen & Thomas, 2008; Güney, 2004).

The ability to forge a partnership that effectively provides for student learning is a necessary, but often difficult, aspect of service-learning (Abes et al., 2002; Sandy & Holland, 2006). The process requires faculty and community partners to engage in "boundary crossing" or "boundary work" (Hayes & Cuban, 1997) in which they cross back and forth between academic and nonacademic worlds that may have different norms, cultures, and expectations (Carriere, 2006). Boundary-spanners are organizational representatives who are "intimately involved in the day-to-day relationship-building activities and operations within the developing partnership" (Noble & Jones, 2006, p. 897). Organizations have norms about whether boundary-spanners should act competitively or collaboratively, for how long, as well as the degree of flexibility they have in negotiating the relationship and relevant issues (Kahn, Wolfe, Quinn, Snoek, & Rosenthal, 1964). Child and Faulkner's (1998) study of boundary-spanners suggests that organizational representatives may experience role tension as they work between two or more different organizations. Boundary-spanners may experience a "sense of separateness" (1998, p. 240) as a result of not knowing or understanding the organizational norms of their partners. In some instances, however, boundary-spanners' loyalties may expand to include the partnership as an entity in its own right to the "point where their loyalty 'rolls over' to the (partnership) ... and they find themselves representing the (partnership) as an entity within their own organization" (p. 913). In such instances, the boundary-spanner is becomes a member of both the host organization and the partnership.

Identity is a term that has received substantial attention from scholars for many decades (see for example, Albert & Whetten, 1985; Ashforth & Mael, 1989; Corley & Gioia, 2004; Erikson, 1970; Gioia, Shultz & Corley, 2000; Haslam, 2004; Ibarra, 1999; Tajfel, 1972, 1974; Tajfel & Turner, 1979). In the most basic sense, identity is who somebody knows her or himself to be. It is the answer to the age old question, "Who am I?" and is important because of its implications for how people perceive and behave in the world (Ibarra, 1999). For example, Erikson (1970) coined the term "identity crisis" to explain why people struggle and feel disoriented when their roles change. Erikson suggested that soldiers returning from war experienced an identity crisis when they traded their uniforms for civilian clothes and returned to the roles they held before their service. Writing on the identity of graduate students in their academic careers, Colbeck (2008) suggests that identity is important because it provides a "cognitive framework for interpreting new experiences" (p. 10). Identity, Colbeck suggests, affects the roles people take on, the relationships they develop, and the goals they set for themselves and others.

This paper explores three types of identity: Social, organizational, and partnership. In planning my research, I hypothesized that identity could be a useful concept in understanding faculty-community partnerships because who people believe themselves to be may significantly affect how they perceive partnerships, their roles in the partnerships, and the legitimacy of the partnerships. My exploration of identity in faculty-community partnerships is rooted in two areas of identity theory and research: Social identity—"Who am I?" (Tajfel & Turner, 1979)—and organizational identity—"Who are we as an organization?" (Albert & Whetten, 1985). According to social identity theory, one's identity is intimately tied to and affected by group membership (Haslam, 2004; Tajfel & Turner,

1979). According to organizational identity theory, the identity of an organization, those features that members believe are core, distinct, and enduring to the organization, influences how members perceive their roles and relationships with others inside and outside of the organization (Albert & Whetten, 1985; Clark, et al., 2008; Güney, 2004).

Social Identity

Social identity theory posits that individuals define themselves in terms of formal or informal group memberships (soccer fan, Penn State alumna), as well as in terms of their individual characteristics (tall/short, young/old, extroverted/introverted) and preferences (reading, traveling, cooking). Colbeck and Weaver's (2008) study of faculty members who were engaged in public scholarship supports a view of multiple simultaneous social identities: Faculty recognized multiple professional identities with regards to discipline, roles, and professions.

Social identity theory was first conceptualized by Tajfel and Turner (1979) in their studies of individual and group behavior. They found that persons randomly assigned to groups tend to see their own group members in a more favorable light than those in another group. The mere act of naming or assigning a person to a group had the effect of creating an in-group identity and fostering in-group favoritism (Tajfel, 1972). The perception of membership is a sufficient condition for individuals to display favoritism to members of their group over others outside of their group. However, researchers found that in-group identification does not depend on the existence of an out-group (such as a another team or competitor); it may exist independent of intergroup competition.

It appears that in-group membership has an emotional component (Tajfel, 1972) that may help persons to work well together (Ouwerkerk, Ellemers, & de Gilder, 1999). Turner, Hogg, Oakes, Reicher, and Wetherell (1987), in their review of empirical studies about social identity, suggest that shared in-group identities may improve work outcomes (increase productivity and performance, improve morale and job satisfaction), enhance group interactions (increase conformity to group norms, facilitate communication, improve perceptions of members as flexible, kind, and fair, and reduce hostility), and increase personal feelings of security and self-worth. Similarly, Haslam (2004) showed that communication is more effective among in-group members because of reduced uncertainty and increased feedback and coordination than is communication with those who do not share a social category.

Extending social identity theory into the realm of faculty-community partnerships for service-learning and other forms of community-engaged scholarship, one may view the partnership as an opportunity for the development of in-group affiliations and the positive attributes associated with membership in a defined group.

Organizational Identity

Organizational identity was first defined by Albert and Whetten (1985) to describe members' collective sense of "who we are as an organization." Whereas social identity is defined as how the individual perceives him/herself, organizational identity is defined by members' collective perceptions of those features that are central, distinctive, and enduring to the organization. Whetten (2006) emphasizes that the "core point here is that organizations are best known by their deepest commitments—what they repeatedly commit to be, through time and across circumstances" (p. 224).

The identity of an organizational entity is relevant to faculty-community partnerships because it is possible that they may develop into groups that share features similar to formal organizations. That is, partnerships may develop core, distinctive and enduring features that define the partnership through time and across changing circumstances. Organizational identity has been shown to focus members' attention and resources in a particular direction (Tajfel, 1972). Members of organizations use their organizations' identities as guides for directing their own behavior and resources (Pratt, 2000). An organization's identity may influence individuals' perceptions of what is most essential to the organization, and, by extension, what is most essential for their own work roles.

Defining and Characterizing Partnership Identity

A key purpose of the present study was to explore whether faculty-community partnerships are capable of developing organizational identities (herein referred to as Partnership Identity), and if so, to define the core characteristics of Partnership Identity. This study followed a multiple case study approach (Eisenhardt, 1989; Yin, 2003), and involved intensive data collection from members of five campus-community partnerships. Case studies are appropriate to answer "how" or "why" questions in naturalistic settings and when the focus is on a contemporary phenomenon within some real-life context (Yin, 2003). Multiple-case sampling strengthens the precision, validity, and confidence in findings because it allows for comparisons across similar and dissimilar cases (Miles & Huberman, 1994). Findings from small samples may be transferable to other partnerships

(Lincoln & Guba, 1985), illuminating key aspects of partnership identity. Purposive samples permit the researcher to select participants based on the qualities that may be relevant to answering the research question. The aim of the present study was to identify core characteristics of five campus-community partnerships in order to determine the extent to which each had achieved a Partnership Identity.

METHOD

Research Participants

The unit of analysis for this study is service-learning partnerships between faculty and community boundary-spanners. The study included five partnerships, two from a large, public land-grant university and three from a small liberal arts college. I sampled partnerships that (1) were currently ongoing, (2) had lasted 1 or more years, and (3) consisted of faculty members and community agents who worked together to facilitate service-learning opportunities for college and university students.

I studied on-going partnerships to gain a sense of how faculty and community members experienced the partnership while they were actively involved in partnership-related activities, such as providing service-learning experiences. I sampled partnerships that had been in existence for 1 or more years in order to explore partnerships that are relatively long lasting. Selection of partnerships based on longevity of the partnership follows in the tradition of Lawrence and Lorsch (1967) and Dorado and Giles (2004). While recognizing that financial limitations may limit the longevity of partnerships (Bringle & Hatcher, 2002), a partnership that has lasted for more than 1 year may be likely to have sufficiently met certain conditions and expectations of each of the parties involved. Each of the partnerships I studied included at least one tenure-line faculty member, but may also have included staff and graduate students who served boundary-spanning roles on behalf of the partnership. Community teams included one or more employees or volunteers from a not-for-profit organization.

Exhibit 4.1 provides an overview of the partners' pseudonyms, employers, job titles, and partnership acronyms for each of the five partnerships. The Township Energy Partnership (herein referred to as the Energy Partnership) involved two university members, two township members, and undergraduate students enrolled in a 300-level geography course on greenhouse gas emissions. At the time of the study, the partnership was in the third semester of a four-semester project in which students identified and measured local sources of greenhouse gas emissions and developed a proposal for the reduction of the township's energy use. The university

**Exhibit 4.1.   Partnership Names,
Members' Job Titles, and Their Employers**

Partnership	Partner	Employer
Energy	Geography professor	Eastern State University
	Senior research associate	Eastern State University
	Manager of public works	Shafer Township
	Elected councilperson	Shafer Township
Immigration	Geography professor & institute director	Wilken College
	Director of adult education	City Schools
Building	Engineering professor	Eastern State University
	Architecture professor	Eastern State University
	Landscape architecture professor	Eastern State University
	President	Red Clay Tribal College
	Vice president & facilities director	Red Clay Tribal College
Tax credit	Economics professor	Wilken College
	Executive director	United Way of Umpachene
	Director, financial fitness	Opportunities for Umpachene
	Administrative assistant & tax credit partnership coordinator	Opportunities for Umpachene
	Finance & office manager	Cooperative Extension Services
Tax assistance	Economics professor	Wilken College
	Director of administrative services	Department of Social Services
	Manager of family & youth services	Community Action Program
Acronym or Pseudonym		
ESU	Eastern State University	
GU	Grasslands University	
RCTC	Red Clay Tribal College	
WC	Wilken College	

partners included a senior research associate and a geography professor who co-taught the course, and the township partners included the manager of public works and an elected councilperson.

The Tribal College Building Initiative (herein referred to as the Building Partnership) involved, primarily, two professors from Eastern State University (ESU), one professor from Grasslands University (GU), two senior level administrators at Red Clay Tribal College (RCTC), and undergraduate and graduate students from ESU and GU enrolled in architecture, engineering, and landscape architecture courses. Each summer for 6 years, students traveled to the Native American reservation on which RCTC was located to construct buildings from the sustainable designs and materials developed during the fall and spring semesters. Students and faculty partners camped on the reservation's land for approximately three weeks each semester as they worked to complete the construction projects.

The Volunteer Income Tax Assistance Partnership (herein referred to as the Tax Assistance Partnership) involved one economics professor, two staff members of nonprofit agencies, and undergraduate students at Wilken College (WC) who provided tax assistance to low-income families through an anti-poverty program developed by the Internal Revenue Service (IRS). Although most students involved in the Tax Assistance program were or had been enrolled in the economics course taught by the faculty partner, their service to the Tax Assistance program was not credit-bearing. The partnership was initially developed by another economics professor and a director of a nonprofit agency who were no longer directly involved in the partnership at the time of this study.

The economics professor who was involved with the Tax Assistance Program at the time of the study also was involved with the Earned Income Tax Credit Partnership (herein referred to as the Tax Credit Partnership). The Tax Credit Partnership was similar to the Tax Assistance Partnership in its purpose and connection to the IRS, but was located in an adjacent county and involved approximately six nonprofit agencies. WC students provided tax assistance to low income families but did not receive academic credit for their service.

The Immigrant and Refugee Partnership (herein referred to as the Immigration Partnership) included only two partners: A geography professor and the director of adult education at City School who supervised education programs for immigrants and refugees. The partnership was initiated by the geography professor nearly a decade before this study with the intent of providing students at WC with opportunities to learn about and serve the refugee and immigrant community. Over the years, the professor and director developed service-learning and internship opportunities for dozens of WC students including ESL (English as a Second Language) tutoring, portrait projects, facilitating focus groups to evaluate programs, and assisting administrative staff.

Data Collection

The data collection strategies used in this study included interviews with faculty and community partners, observations of partners' utterances and interactions, and analyses of documents. The interview protocol included questions about how partners experienced and perceived the partnership. Because this project was part of a larger study that explored the factors that may affect the longevity of partnerships, I also asked questions about participants' social identities, the organizational identities of partners' employing organizations, and questions about the content and style of conversations between partners.

To discover the presence and character of the partnerships' identities beyond the interviews with its members, when possible, I observed partnerships at the times when the partnership was active. This included times during which the community representatives were on campus talking to and working with students, as well as during meetings in which faculty and community partners planned their activities. During these occasions, I took field notes, paying particular attention to how and what partners negotiated, as well as to the words partners used to describe themselves, each other, their interpersonal relationships with each other, and their partnership. All interviews were transcribed verbatim and entered into NVivo, a qualitative data software program to identify themes according to the interview guide questions and topics.

Data Analysis

Data from the interviews, observations, and documents were analyzed to begin to develop theory about faculty-community partnerships from the five case studies. Although I used conceptions of organizational identity to guide my exploration of Partnership Identity, I sought to understand how partners' descriptions of the partnership may have informed the key components of partnership identity. Data analysis included both within- and cross-case analysis (Eisenhardt, 1989) of partnerships. Within-case analysis was used to explore how partners experienced and perceived the partnership. Cross-case analyses explored similarities and differences between the partnerships.

RESULTS

Defining the Characteristics of a Partnership Identity

Partnership Identity is defined in this study as how faculty and community partners perceive "who we are" as a partnership entity. Some partnerships did not extend beyond partners' interpersonal relationships with each other, or beyond the temporary cooperative relationship required to complete the project, and therefore, were not categorized as having established a Partnership Identity.

Partnerships that developed Partnership Identities shared four characteristics:

1. Partners held unified beliefs regarding that which was core to the mission of the partnership;
2. Partners self-categorized themselves as members of a distinctive entity;
3. Partners had developed organizational structures to facilitate the work of the partnership; and
4. Partners believed the partnership would endure in the face of changing partners or resources.

Three of the five partnerships (Building, Tax Assistance and Tax Credit) exhibited all four characteristics, as shown in Exhibit 4.2. Neither the Immigration Partnership nor the Energy Partnership exhibited all of these characteristics. Below, I describe these characteristics in more detail and provide evidence of each as seen in interviews and observations.

Unified Missions

In partnerships with strong Partnership Identities, partners embraced one or a unified set of core reasons for the partnership's existence—why they were working together. I labeled partnerships as having unified missions if faculty and community partners articulated the same missions or purpose. For example, in response to my questions, partners with unified

**Exhibit 4.2.   Key Characteristics
of Partnership Identity Shown by Participants**

Partnership Identity (Key Characteristics)	Energy Partnership	Immigration Partnership	Building Partnership	Tax Credit Partnership	Tax Assistance Partnership
Unified missions		X	X	X	X
Membership in a distinctive entity			X	X	X
Organizational structures			X	X	X
Expectation to endure			X	X	X

missions spoke both of their primary purpose and their partners' primary purpose as justifications for why they worked together.

In the Immigration Partnership, the faculty and community partner embraced each other's missions and had a unified vision for the partnership. Both wanted to enhance WC students' education and the adult education program for refugees. In the faculty partner's words, they even "contested" over whose mission should guide their decisions about projects that students could pursue through the program.

I concluded that the Building Partnership had a unified mission. Faculty and community partners mentioned two core reasons as comprising the mission of the Building Partnership; (1) to provide educational opportunities for students enrolled in the Building Partnership-affiliated courses, and (2) to improve the physical infrastructure of RCTC's campus as a common good for the Tribal community. Faculty and community partners spoke about the importance of hands-on experiences for students' learning, as well as the importance of addressing the structural needs of the tribal college and community. One community partner suggested that partners' individual missions had evolved into one holistic mission. He said,

> as the partnership has evolved, I'd have to say they're shared goals.... I think the goals initially were pretty institutionally driven for each institution. I think that has evolved. I think there is more of a shared goal of doing these projects benefiting all of us, not just working in the facility to get training for [ESU and GU students]. I see it more as a single purpose in mind for all of us. That's how I see it.

Another community partner also described both purposes as being core to the partnership. In response to my asking, "How would you describe what the partnership is about, its essence?" he said "getting something mutual out of it. Sort of like a symbiotic relationship where we exist for each other." Later in the interview he suggested that he and his partners had "found a commonality of purpose" in meeting "the needs of the [Tribal] community" and the "educational value" of the project for undergrads involved in the design-build project. Although educating college students was not their initial reason for becoming involved in the Building Partnership, the community partners viewed the partnership as being about both education and meeting community needs.

In the Tax Credit and Tax Assistance partnerships, the faculty and community partners spoke about a single purpose, to improve the financial future of low-income families by providing assistance with tax returns. The faculty member spoke of how her perspective of the partnerships' purposes shifted as a result of her experience. The learning experience for her students was part of the reason she decided to become involved in the partnership. The faculty member described the economic assistance the partnership provided to low-income individuals and families as the abiding reason for her continued involvement. Hence, the faculty member's view of the mission was almost solely focused on serving low-income community members. The community partner noted that she had not before thought explicitly about the purpose of the partnership, but that "at its basic level, the main purpose is to have people file their income taxes and get returns and to have that resource given to them for free in an ethical, friendly and professional manner." Likewise, another community partner told me, "our mission [is] to try to help the low-income so they [don't] have to search out places ... that charge two [to] five hundred dollars to get their taxes done."

Partners with unified missions in the Immigration, Building, Tax Credit, Tax Assistance partnerships often spoke of having their own reasons for entering the partnership, but also spoke of having come to embrace their partners' objectives as essential justifications why they remained involved. Although they initially embraced separate individual missions, the partners voiced a unified vision of the partnership.

In contrast, faculty and community partners in the Energy Partnership emphasized different priorities in their articulations of the partnership's mission. In response to my question, "What is the purpose of the partnership?" one faculty partner admitted, "[w]e never really talked about that sort of thing." When I asked [a community partner] whether the partnership had developed a shared vision or mission, she told me "[We] (community partners) feel the constraints and needs of our bureaucracy, whereas [the faculty partners], I think, feel the push of wanting to get this going for their students." Likewise, [another community partner] discussed his interests in developing an energy management plan, but did not talk about student learning as key to the mission of the partnership. University partners spoke about the partnership primarily from the perspective of educators. One faculty partner told me that in his first meeting with the community partners, he told them, "from our point of view, this was a service-learning project for our students. If it had no value [to the Township], then it was their decision. We were not getting into the planning process." Likewise the other faculty partner told me that although he "want[ed] to do environmental good" he was "coming at it from an educator's point of view. I want to see what I can do for my students."

Membership in a Distinctive Entity

Albert and Whetten (1985) suggest that organizational members assign importance to the ability to distinguish one's organization from others—to stand apart from others in a meaningful way, such as through reputation or types of services and products. However, the present study showed that faculty-community partnerships were not characterized by comparisons (one partnership from another), but rather by cohesiveness (feeling a part of an identifiable entity). Partnerships that had Partnership Identities were characterized by partners' articulation of themselves and their partners as members of a single team. They spoke of their work as contributing to the collective work of the partnership, rather than solely serving their own interests or those of their institutions. Therefore, my definition of distinctive as a characteristic of Partnership Identity is tied to whether members categorize themselves and their partners as part of an interdependent team, not how they categorize themselves as different from other partnerships.

All partners in the Building Partnership characterized themselves as members of a team. One community partner was very explicit about his perceptions that he and his partners were members of a partnership. He said, "I talk in terms of partnerships and I talk about these projects." Later he told me, "I think there is a shared identity ... there is equality in [the building Partnership]." Another community partner also told me that he told others "we're in a partnership" with the faculty partners.

Faculty and community members of the Energy Partnership did not speak of themselves as members of a partnership entity. Instead, they appeared to view themselves and their partners as members of a temporary work group (Robbins & Judge, 2007). Unlike a team in which members' individual contributions are integral to the functioning and effectiveness of all involved, a work group consists of persons who share information for the sole purpose of developing or advancing progress on a specific project. Partners in the Energy Partnership tended to discuss serving their own interests or needs, rather than serving the partnership.

Although one community partner described the Energy Partnership as a "partnership," she spoke as though the faculty and community partners were on different teams that were working together to meet their respective interests. She talked about the partners being open to working with each other, though from different "sides of the street." The other community partner described working with the faculty partners as a "good working relationship" and included it as one of many relationships he had with ESU employees (e.g., faculty members, researchers, director of facilities). I asked him, "How do you talk about your relationship? Do you call it a partnership, a collaboration, a project?" He responded, "collaboration or project would be a better" way to describe the relationship rather than a partnership.

One faculty member told me,

> I would characterize it as loose; the partnership as loose (pause)… we have a jointly perceived goal in general outline…. They are trying to take advantage of what we have to offer, which is person power, student power, some knowledge, and they can pick our brains.

The other faculty member described the partnership as "a very good relationship," but one in which "they see it as the university providing a free service and we're doing it willingly, and gratefully even, and they're grateful for us helping them out."

I also labeled the Immigration Partnership as not having a distinct group identity because the faculty and community partner each expressly stated that the relationship between "her" and "me." As noted above, the partners believed they had an interpersonal relationship—not a separate group to which they belonged.

Organizational Structures

Partnerships with Partnership Identities were characterized by the presence of formal and informal structures that coordinated partners' work and established partners' roles and responsibilities within the partnership. The Building and Tax Credit partnerships developed formal social structures in which social positions and relationships were explicitly specified and were defined independently of partners' personal characteristics and relations of persons occupying the positions (Scott, 2003). For example, at the Tax Credit Partnership meeting I observed, partners discussed the positions of chair, secretary, and treasurer. Partners nominated one another and agreed on persons to fill each of the positions. In the Tax Assistance partnership, each partner had a task identity (Hackman & Oldham, 1976), involving identifiable pieces of work, rather than a position title. For example, in the Building Partnership, one faculty member was responsible for writing and submitting grants and supervising construction, another faculty member was responsible for designing and constructing the landscape, and two RCTC representatives were responsible for coordinating logistics at the tribal college. In the Tax Assistance Partnership, the partners each spoke of their specific tasks: A community partner was responsible for coordinating the training of volunteers and supervising and filing tax returns; a second community partner was responsible for scheduling clients' appointments, publicizing partnership services to potential clients, and writing grants to support the work of the partnership; while the faculty member was responsible for coordinating students and providing computers and printers for the sites. Blau and Scott (1962) write that "the conception of a structure or system implies that the component units stand in some relation to one another and, as the popular expression 'The whole is greater than the sum of its parts' suggests, that the relation between units add new elements to the situation" (p. 206). In groups with Partnership Identities, partners had developed task identities, whether formally recognized in the form of titles or informally recognized in the form of assuming responsibility for whole tasks.

The three groups with Partnership Identities had accounting systems to manage grant monies and support staff that coordinated and facilitated the partnership work. In each case, at least one partner used the financial services department of their employing institution to deposit, manage, and allocate money on behalf of the partnership, and at least one person was paid a wage or stipend for specific work with the partnership. In the Building Partnership, a private contractor, graduate students, and summer support staff were hired on grants that funded the partnership. In the Tax Assistance Partnership, a community partner and two student leaders were paid stipends for their work for the partnership. In the Tax Credit, a community partner received a salary for her part-time work coordinating clients' schedules for each of the sites.

The Energy and Immigration Partnerships did not contain organizational structures to fund, support, or coordinate the partnership's activities. Partners did not have positions, either formally or informally, within the partnership that were separate from their roles as members of their employing institutions. For example, the councilperson's position in the Energy Partnership was tied to her governmental position. Her own advocacy and political interests defined her role in the partnership. The two members of the Immigration Partnership did not have systems to support their work. They worked with each other and did not create systems that could allow others to facilitate or coordinate the work of the partnership.

Expectations That the Partnership Will Endure

Partnerships with Identities were characterized by partners' expectations that the partnership could and would continue despite changes in persons and resources. These partners felt that even if certain members were no longer involved, the partnership would continue—partners would find a way to sustain it. I found that partners who perceived a shared sense of "we" also sensed that the partnership itself would continue. Three partnerships (Building, Tax Credit, Tax Assistance) were characterized as expected to endure despite (potential) changes in their memberships.

One community partner felt quite certain that the Building Partnership would continue; he told me "the partnership is not determined by the individuals within the partnership. You can change the faces of the players in the partnership, and hopefully, the partnership will continue." Likewise, each of the other community and faculty partners explained that they were developing ways to remain connected after there was no longer any space left to build on RCTC's campus. They discussed developing a summer workshop program in which ESU students provided workshops on how to build and maintain sustainable homes. Although the activities of the partnership might change, partners were committed to continuing to find ways to extend and expand their work together. As one faculty partner put it

> I know on paper, it's all about sustainable housing technologies, but I don't think that's what it's about. I think it's the commitment to the partnership. I think that's why [faculty member] has been here for so long as a designer; it's not because there are a lot of new techniques he gets to try out as a sustainable designer. It's more because he gets to be a part of this organization.... You know, so it's this commitment to *this* partnership [faculty partner's emphasis] ... we could do [these projects near ESU]. There are other underserved areas.

Community and faculty partners believed they would continue to find ways of working together within the context of the partnership, even if they had to find new types of projects on which to collaborate.

Partners in the Tax Assistance Partnership agreed that the partnership would endure changes in persons, primarily because it already had. In response to my question about whether the partnership was an entity that was capable of sustaining itself over time and through different iterations of people, one community partner responded,

> I think so. I mean, right now this partnership has been going on for 6 years and it just seems to get stronger. I think that it had a lot to do with everybody involved, but [faculty member] left and [another faculty member] filled right in. [The IRS representative] has stayed in it, and [community partner] left for a little and then came right back into it. It just seems to stand on its own and get stronger.

The faculty partner also believed that "someone" at WC would step in to facilitate students' involvement in the program. Although she did not indicate who would replace her, should she leave, she had a sense that she could find someone who would.

Partnerships without identities were characterized by partners' expectations that the partnership would not continue past the current project or if partners left the partnership. Partners in the Energy and Immigration partnerships did not expect the partnership to endure their leaving of the project and were not committed to sustaining the partnership for its own sake.

Although partners in Energy Partnership acknowledged that they could find additional projects to benefit each other, they did not expect the partnership to continue beyond the 2-year commitment. One faculty partner noted, "This partnership was designed for a finite mission, to cover four [semesters]." The other faculty partner told me,

> At the end of the next spring semester, we should be able to turn over things to the [Township] so that they really have a great solid foundation to get their mitigation process going. Of course, we'll be looking over their shoulder and keeping in contact with them, but we're not going to work on it anymore. The idea is to move onto other entities, like maybe the townships [near Shafer Township].

The faculty partners discussed wanting to find other townships throughout the region to serve as case studies for future class projects. One faculty partner talked about "partnering" with other municipalities "to do ... inventor[ies]" and the potential of working with an intergovernmental group "to grow an inventory and plan to cover the whole region."

The faculty partner in the Immigration Partnership did not believe her service-learning partnership with the community partner would continue if she were to stop participating. "It is really so contained in the form of *my* work up there and nobody else's" (faculty partner's emphasis). The partners did not feel that they had a partnership that needed to be preserved or extended to new areas. The faculty partner worked with her community partner to identify projects only when she was teaching a course in which she wanted to integrate service-learning experiences, which was sometimes only once a year. They may not have felt it necessary that their partnership continue because the faculty partner maintained what she called "a partnership" with the Center for Immigrants and Refugees, the employer of the community partner when their partnership began and where many of the educational and cultural programs were held. She developed relationships with several staff members at the center, including the executive director, and served on the board of directors. The fate of her service-learning partnership with that particular community partner, therefore, affected neither her friendship with the partner nor her other roles or relationships in the center. In both the Energy and Immigration partnerships, it was unlikely that any of the partners' roles could or would be filled if they left the partnership because their roles were specifically tied to particular professional interests and responsibilities, not to positions established within the partnership.

Nurture Norms

The development of nurture norms, informal but clear expectations of how partners were to behave as members of the partnership, may be an outcome of Partnership Identity development. To explore norms in partnerships, I observed partner's interactions and analyzed participants' interview transcripts for comments about how they perceived that they or others should act toward others within the partnership. I asked participants, "If you were introducing a newcomer to the project, what are some of the implicit rules or guidelines that you would tell them to follow?" Borrowing from Dorado and Giles' (2004) definition of nurturing behaviors between faculty and community partners, I define a nurture norm as the expectation that partners will engage in conversations and activities that can be described using the verbs *nurture, cultivate, support, encourage, cherish, celebrate, develop, care for, foster,* and related synonyms.

I found that all the partnerships with Partnership Identities exhibited norms about nurturing the relationship, whereas only one of the two partnerships without Partnership Identities did. The Building, Immigration, Tax Credit, and Tax Assistance partnerships were characterized by nurture norms. For example, nurture norms were exhibited in the Building Partnership by faculty and community partners visiting each other throughout the year, despite the considerable distance between campuses. Faculty partners spoke about the importance of meeting face-to-face with their community partners to discuss aspects of the projects and students' learning, but perhaps, more importantly to foster open communication and trust. In monthly meetings, members of the Tax Assistance Partnerships asked about each other's families and vacations. Several members often shared meals together after the meetings and offered to help each other with their responsibilities and activities related to the partnership.

DISCUSSION

The definition of Partnership Identity presented in this chapter contributes a working definition that suggests key components of a group identity that may be shared by faculty and community partners. The definition looks beyond interpersonal relationships, which though important, are not sufficient for developing a lasting sense of "who we are" as an organization-like entity. Partnerships in the service-learning and community engagement literature are frequently conceptualized and studied as relationships between individuals. For example, Bringle and Hatcher (2002) use psychological theories of friendships and romantic relationships to explain service-learning partnership development and their characteristics in recognition that partnerships tend to be individualistic and commonly arise from one-on-one relationships.

The exploration of Partnership Identity contributes to a growing number of studies that use partnerships as the unit of analysis. Several reports and guidebooks for partnerships suggest the practice of developing an identity for the partnership, but the term is not clarified and it remains to the reader to infer what identity means. A possible reason for the lack of explication of identity as it pertains to partnerships may be the difficulty of "properly accounting for the subjective ('I') frame of reference" (Whetten, 2006, p. 229). Specifically, who speaks for the partnership? Who gets to specify its identity, those features that are central, distinctive, and enduring?

A number of writers have been concerned with factors influencing the development of partnerships and partnership identities. Giddens' (1984) theory of structuration suggests that partnerships are cognitive and socially developed structures. That is, partnerships are not brought into existence at the moment that formal procedures, positions, and resources are set in place, but rather, when members perceive the presence of a partnership. Therefore, partnerships may be brought into existence through members' assumptions and adoptions of rules (expectations) and resources, as well as by formal organizational structures as partners collectively make sense of their perceived reality, and in so doing, establish seemingly externally imposed sociocognitive and behavioral norms.

Interactions between faculty and community partners may serve as the medium through which partners develop a Partnership Identity. Beech and Huxham (2003) suggest that partners may progress through interlocking cycles in which collaborators view each other as partners and subsequently treat each other as partners. The cycle of forming a Partnership Identity may begin, for example, when Person X identifies herself as a member of the partnership. Person X, through conversations with Person Y (the individual with whom Person X is collaborating), may indicate the belief that she is a member of the partnership. If Partner Y interprets Partners X's identity as a member of the partnership, then Partner Y is likely to treat Partner X as a member. Ultimately, partners' individual perceptions of a shared Partnership Identity will become crystallized as partners reinforce their notions of each other as members of the same group through their conversations and interactions. Beech and Huxham's model of cyclical identity formation highlights the significance of one's perceptions of self and others in how she or he communicates with others.

Consistent with the emphasis on the importance of interaction, Dorado and Giles (2004) found that partnerships in the first few semesters tended to spend a great deal of time getting to know one another: Brainstorming ideas, discussing goals or needs, and gathering information about each other, in general. The authors found that these behaviors were dominant in early stages of partnering, when partners were learning about each other and identifying ways to work together, but they also occurred throughout the lives of some partnerships. Beech and Huxham's (2003), as well as Hardy, Lawrence, and Grant's (2005) theories about perception and communication in collaborations, suggest that faculty and community partners are not only communicating about procedures, but also about identities. How faculty and community partners interact is part of the process whereby partners develop a Partnership Identity.

Enos and Morton (2003) observe that it is difficult to predict how partnerships will develop—whether they will be transactional or transformative. In some cases, transformative relationships may result in partners developing a shared sense of "we" at an organizational partnership level. Partners' ability and willingness to transform their ways of thinking about roles, partnerships, and the organizations they represent may stem from a cognitive shift that takes place when partners see themselves and their partners as members of a distinct partnership, rather than as individuals, or, as was the case in the Energy Partnership, as colleagues working from "different sides of the street."

Nurture norms appear to be an important outcome of Partnership Identity. This finding is consistent with findings from social identity research that persons who participate in groups tend to see their own group members in a more favorable light than others. They are more likely to favor other group members, feel emotionally attached to the welfare of group members and the outcomes of the group, work more efficiently, communicate better, and feel a greater sense of morale and job satisfaction with members of their group. Partners in Partnerships with Identity held implicit expectations that they should nurture the partnership beyond that which was required to complete specific tasks. Palmero, McGranaghan and Travers (2006) suggest that in their very first meeting together, partners should establish "operating norms," a set of ground rules that partners jointly develop to "get the partnership off to a good start" (section 3.5). Examples of operating norms provided by the authors include mutual respect, listening to one another, agreeing to disagree, and decisions making by consensus. That partners should explicitly discuss expectations regarding communication, processes, and outcomes is a common theme that runs through nearly every study of or guidebook for inter organizational collaboration (Mattessich, Murray-Close, & Monsey,

2001). Operating norms not only help to avoid misunderstandings, but also help to increase the efficiency and effectiveness of interorganizational partnerships because partners have a sense of each others' interests, preferences, and desires.

Creating new organizational structures can be an important and essential activity developing interinstitutional partnerships. In their review of organizational structures that facilitated the development and functioning of a community partnership for health, Meservey and Richards (1996) describe the creation of formal structures that "that have achieved some apparent influence and permanency" and which have also "established a collective sense of purpose beyond the immediate interests of the partner" (p. 114). The authors suggest that the organizational structures, such as clearly defined roles and responsibilities, and access to shared resources, helped provide autonomy for the partnership and guided partners' attentions and actions toward developing the vision and goals of the partnership, rather than reverting back to the separate though complementary interests of their particular institutions, disciplines, or constituencies.

In several of the partnerships I studied, however, partners did not necessarily talk about their expectations for how the partnership would be "operated," but rather, had developed implicitly understood expectations. Four of the five partnerships (Building, Tax Credit, Tax Assistance, Immigration) established nurture norms, or implicit expectations that partners would treat one another in ways that fostered their relationship. Implicit norms may influence partners' actions even more than explicit ground rules that are established at the start of the relationship, because they are often assumed or taken for granted (Hogg & Abrams, 1988). That is, partners enact norms without consciously being aware that they are following any particular rules for behavior. In contrast to the partnerships with nurture norms (Building, Tax Credit, Tax Assistant partnerships), Energy Partnership faculty and community partners did not contact or see each other beyond that which was required to facilitate the project. They appreciated one another's work, but did not seek to further develop the relationship. The partners maintained separate responsibilities (and identities)—the community partners as service providers and the faculty partners as educators.

The concept of Partnership Identity, and its presumed value or benefit, follows in the tradition of research that explores the role of individuals' and organizations' identities in partnership effectiveness (Clark et al., 2008; Gray, 1989; Güney, 2004; Hardy et al., 2005;). According to this approach, partners initially draw on the identities of the organizations they represent to establish whether they will partner, but must come to a new and shared agreement on the identity of their partnership if the collaborative effort is to be successful. By extension, the success of faculty-community partnerships may depend on boundary-spanners' abilities to relinquish existing ways of thinking of themselves as members of separate organizational entities and to forge, instead, new consensually shared ways of making sense of the partnership's identity.

Partnership Identity may help partners make sense of what it means to be partners with each other. Clark et al.'s (2008) study of transitional identity formation in organizational mergers between hospitals suggests the importance of sociocognitive features in facilitating or inhibiting the integration of partners' visions for the organization. Transitional identity is the "interim sense" of how partners perceive what the host organizations "are becoming" (p. 19) as they merge together. In their study, the construction of a temporary identity helped members to overcome a long history of distrust and disagreements because it provided the "freedom" (p. 21) for members to cognitively detach themselves from a previous organizational identity and to realign themselves as members of a new organization. Future research should study the process or stages by which Partnership Identity is formed, as well as whether and how members of partnerships develop tentative understandings of "who we are as a partnership." Such studies will further the understanding of how and when various characteristics of Partnership Identity are established.

Longevity or the expectation to endure past the present project appears to be associated with partners sharing a Partnership Identity. Persons who share an in-group identity are likely to feel emotional ties toward other members of their group, or at the very least, feel that they share some responsibility for the welfare of the group. In my study, I found that partners who categorized themselves and their partners as "we" also were committed to the success and longevity of the partnerships. Clark et al. (2008) found that the "erosion of two merging organizations' former identities and the emergence of a distinct and shared identity was crucial" (p.1) to the success of the merger they studied. The authors suggest that language may have played an important role in how partners perceived each other as part of the same or separate team or organization. Future research with larger samples of partnerships should explore the connection between the partnership being a distinct entity and partners' feelings of commitment to continuation of the partnership.

Partnerships that were expected to endure changes in partner involvement were also those that established organizational structures. The presence of organizational structures may be important for helping newcomers to the partnership understand how they can join the partnership, what roles need to be filled or developed. Clear organizational structures allow newcomers to assess the partnership and to determine whether and how they can become involved. The extent to which interorganizational structures are created and sustained by partners may significantly affect the long-term sustainability of such voluntary, joint initiatives, as well as their effectiveness (Salk & Shenkar, 2001). Therefore, faculty and community partners who discuss ways to structure the partnership so that it may incorporate others may be able to sustain the loss of a partner or adopt partners into the partnership.

IMPLICATIONS AND FUTURE RESEARCH

This chapter provides a definition of Partnership Identity, but additional research is necessary to clarify and deepen understanding of the factors that contribute to the development of Partnership Identity, as well as the benefits of Partnership Identity. For example, what is the role of communication? Clark et al. (2008), Hardy et al. (2005), and Huxham and Vangen (2005) suggest that how partners interact, and particularly their style of communication (cooperative as opposed to collaborative), may be linked to whether partners from different groups view themselves as part of a collective entity. In particular, Hardy et al. (2005) suggest that collaborative styles of talk may be important in the development of a shared group identity. Future research should address whether partnerships in which most faculty and community partners follow a truly collaborative style of communication are more likely to develop a Partnership Identity than partners who simply cooperate and share information.

This study portrayed five partnerships during a brief moment in time. Therefore, it was not possible to see how the partnerships evolved and the factors that affected whether they developed a Partnership Identity. A longitudinal study would greatly inform scholars and practitioners understanding of the crucial processes and patterns involved in establishing effective and enduring service-learning partnerships. For example, a longitudinal study of multiple partnerships may help us understand the extent to which partnerships should be nurtured and what types of nurturing activities are most effective in fostering the partnership. When is it most important to nurture the partnership and how do the types of nurturing activities change over the course of the partnership?

Finally, it is important to explore partnership identity as an independent variable: What effect does Partnership Identity have on the effectiveness, success, or longevity of the partnership for the students, faculty and community members involved? Do partnerships that have Identities achieve their goals more effectively or more efficiently than those that do not have Identities? I did not find obvious differences between partnerships with and without Partnership Identities in the extent to which each facilitated meaningful service to the community partners, student learning, and the scholarly development of faculty partners. The partners in the Energy and Immigration partnerships appear to have been successful in enhanced students' learning and helping the community agencies serve their missions—yet neither developed Partnership Identities. The absence of a Partnership Identity, therefore, did not appear to affect the success of the programs. This finding is significant, in large part, because it was unexpected: Partners who maintained transactional relationships were as successful as those partners who developed transformational partnerships in providing a useful service to the community partner, educating students through service-learning, and enhancing the faculty members' scholarship. This finding highlights (perhaps wrongly held) assumptions that those partnerships that transcend individual interests to develop shared missions, organizational structures, and indeed, identities, are preferable to exchange-based and utilitarian partnerships that focus almost exclusively on the project and not the partnership. Further study and discussion of the differences between transactional and transformative partnerships with regards to successful outcomes is needed, especially if transformative partnerships are to be held up as the gold standard of service-learning partnerships. Future research should rigorously assess the outcomes that are associated with partnerships having Identities, and in particular, seek to understand what types of partnerships are most effective for which types of outcomes.

ACKNOWLEDGMENTS

The author gratefully acknowledges the contributions of those who have influenced her approach and explorations of Partnership Identity: Most especially Carol Colbeck, as dissertation advisor, Lisa Lattuca, Jeremy Cohen, and Dennis Gioia as teachers and dissertation committee members, and each participant who shared her/his experience and perspective to inform this study. The author also wishes to thank the editors of this volume for their thoughtful and careful review and editing of this chapter.

REFERENCES

Abes, E. S., Jackson, G., & Jones, S. R. (2002). Factors that motivate and deter faculty use of service-learning. *Michigan Journal of Community Service Learning, 9*(1), 5-17.

Albert, S., & Whetton, D. A. (1985). Organizational identity. In L. L. Cummings & B. M. Staws (Eds.), *Research in organizational behavior* (Vol. 7, pp. 263-295). Greenwich, CT: JAI Press.

Ashforth, B. E., & Mael, F. E. (1989). Social identity theory and the organization. *Academy Management Review, 14*, 20-39.

Beech, N., & Huxham, C. (2003). Cycles of identity formation in collaboration. *International Studies of Management and Organization, 33*(3), 28-52.

Blau, P., & Scott, W. R. 1962. *Formal organizations*. San Francisco: Chandler.

Bringle, R. G., & Hatcher, J. A. (2002). Campus-community partnerships: The terms of engagement. *Journal of Social Issues, 58*(3), 503-516.

Carriere, A. (2006, September). *Community engagement through partnerships*. Paper presented at the HEQC/JET Conference on Community Engagement in Higher Education, Cape Town, South Africa.

Child, J., & Faulkner, D. (1998). *Strategies of cooperation: Managing alliances, networks, and joint ventures*. Oxford, England: Oxford University Press.

Clark, S. M., Gioia, D. A., Ketchen, D., & Thomas, J. B. (2008). *Transitional identity as a facilitator of the merger process*. Unpublished manuscript, The Pennsylvania State University.

Colbeck, C. L. (2008). Professional identity development theory and doctoral education. *Educating Integrated Professionals: Theory and Practice on Preparation for the Professoriate. New Directions for Teaching and Learning, 113*, 9-16.

Colbeck, C. L., & Weaver, L. D. (2008). Faculty engagement in public scholarship: A motivation systems theory perspective. *Journal of Higher Education Outreach and Engagement, 12*(2), 7-32.

Corley, K. G., & Gioia, D. A. (2004). Identity, ambiguity and change in the wake of corporate spin-off. *Administrative Science Quarterly, 49*, 173-208.

Dorado, S., & Giles, D. E., Jr. (2004). Service-learning partnerships: Paths of Engagement. *Michigan Journal of Community Service Learning, 11*(1), 25-37.

Eisenhardt, K. M. (1989). Building theories from case study research. *Academy of Management Review, 14*(4), 532–550.

Enos, E., & Morton, K. (2003). Developing a theory and practice of campus-community partnerships. In B. Jacoby and Associates (Eds.), *Building partnerships for service-learning* (pp. 20-41). San Francisco: Jossey-Bass.

Erikson, E. H. (1970). Autobiographic notes on the identity crisis. *Daedalus, 99*(4), 730-759.

Giddens, A. (1984). *The constitution of society: Outline of the theory of structuration*. Cambridge, England: Polity Press.

Gioia, D. A., Schultz, M., & Corley, K. G. (2000). Organizational identity, image, and adaptive instability. *Academy of Management Review, 25*, 63-81.

Gray, B. (1989). *Collaborating: Finding common ground for multiparty problems*. San Francisco: Jossey-Bass.

Güney, S. (2004). *Organizational identity and sensemaking in collaborative development of technology: An ethnographic case study of building the box*. Unpublished doctoral dissertation, University of Texas at Austin.

Hackman, R. J., & Oldham, G. R. (1976). Motivation through the design of work: Test of a theory. *Organizational Behavior and Human Performance, 16*, 250-279.

Hardy, C., Lawrence, T. B., & Grant, D. (2005). Discourse and collaboration: The role of conversations and collective identity. *Academy of Management Review, 30*(1), 1-20.

Harkavy, I. (2003). Foreword. In B. Jacoby and Associates (Eds.), *Building partnerships for service-learning* (pp. xi-xv). San Francisco: Jossey-Bass.

Haslam, S.A. (2004). *Psychology in organizations: The social identity approach* (2nd ed.). Thousand Oaks: SAGE.

Hayes, E., & Cuban, S. (1997). Border of pedagogy: A critical framework for service-learning. *Michigan Journal of Community Service Learning, 4,* 72-80.

Hogg, M. A., & Abrams, D. (1988). *Social identifications: A social psychology of intergroup relations and group processes.* London: Routledge.

Huxham, C., & Vangen, S. (2005). *Managing to collaborate: The theory and practice of collaborative advantage.* New York: Routledge.

Ibarra, H. (1999). Provisional selves: Experimenting with image and identity in professional adaptation. *Administrative Science Quarterly, 44,* 764-791.

Kahn, R. L., Wolfe, D. M., Quinn, R. P., Snoek, J. D., & Rosenthal, R. A. (1964). *Organizational stress: Studies in role conflict and ambiguity.* New York: John Wiley & Sons.

Lawrence, P., & Lorsch, J. (1967). Differentiation and integration in complex organizations. *Administrative Science Quarterly 12,* 1-30.

Lincoln, Y., & Guba, E. (1985). *Naturalistic inquiry.* New York: Sage.

Mattessich, P. W., Murray-Close, M., & Monsey, B. R. (2001). *Collaboration: What makes it work* (2nd ed.). Saint Paul, MN: Amherst H. Wilder Foundation.

Meservey Maguire, P., & Richards, R. W. (1996). Creating new organizational structures. In R. W. Richards (Ed.) *Building partnerships: Educating health professionals for the communities they serve* (pp. 105-120). San Francisco: Jossey-Bass.

Miles, B. M., & Huberman, A. M. (1994). *Qualitative data analysis: An expanded sourcebook.* Thousand Oaks, CA: SAGE.

Noble, G., & Jones, R. (2006). The role of boundary-spanning managers in the establishment of public-private partnerships. *Public Administration, 84,*4, 891-917.

O'Meara, K. (2002). Uncovering the values in faculty evaluation of service as scholarship. *Journal of Higher Education, 26*(1), 57-80.

Ouwerkerk, J. W., Ellemers, N., & de Gilder, D. (1999). Group commitment and individual effort in experimental and organizational contexts. In N. Ellemers, R. Spears, & B. J. Doosje (Eds.), *Social identity: Context, commitment, content* (pp. 184-204). Oxford, England: Blackwell.

Palermo, A. G., McGranaghan, R., & Travers, R. (2006). Unit 3: Developing a CBPR Partnership—Creating the "glue." In The Examining Community-Institutional Partnerships for Prevention Research Group (Ed.), *Developing and sustaining community-based participatory research partnerships: A skill-building curriculum.* Retrieved April 23, 2007, from www.cbprcurriculum.info.

Park, S. H., & Ungson, G. R. (1997). The effect of national culture, organizational complementarity, and economic motivation on joint ventures. *The Academy of Management Journal, 40*(2), 279-307.

Pratt, M. G. (2000). The good, the bad, and the ambivalent: Managing identification among Amway distributors. *Administrative Science Quarterly, 45,* 456-493,

Robbins, S., & Judge, T. (2007). *Organizational behavior.* Upper Saddle River, NJ: Pearson/Prentice Hall.

Salk, J. E., & Shenkar, O. (2001). Social identities in an international joint venture: An exploratory case study. *Organizational Science, 12(2), 161-178.*

Sandy, M., & Holland, B. (2006). Different worlds and common ground: Community partner perspectives on campus-community partnerships. *Michigan Journal of Community Service Learning, 13*(1), 30-43.

Scott, W. R. (2003). *Organizations: Rational, natural, and open systems* (5th ed.). Upper Saddle River, NJ: Prentice Hall.

Sebring, R. H. (1977). The five-million dollar misunderstanding: A perspective on state government-university interorganizational conflicts. *Administrative Science Quarterly, 22*(3), 505-523.

Tajfel, H. (1972) Experiments in a vacuum. In J. Israel & H. Tajfel (Eds.), *The context of social psychology: A critical assessment* (pp. 69-121). London: Academic Press.

Tajfel, H. (1974). Social identity and intergroup behaviour. *Social Science Information, 13,* 65-93.

Tajfel, H., & Turner, J. C. (1979). An integrative theory of intergroup conflict. In W. G. Austin & S. Worshel (Eds.), *The social psychology of intergroup relations* (pp. 56-65). Monterey, CA: Brookes/Cole.

Turner, J. C., Hogg, M. A., Oakes, P. J., Reicher, S. D., & Wetherell, M. S. (1987). *Rediscovering the social group: A self-categorization theory.* New York: Basil Blackwell.

Whetten, D. A. (2006). Albert and Whetten revisited: Strengthening the concept of organizational identity. *Journal of Management Inquiry, 15*(3), 219-234.

Yin, R. K. (2003). *Case study research: Design and methods.* London: SAGE.

CHAPTER 5

TWO-DIMENSIONAL APPROACH FOR ASSESSING TRANSFORMATIVE CAMPUS/ COMMUNITY SERVICE- LEARNING PARTNERSHIPS

Jason T. Phillips and Cynthia V. L. Ward

ABSTRACT

Research on campus/community service-learning is often bounded by linear approaches that do not do justice to the complexity of the construct. This study addressed the issue by designing and testing a 2-dimensional instrument for assessing the transformational qualities of service-learning partnerships from the 2 perspectives: type and extent and from the 2 sides of the divide—campus and community.

INTRODUCTION

Because campus/community service-learning partnerships can help to revitalize communities, as well as campuses, the popularity of the community engagement movement continues to grow and to attract new advocates. Evidence of this growth can be gauged by interest in Campus Compact, the national organization dedicated to promoting service-learning, which has attracted more than 1,100 member colleges and universities (Campus Compact, 2009). To complement this expansion, research concerning campus/community partnerships, and the mutual benefits that can accrue to each as the result of partnering, needs to be more inclusive, more empirical, and more structured.

Campus/community service-learning partnerships differ greatly in the level of commitment of the partners and the depth of the engagement. Committed paths of engagement involve partners who value the service-learning partnership beyond individual projects and who are committed to protecting and extending the relationship (Dorado & Giles, 2004). Such commitment requires support at all levels of the academy (Plater, 2004); in addition, multilevel support enhances the possibility for institutionalization (Furco & Holland, 2004). When both leaders and other stakeholders are engaged in campus/community service-learning partnerships, institutions are more open to the possibility of transformation because of the continuous, dynamic exchange of ideas and opportunities (Enos & Morton, 2003). When exchange is present, the transformative power of partnerships is enhanced. However, little research has been done for the purpose of determining whether and, if so, how transformation occurs for campuses and communities engaged as partners in service-learning.

During most of the twentieth century, colleges and universities tended to adopt an attitude of privilege in relation to their surrounding communities by interacting, if at all, from the position of detached experts applying knowledge to needy clients. The twenty-first century has brought a shift from the culture of detached privilege to one in which colleges and universities are increasingly interested in at least exploring the possibility of transformative relationships with their community counter-parts (Bringle, Games, & Malloy, 1999; Jacoby, 2003; Langseth & Plater, 2004; Percy, Zimpher, & Brukardt, 2006). Transformative campus/community service-learning partnerships are defined as ones that establish a communal identity designed to mobilize and share strengths, assets, and resources among participating partners (Enos & Morton, 2003; Harkavy, 2005; Percy et al., 2006). Such partnerships can result in an identity that challenges policy and practice, that creates new knowledge, that invents new ways to improve service and learning, and that improves the quality of life for the shared community (Enos & Morton, 2003). The shift to a transformative culture requires higher education institutions to become socially and geographically engaged in the community (Bringle et al., 1999). Establishing a partnership with a communal identity not only requires commitment from institutional leaders, but also from individual faculty members, who must extend their priorities to include issues of community concern (Boyer, 1990; Enos & Morton, 2003).

Although the transformative potential of campus/community service-learning partnerships has been recognized and discussed, little guidance has been offered in the literature as to how to identify and to assess transformative partnerships. This study was designed to address these short-comings. The campus/community service-learning partnership was selected as the unit of analysis for the study, because as noted by Cruz and Giles (2000), "Properties of the partnership can be known and examined for changes or impacts in service and learning" (p. 31), and because focusing on the partnership as the integral unit recognizes the importance of the interdependence between the campus and the community in a transformative relationship. A mixed methods approach was used, because it is an effective means of gathering data in cases where the priority is to "explore the research problem from a wide variety of angles" (Creswell, 2003, p. 11).

To conduct the research, a three-phase sequential explanatory strategy was employed. First, an assessment instrument, which consisted of a questionnaire and a matrix, was designed and pilot-tested. The instrument was intended to assess the degree to which campus/community service-learning partnerships experienced transformation. Second, transformative campus/community service-learning partnerships were identified using questionnaire responses from both campus and community coordinators of exemplary partnerships. Third, campus and community coordinators, who were engaged in transformative partnerships or in partnerships using transformative practices, were interviewed to determine the defining processes that promoted transformation.

The purposes of the study were:

- To develop an assessment instrument to measure the degree of transformation for campus/community service-learning partnerships; and
- To use the instrument for identifying and describing transformative partnerships within a single New England state.

METHOD

Identifying Participants

To identify potential transformative campus/community service-learning partnerships, the campus service-learning directors in one New England state ($N = 11$) were asked to identify up to five partnerships that they viewed as having had the greatest influence on educational practices at the institution and service to the community. Because of the rarity of transformative partnerships, only those partnerships identified as having some potential for transformation were included in the study. The directors were asked to provide the names and contact information for the campus coordinators involved most directly with these exemplary partnerships. The identified campus coordinators ($N = 20$) were contacted by e-mail and telephone and were asked to participate in the study. Those who agreed were e-mailed the campus coordinator version of the questionnaire. At the end of the questionnaire, the campus coordinators were asked to provide the names and contact information of their community counterparts. Those community coordinators ($N = 21$) were contacted by e-mail and telephone and asked to complete and return the community coordinator version of the questionnaire, which was e-mailed to them. Completed questionnaires were received from 15 campus coordinators and 14 community coordinators, which resulted in 14 partnerships that could be compared from both the campus and the community points-of-view.

Subsequently, telephone interviews were conducted with selected campus coordinators and community coordinators.

Developing the Conceptual Model

The decision to describe partnerships in terms of more than one dimension resulted from the complexity of the construct, conclusions drawn from the literature, and discussions with experts in the field. Two dimensions emerged from the literature to describe campus/community service-learning partnerships: *type* of transformation and *extent* of transformation (Bringle et al., 1999; Dorado & Giles, 2004; Enos & Morton, 2003; Percy et al., 2006; Torres, 2002; Zimpher, Percy, & Brukardt, 2002). Type of transformation was defined as the degree to which practices and services engaged in by campus/community partnerships embrace and utilize the skills of both partners, so that each has a stake in the outcomes (Enos & Morton, 2003). Extent of transformation was defined as the degree to which campus/community partnerships move toward a joint communal identity (Phillips, 2007). These dimensions were combined into a taxonomy for assessing campus/community partnership transformation. A taxonomy is defined as a framework in which the categories lie along a continuum and "become one of the major organizing principles of the framework" (Anderson & Krathwohl, 2001, p. 4). These two dimensions were combined to create the *Transformative Partnership Matrix*.

The X axis of the matrix, labeled *type* of transformation, evolved from the stages of the transformation proposed by Enos and Morton (2003), who described service-learning relationships as moving on a continuum from transactional to transformative. The continuum was segmented into four stages: *static, alters, expands,* and *transforms* (Phillips, 2007).

The *static* stage represents partnerships in which service-learning is part of the regular practice of institutions and organizations. However, in this stage the institution has no stake in any particular community agency and the community agency does not distinguish between students involved in service-learning and other volunteers. There may be regular communication between service-learning partners but the communications involve the logistics of accomplishing short-term project goals with no intent of changing existing educational practice or service provided. Service-learning experiences are seen as useful and may supplement traditional coursework, but not much change happens as a result of the partnership (Cone & Harris, 2003; Cruz & Giles, 2000; Enos & Morton, 2003; Holland & Gelmon, 2003; Howard, 2003; Zlotkowski, 2003).

The *alters* stage represents the beginning of transformation in pedagogy and community service for partnerships. In this stage, the fundamental ways of conducting business in both the campus and the community have become altered due to the partnership. Claims of academic expertise as well as academic neutrality become problematic. The concept of what knowledge is, how it is derived, and how it should be used is questioned and informs the direction of pedagogy and service (Enos & Morton, 2003; Howard, 2003; Strand, Marullo, Cutforth, Stoeker, & Donahue, 2003a; Winer & Ray, 1994; Zlotkowski, 2003).

The *expands* stage represents partnerships engaged in multiple ways in which members seek new opportunities to connect efforts, skills, and resources. In this stage, educational practices and services to the community break out of the limits traditionally assigned to specific discipline and service specialists. Those involved in the partnership creatively work to pool resources and administer available assets for the benefit of the shared community. An increased sense of synergy is seen in this stage (Enos & Morton, 2003; Harward, 2004; Holland & Gelmon, 2003; Jacoby, 2003; Strand, Marullo et al., 2003a; Winer & Ray, 1994; Zlotkowski, 2003).

In the *transforms* stage, no distinction is made between traditional educational experiences and service-learning experiences, because the tripartite focus of the academy on learning, research, and service is fulfilled. Some key identifiers of the this stage are that the partnership fulfills educational, research, and scholarly goals; the community is as viable a learning environment as the campus; community partners are co-creators of knowledge; knowledge created is shared among all members of the partnership; knowledge created directly benefits the community partner; service experiences of the partnership inform and transform learning; and attracted resources expand the scope and influence of educational practice and service to the community (Enos & Morton, 2003; Harward, 2004; Howard, 2003; Singleton, Hirsch, & Burack, 1999; Strandet al., 2003a; Zlotkowski, 2003).

The Y axis on the matrix, labeled *extent* of transformation, was designed to measure the degree to which campus/community service-learning partnerships have developed joint communal identities in order to improve the quality of life for the shared community. The extent to which campuses and the communities have been transformed due to participation in partnerships also encompasses four stages: *individual relationships, institutional/organizational support, community mobilization,* and *communal identity* (Phillips, 2007).

The *individual relationships* stage represents limited interactions between one or two faculty members and one or two members within the community. There may be very strong relationships between these partnering members; however, such relationships are an anomaly within the host institution and organization (Strand, Marullo, Cutforth, Stoeker, & Donahue, 2003b; Torres, 2002; Winer & Ray, 1994).

The *institution/organization support* stage represents a situation in which institutional and organizational leaders are aware of and involved in the practice, promotion, and planning of partnerships, and administrators, faculty, staff, and students at different levels are familiar with the work of the partnership. The partnering institutional and organizational mission statements reflect the vision of the campus/community partnership and there is an established campus/community center to organize efforts (Bringle et al., 1999; Dorado & Giles, 2004; Furco & Holland, 2004; Harward, 2004; Holland, 1999; Holland & Gelmon, 2003; Torres, 2002; Zimpher et al., 2002).

The *community mobilization* stage represents the point at which the initiatives, practices, and services of partnerships are known and are visible on campuses and in local communities. There is a conscious effort on the part of partnerships to seek out and mobilize community assets and leadership. Members of the partnerships are committed to promoting civic engagement and service-learning. Partners are brought together to plan, discuss, and address areas of common concern, and resources are shared to accomplish mutual goals (Bringle et al., 1999; Harward, 2004; Holland, 1999; Holland & Gelmon, 2003; Kretzmann & McKnight, 1993; Maurrasse, 2003; Singleton et al., 1999; Torres, 2002; Winer & Ray, 1994; Zimpher et al., 2002).

The *communal identity* stage represents partnerships that have transformed the identities of both the institutions and the organizations. The partners work together to deepen and expand the partnerships through long-range plans in order to improve the quality of life for the shared community. The institution and organization are equal partners, each with resources that are extended to achieve partnership goals. Some of the key identifiers of this culminating stage are that the campus/community service-learning partnerships have a name, structure, mission, and vision statement independent of any one partnering member; a memorandum of understanding has been developed and signed by partnering members; the partnerships seek ways to attract funding and resources; literature and advertisements for the partnerships are available; the partnerships make decisions for resource allocation; and the partnerships have a process for promoting new membership and leadership (Bringle et al., 1999; Enos & Morton, 2003; Harward, 2004; Holland, 1999; Maurrasse, 2003; Singleton et al., 1999; Torres, 2002; Winer & Ray, 1994; Zimpher et al., 2002).

On the matrix created by combining these two dimensions, four transformational zones were identified; the zones loosely correspond to Dorado and Giles (2004) three paths of engagement: *tentative, aligned,* and *committed,* plus a fourth zone, *transformative* (see Exhibit 5.1).

Designing the Questionnaire and Matrix

To provide data for placement on the matrix, a questionnaire was designed in two parallel forms: one for campus coordinators and the other for community coordinators, with slightly different statements tailored to the respondent type. The questionnaire asked coordinators to respond, using a 6-point Likert-type scale ranging from *never* (0) *to always* (5), to 32 statements regarding the transformative practices of their campus/community service-learning partnerships. The statements were designed based on indicators of partnership practice extracted from the literature concerning service-learning, institutional change, civic engagement, and campus/community partnerships. (See Exhibit 5.2 for a list of the references from which the statements were derived.) One of the most challenging aspects of the study was converting material from various qualitative case studies, which reported on successful campus/community

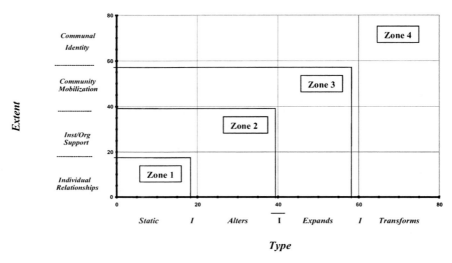

Note: Zone 1: tentative; Zone 2: aligned; Zone 3: committed; Zone 4: transformative.

Exhibit 5.1.   Transformative partnership matrix.

service-learning partnerships, into usable statements for incorporation into the questionnaire. (See Exhibits 5.3 and 5.4 for statements used in the two forms of the questionnaire.)

To increase the validity of the questionnaire and the matrix, three pilot tests were completed sequentially using a group of doctoral graduates and students ($n = 16$), a subset of the initial group ($n = 4$) to react to changes resulting from the first trial, and a group of national experts in the field of campus/community service-learning partnerships ($n = 6$). Extensive feedback from all three pilot tests resulted in changes that produced a tighter, clearer, more user-friendly questionnaire and a clarified matrix. Content validity of the questionnaire was determined by utilizing two strategies: evidence from existing literature (Creswell, 2003) and feedback from experts in the field (Gall, Gall, & Borg, 2003). After each pilot test, modifications were made.

Implementing the Procedures

Questionnaire and Matrix

To plot each set of coordinators on the matrix, scores were assigned to the questionnaire responses of the coordinators to the four statements for each of the four stages and summed for each of the two dimensions (see

**Exhibit 5.2.   References for Stages and
Statements on Transformative Partnership Questionnaire**

Stages for X Axis: Type	Supporting References
Static	Cone & Harris, 2003; Cruz & Giles, 2000; Enos & Morton, 2003; Holland & Gelmon, 2003; Howard, 2003; Zlotkowski, 2003
Alters	Enos & Morton, 2003; Howard, 2003; Strand, Marullo, Cutforth, Stoeker, & Donahue, 2003a; Winer & Ray, 1994; Zlotkowski, 2003
Expands	Enos & Morton, 2003; Harward, 2004; Holland & Gelmon, 2003; Jacoby, 2003; Strand, Marullo, Cutforth, Stoeker, & Donahue, 2003a; Winer & Ray, 1994; Zlotkowski, 2003
Transforms	Enos & Morton, 2003; Harward, 2004; Howard, 2003; Singleton, Hirsch, & Burack, 1999; Strand, Marullo, Cutforth, Stoeker, & Donahue, 2003a; Zlotkowski, 2003

Stages for Y Axis: Extent	Supporting References
Individual relationships	Strand, Marullo, Cutforth, Stoeker, & Donahue, 2003b; Torres, 2002; Winer & Ray, 1994
Institutional/organizational support	Bringle, Games, & Malloy, 1999; Dorado & Giles, 2004; Furco & Holland, 2004; Harward, 2004; Holland, 1999; Holland & Gelmon, 2003; Torres, 2002; Zimpher, Percy, & Brukardt, 2002
Community mobilization	Bringle, Games, & Malloy, 1999; Harward, 2004; Holland, 1999; Holland & Gelmon, 2003; Kretzmann & McKnight, 1993; Maurrasse, 2003; Singleton, Hirsch, & Burack, 1999; Torres, 2002; Winer & Ray, 1994; Zimpher, Percy, & Brukardt, 2002
Communal partnership identity	Bringle, Games, & Malloy, 1999; Enos & Morton, 2003; Harward, 2004; Holland, 1999; Maurrasse, 2003; Singleton, Hirsch, & Burack, 1999; Torres, 2002; Winer & Ray, 1994; Zimpher, Percy, & Brukardt, 2002

Exhibit 5.5). The resulting values for each dimension were used as the coordinates for plotting coordinator pairs on the matrix with different symbols for campus (■) and community (●) coordinators. Placement on the matrix of the pair of coordinators for each partnership was used to determine congruence between the responses of partners and the degree of transformation for that partnership. (See Exhibit 5.6 and Exhibit 5.8 for the display of the zone-congruent partnerships on a common matrix.)

**Exhibit 5.3.   Transformative Partnership
Questionnaire Statements for *Type* of Transformation**

Stages on X Axis: Type of Transformation

Static

Service-learning is an integral component.

Service-learning occurs throughout the semester/term.
Service-learning programs support community throughout semester/term.

Interdisciplinary approaches are used.
Students are a reliable source of support to the community.

College/university learning goals are addressed.
Community partner goals are valued and addressed.

Alters

Activities fulfill the educational goals of college/university.
Activities fulfill the service goals of the community partner.

Students contribute unique skills to the community.
Students contribute unique skills to the community partner.

Students discuss their work with community partner.

The community is recognized as a meaningful learning site.

Expands

Faculty work with community partner to design and assess activities.
Community partner works with faculty partner to plan activities.

Community partner participates in campus activities.
Faculty partner participates in community activities.

Services to the community have been expanded.

New academic programs have emerged.
New services or programs in the community have emerged.

Transforms

Community partner initiates ideas for new educational opportunities.

Campus facilities are used to support community services.
Community partner facilities are used to support student learning.

External resources have been attracted to support the work.

Knowledge produced is shared by campus and community partners.

Note: For grouped statements, the first appeared on campus coordinator version of the questionnaire and the second on the community coordinator version.

Visual inspection of the resulting placements indicated the extent of agreement between the campus and community coordinators, and whether the plots were within the same transformative zone. From this information, the number and degree of transformation of campus/community service-learning partnerships were determined.

Exhibit 5.4.   Transformative Partnership
Questionnaire Statements for *Extent* of Transformation

Stages on Y Axis: Extent of Transformation

Individual Relationships

Campus partner communicates regularly with community partner.

Campus and community partners discuss goals, constraints and expectations.

Campus and community partners establish processes to address challenges.

Campus and community partners work to expand scope of the partnership network.

Institutional/Organizational Support

There is a campus center established to support partnership projects.

College/university mission supports the partnership.
Mission statement of the community partner supports the partnership.

Campus leaders support the partnership.
Community partner agency leaders support the partnership.

Campus resources are dedicated to sustaining the partnership.
Community agency resources are dedicated to sustaining the partnership.

Community Mobilization

Community partner members mentor campus partner students.
Campus partner members mentor community members.

Brochures/advertisements promote campus involvement in the partnership.
Brochures/advertisements promote community involvement in the partnership.

Campus resources are dedicated to mobilize community skills and assets.
Community partner resources are dedicated to mobilize student skills and assets.

Processes allow for feedback and suggestions from community partner.

Communal Identity

Partnership mission statement reflects both campus and community partners.

Written partnership agreement has been developed and signed by both partners.

Partnership has its own organizational structure.

Partnership controls the allocation of shared resources.

Note: For grouped statements, the first appeared on campus coordinator version of the questionnaire and the second on the community coordinator version.

In order to provide evidence for testing the validity of the questionnaire and for assessing the four stages of the two dimensions on the matrix, means scores were calculated from the questionnaire responses. For each stage, means were determined by averaging separately the scores of campus coordinators and community coordinators for each the four statements that composed each stage. (See Exhibits 5.7 and 5.8 for the resulting mean scores.)

Exhibit 5.5. Characteristics of Campus/Community Partnership and Questionnaire Scores by Dimension for Campus Coordinators and Community Coordinators (N =14)

#	Descriptions of Institution of HE	Campus Coordinator		Community Coordinator		Transformative Zone	Coordinator Interviewed	
		X	Y	X	Y		Cam.	Com.
1	Midsized urban private college	60	64	52	60	Trans.	X	X
2	Midsized urban private university	39	42	70	76			X
3	Small private institution	60	49	42	40	Trans. Pract.		X
4	Large public university	52	56	28	36		X	X
5	Midsized urban private university	39	42	64	68			X
6	Large public university	70	61	46	30		X	
7	Small private university	60	43	25	43	Committed		
8	Midsized private university	58	40	60	70	Trans.		
9	Midsized urban private institution	32	23	52	60			
10	Midsized urban private university	34	47	62	56			
11	Midsized urban private university	49	42	42	6	Committed		
12	Large public university	52	56	50	36	Trans. Pract.		
13	Large public university	52	56	52	56	Trans. Pract.		
14	Large public university	49	63	54	63	Trans.		

Notes: Trans. = Transformative; Trans. Pract. = Transformational Practices.

X = Sum of total scores for coordinators on the 16 statements for the *type* of transition dimension.

Y = Sum to total scores for coordinators on the 16 statements for the *extent* of transition dimension.

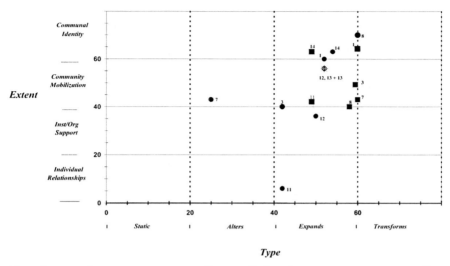

Exhibit 5.6.   Congruent partners plotted on transformative partnership matrix.

Notes. Squares (■) represent campus coordinators. Circles (●) represent community coordinators. For the 8 congruent partnerships (16 plots), numbers represent paired coordinators. Three coordinators shared the same position: two campus coordinators (#12 and #13) and one community coordinator (#13) at *X* = 52 and *Y* = 56.

**Exhibit 5.7.   Transformative Partnership
Questionnaire Means for Coordinators by Stage: Type**

Stages on X Axis - Type	*Campus Mean Score*	*Community Mean Score*
Static	3.34	3.45
Alters	3.30	3.34
Expands	2.59	2.70
Transforms	2.98	2.73

Interviews

In order to add richness and depth to the questionnaire results, partnership coordinators were contacted and asked for interviews. In all, three campus coordinators and five community coordinators were interviewed. Semistructured telephone interviews were conducted with these coordinators over a 2-week period in December 2006. The interviews lasted on average 45 minutes. The primary focus of the interviews was on the pro-

**Exhibit 5.8.   Transformative Partnership
Questionnaire Means for Coordinators by Stage: Extent**

Stages on Y Axis—Extent	Campus Mean Score	Community Mean Score
Individual relationships	3.23	3.08
Institutional/organizational support	3.50	3.30
Community mobilization	3.08	2.82
Communal identity	2.13	2.86

cesses that led to the success of the partnership. Analysis of the interview information was accomplished through coding to identify themes and patterns, which provided the context and description of the factors that contributed to transformative relationships.

RESULTS

One set of findings from the study dealt with identifying and describing the salient features of transformative partnerships, or at least ones headed toward transformation; another with the viability of an instrument and process for assessing transformation of campus/community service-learning partnerships; and a third with identifying the processes and challenges in developing transformative partnerships.

Identifying Transformative Partnerships

As a result of reviewing the placement on the matrix of the eight partnerships with zone-congruent scores by the campus coordinator and the community coordinator, three partnerships were identified as being transformative (#1, #8, and #14) by being located primarily in zone 4. Three other partnerships were identified as being engaged in practices headed toward transformation (#3, #12, and #13) by being in zones 3 and 4. The last two relatively congruent partnerships (#7 and #11) averaged out to be solidly in zone 3. The remaining six partnerships, which exhibited little agreement between campus and community coordinators, could not be described by a single zone.

Identifying only a few of the exemplary partnerships as being transformative was consistent with the work of Dorado and Giles (2004), who found that a limited number of partnerships progress into committed paths of engagement and with the work of Brukardt, Holland, Percy, and

Zimpher (2006), who noted that transformed institutions with engagement as their defining characteristic are rare. Therefore, the definition of transformative partnerships was stretched to include those partnerships engaging in transformative practices, as determined by placement on the matrix and from explanatory comments added on the questionnaire.

Evaluating the Transformative
Partnership Questionnaire and Matrix

Responses to the questionnaire were used to test whether the assumption that the stages used to define the dimensions of the matrix were sequential and progressive. If this were the case, means for the stages should move from high to low from the first stage to the fourth stage of each dimension. Exhibits 5.7 and 5.8 present the response means by stage for the two dimensions. As indicated by these values, the progression is good, but not perfect, and in the right direction, which adds credence to the underlying assumption. However, more consideration should be given to certain stages on each dimension: *type - expands* and *transforms* and *extent - institution/organizational support.* The mean responses to the statements within these stages did not follow the anticipated pattern. In retrospect, one of the problems with the statements contained within the *expands* stage may be that they are very specific regarding work performed, while the statements for the *transforms* stage are more general. The original reason for this development stemmed from the premise that the *transforms* stage, and the statements which go with it, represent the ideal. Although good in theory, respondents seemingly gave their partnerships the "benefit of the doubt" and scored these more general statements higher than the more specific ones. As for the *extent-institutional/ organizational support* stage, this may be more a function of the state in which the study was conducted than anything else. The statements in this stage are related to a set of interrelated themes concerning support of service-learning partnerships through institutional goals and mission, recognition of the community as meaningful learning sites, establishment of a campus center, and dedication of leaders and other resources to service-learning. In the state used for the study, considerable money and attention have been expended statewide to ensure that colleges and universities are involved in and committed to service-learning. In other states these statements might work better to discriminate between stages of transformation.

Because the literature, as well as experts in the field, supported the selected statements and the correspondence to the stages on the matrix, the statements should be tested on a larger target population to determine whether the results would persist. However, it appears that further refinement of the statements is necessary for use in the study state and perhaps in other states, as well, and for testing these statements in states with lower statewide dedication to service-learning.

Describing Transformative Processes and Challenges

From the interviews conducted with campus and community coordinators, three major processes were seen as prevalent in transformative partnerships or partnerships using transformative practices. These factors were consistent with the literature on successful campus/community partnerships and included *consistency in relationship, proactive pursuit*, and *campus/community fusion*.

Development of *consistency in the relationships* was considered to be the responsibility of many different partnership participants, especially because of the constantly changing mix of individuals involved. Students in particular, who may come and go on a semester or term basis, must be grounded in a common understanding of the purposes, processes, and practices of the partnership. Consistency within a partnership can be achieved in a number of ways, but primarily by using key partnership members: student leaders should transmit familiarity with the culture and mission of the partnership to other students; campus coordinators should maintain constant contact through multiple means of communication with various partnership members; and community partners and community leaders should verbalize what they want the partnership to achieve. Campus service-learning directors are excellent points of contact, because they usually have a wider scope of understanding of partnerships and can provide consistency regarding theory, expectations, goals, strategies, and resources for campus/community service-learning partnerships.

Proactive pursuit was defined as active engagement on the part of campus and community coordinators in the partnerships in order to ensure success and to seek ways to broaden the partnership by connecting mutual interests. Promoting action depends heavily on personal interests, on meaningful institutional/organizational collaborations, on excellent communication between partners, and on deepening opportunities to interact. The logistical challenges of sustaining successful partnerships were recognized, as were the requirement for dedicated coordinators to work proactively to recognize and address these challenges.

Campus/community fusion can be enhanced through multiple campus and/or community projects in order to improve synergy, as opposed to simply providing services for meeting immediate needs. Part of deepening relations with the neighboring community depends on establishing the campus as a place that brings people together, mobilizes assets, and establishes networks among interested stakeholders. However, community members often do not feel comfortable utilizing campus facilities or attending campus events. To move toward campus/community fusion, both campus and community coordinators should attend events, on and off the campus, to celebrate partnership accomplishments; form networks to broaden partnership connections; and ensure that community members become part of team teaching-learning strategies. By emphasizing the campus/community relationship, partnerships can shift from service-learning to more comprehensive engagement.

Several challenges were also identified in regard to the evolution of transformative campus/community service-learning partnerships: *logistics*, *sustainability*, and *deepening engagement*. Being unable to overcome any one of these barriers could be sufficient to keep a partnership from realizing long-term transformation.

Logistical challenges often present a major obstacle for campus/community partnerships and keep these partnerships from evolving. Logistical difficulties included transportation for individuals desiring to participate in partnership events; availability of facilities on and off the campus for partnership meetings and events; scheduling conflicts for those on the campus and in the community; and, most importantly, insufficient time for planning, execution, and reflection. The authors of *The Dance of Change* noted that creating change within organizations requires time for thought and reflection; they coined the term *white space* for this necessity (Senge, Kleiner, Roberts, Ross, Roth, & Smith, 1999, p. 43). White space was in short supply according to most of the interviewed campus and community coordinators. Lack of time may have contributed to the low average frequencies for both campus and community coordinators to the questionnaire statement concerning communal planning for partnership activities. Support from institutions and organizations, not only financial support but also making time available for partnership activities and planning, is a crucial element for partnerships to succeed and evolve.

To achieve *sustainability*, a campus/community partnership must be built on a solid foundation, beginning with consistency in the relationship. But consistency may be ethereal and insufficient. Partnerships without formal written agreements or shared resources lack the firm grounding needed for sustained transformation; without formal connections between the partners, sustainability may be jeopardized. Statements on the questionnaire concerning written partnership agreement and partnership control over shared resources garnered the lowest mean responses. During the interviews, campus and community coordinators confirmed and elaborated on this finding.

To create and sustain a substantial, meaningful relationship between the campus and community partners requires all members of the shared community, from top to bottom, to be dedicated and active in the process. One key to *enhancing engagement* among partners is to take part in frequent and clear communication. During the course of the study, visits were made to a number of college and university campuses. On each campus a simple question was posed to faculty and students: How do campus/community service-learning partnerships affect life and education on the campus? If the respondents were ignorant of the existence of the partnerships, it was assumed that these institutions probably were not deeply engaged with the community, or if they were that they were not adequately communicating this fact. The same would be true of members of a partnering neighborhood. If neighborhood residents were not aware of the partnerships, this was an indication that the partnerships were not transformative. As is the case in most relationships, partnership engagement can be enhanced by frequent, rich, thoughtful communication. Even though communication is a time-consuming, introspective process, adequate provisions must be made for it if transformative partnerships are to be created and sustained.

DISCUSSION

Transformative campus/community service-learning partnerships break down barriers between the academy and the community by establishing networks of connections throughout and between both, which can change the processes and practices of education and service. Particularly over the last few decades, faculty and students have been encouraged to go beyond the gates of the campus and to engage in civically centered, experiential pedagogy (Benson & Harkavy, 2002; Furco & Holland, 2004). The importance of linking the goals, mission, and vision of colleges and universities with the real-world social challenges facing communities can be realized through service-learning (Eyler, Giles, Stenson, & Gray, 2001). Nonetheless, institutions of higher education, schools within institutions, departments within schools, and faculty within departments have established a practice of narrowly addressing only specific needs within communities, usually based upon the research interests of individual faculty members. The increasing specialization within higher education has widened the chasm between colleges and universities and their surrounding neighborhoods. Despite the social inequities facing many communities that neighbor institutions, critics suggest that academics tend to pursue esoteric agendas with little or no connection to the plight of those who live, literally, next door. Campus/community service-learning partnerships provide a means for institutions of higher education to reach out and work with their neighbors.

Leaders within the service-learning movement have called for less *service* and greater *engagement* in campus/community partnerships (Benson & Harkavy, 2002; Cruz & Giles, 2000; Fisher, Fabricant, & Simmons, 2004; Holland, 1999; Holland & Gelmon, 2003; Torres, 2002; Wolshok, 1999). A long-term commitment on the part of institutions of higher education is required to form deeply engaged, sustainable partnerships focused on holistic approaches to addressing problems in the community. Such partnerships are transformative, but happen infrequently (Brukardt et al., 2006; Dorado & Giles, 2004). The literature describes some institutions that have been transformed through civically engaged partnerships (Andreasen, 2002; Reardon, 2005; Zimpher et al., 2002); however, these institutions are still an anomaly. What is lacking in the literature is a means for gauging the degree to which partnerships are transformative. This study addressed that need by developing an instrument designed to assess the degree to which campus/community service-learning partners synergistically influence one another in daily practice and identity.

Refinement of Study

The transformative campus/community partnership assessment instrument, the questionnaire in two forms and the corresponding matrix, utilized best practices and indicators of transformative partnerships drawn from successful examples and expert opinion. The instrument was subjected to review by academic practitioners and experts inside and outside the field of service-learning, by community activists engaged in campus/ community partnerships, and by campus and community leaders. The result is an assessment instrument based on indicators of successful campus/community service-learning partnerships that holds promise for future use, but needs additional refinements. Modifications should be made to improve the instrument and additional uses should be considered that could extend its applicability. The following points, in particular, need to be addressed:

Reconsideration of Statements

One assumption underlying the assessment instrument was that the dimensions on the matrix were taxonomies and, thus for each dimension the stages were sequential and progressive. Generally this was the case, but it was not uniformly true. As a result, either wording or placement, or both, of some of the statements within stages should be reconsidered in light of the empirical evidence. Use of the instrument also should be extended to produce a greater range of results, which could provide information useful in refining the wording and placement of the statements, thus improving the construct validity of the instrument.

Types of Respondents

Because campus and community coordinators were used as the major source of information, essentially those most responsible for the partnerships were asked to assess the partnerships. To achieve less biased results and a better impact measure of the partnership, other groups, in addition to the coordinators, should be queried. A broader assessment of partnerships could be achieved by using the instrument, but directing the questions to a wider range of stakeholders on the campus and in the community, including the leaders.

Types of Partners

Because this study used as the unit of analysis campus/community service-learning partnerships, the results do not apply directly to the institutions of higher education or to the community organizations that hosted the partnerships. As interesting as it may be to explore the transformative nature of partnerships, the more compelling issues concern the transformation of institutions and organizations. What this study does do, however, is to provide an instrument and a process that could be adapted for broader study of transformation characteristics, not limited to individual partnerships, but encompassing the institutions and organizations that sponsor them.

Implications for Partnership Development

Several suggestions for extending the life and breadth of transformative partnerships emerged from the study. Among these are the following.

Partnership Agreements

To stabilize the working relationship between partners and their corresponding institutions and organizations, the vision, mission, purposes, and expectations of the partnership should be formalized in writing. Although less formal partnerships can be innovative and mutually beneficial, more formal partnerships have a better chance of surviving and thriving. Many of the partnerships in the study were developed and sustained through personal connections and interests. Some partnerships have even grown throughout institutions and organizations by means of personally developed networks. However, personnel turnover, particularly of key individuals, can halt the evolution and threaten the very existence of a partnership. Lack of formal understanding of expectations and goals can lead to frustration and confusion and jeopardize sustainability. One way to address these issues is for the partners to develop a written understanding that is signed not only by the partnership coordinators but also by the institutional and organizational leaders. Because so few partnerships have written agreements, a model agreement template should be designed that campus/community partners could use, but tailor to suit their own situations.

Shared Resources

To solidify partnership bonds, processes should be established through which resources are shared and the power to allocate these shared resources is equitable among partners. Transformative partnerships inspire and mobilize the assets of all members of the shared community. However, to empower the partnership, those involved with oversight should control the assets and assume the task of attracting external resources to support the work.

Providing Time

Institutional and organizational leaders should provide sufficient time for partnerships to flourish. Creative people with far-reaching, innovative ideas about the breadth and depth of partnership possibilities need time to pursue these thoughts. But when individuals are immersed in the day-to-day demands of their work, as well as proactively working on a partnership, they often become overwhelmed and eventually burnt-out. The creative potential of partnership coordinators should be encouraged and allowed to thrive if true transformative social change, which benefits both the campus and the community, is to occur. This takes time and that requires leadership support to ensure that time is available.

Effective Communication

Engagement cannot take place in a vacuum; it requires those within the partnership to exchange ideas, concerns, desires, frustrations, hopes, and fears. The Information Age has made these exchanges easier to accomplish than ever before, but the technology can only provide the means not the substance of communication. To deepen the engagement between partners, so that campus/community fusion can occur, requires insightful and frequent communication that may be daunting, but is an essential component of transformation.

Greater Focus and Fewer Targets

Partnership coordinators reported a variety of socially responsible accomplishments. However, the wide range of activities dissipated a sense of belonging on the parts of both campus and community members. Focusing resources from the campus and community to targeted geographic areas would enhance clarity of purpose, improve campus/community fusion, and develop shared vision. If colleges or universities established deeply engaged partnership networks within specific neighboring communities, it would create greater potential for enhanced economic capacity and positive social change.

CONCLUSION

Transformative campus/community service-learning partnerships require innovative leadership and creative, forward-thinking networks of individuals, who desire positive social change and wish to transform education and service. In order for institutions of higher education to become leaders for social change, they must relinquish their expert role in favor of forming more equitable partnerships with communities. In so doing, they may become followers, as well as leaders, of a transformative process that they have helped to create (DePree, 2006). Leaders of transformative partnerships continually seek and empower individuals and networks to create processes and mindsets that can enhance capacity, see systems holistically, and work towards the greater good of the shared community (Senge, 1996). These are consuming tasks for anyone to shoulder. For leaders of higher educational institutions and community organizations, it may be more responsibility than they care to assume, particularly with their already overburdened agendas. But the time has seldom been more propitious or the needs more apparent than they are at this the beginning of the twenty-first century.

The development of an assessment instrument was intended to move the discussion forward on the transformative nature of campus/community partnerships. Making use of the instrument, even in its evolutionary state, will allow institutions of higher education and community organizations to determine how far along their partnership efforts have moved towards transformation. Being able to locate this point provides an empirical basis for considering whether the partnership is correctly positioned and where it should be going.

For those who want to move forward toward greater transformation, this study identifies some of the processes that help to promote transformation. Transformative partnerships are powerful and carry with them the potential to implement far-reaching change. At this point in the development of the social fabric of the nation, campus and community leaders need to break down the barriers between the two and to adopt transforming practices designed to improve the quality of life on the campus and in the community.

ACKNOWLEDGMENTS

Great appreciation is due to the staff of the Alan Shawn Feinstein Community Service Center at Johnson & Wales University and the director, Susan J. Connery, to members of the Rhode Island Campus Compact, and to the participating campus coordinators and the community coordinators. Without their considerable assistance, continued encouragement, and valuable suggestions, the research would have been impossible to complete.

REFERENCES

Anderson, L. W., & Krathwohl, D. R. (Eds.). (2001). *A taxonomy for learning, teaching, and assessing: A revision of Bloom's taxonomy of educational objectives.* New York: Longman.

Andreasen, N. (2002). Civic responsibility through mutual transformation of town and gown: Service learning at Andrews University. In M. Kenny, L. Simon, K. Kiley-Brabeck, & R. Lerner (Eds.), *Learning to serve: Promoting civil society through service learning* (pp. 67-77). Norwell, MA: Kluwer Academic.

Benson, L., & Harkavy, I., (2002). Academically-based community service and university-assisted community schools as complementary approaches for advancing, learning, teaching, research and service: The University of Pennsylvania as a case study in progress. In M. Kenny, L. Simon, K. Kiley-Brabeck, & R. Lerner (Eds.), *Learning to serve: Promoting civil society through service learning* (pp. 361-378). Norwell, MA: Kluwer Academic.

Bringle, R., Games, R., & Malloy, E. (1999). *Colleges and universities as citizens: Issues and perspectives.* Needham Heights, MA: Allyn & Bacon.

Boyer, E. L. (1990). *Scholarship reconsidered: Priorities of the professoriate.* New York: Carnegie Foundation.

Brukardt, M., Holland, B., Percy, S., & Zimpher, N. (2006). The path ahead: What's next for university engagement? In S. Percy, N. Zimpher, & M. Brukardt (Eds.), *Creating a new kind of university: Institutionalizing community-university engagement* (pp. 242-257). Bolton, MA: Anker.

Campus Compact. (2009). *About Us.* Retrieved May 7, 2009, from http://www .compact.org/about/

Cone, D., & Harris, S. (2003). Service-learning practice: Developing a theoretical framework. In Campus Compact, *Introduction to service-learning toolkit* (2nd ed.) (pp. 27-39). Providence, RI: Campus Compact.

Creswell, J. (2003). *Research design: Qualitative, quantitative, and mixed methods approaches* (2nd ed.). Thousand Oaks, CA: SAGE.

126 J. T. PHILLIPS and C. V. L. WARD

Cruz, N., & Giles, D. (2000). Where's the community in service-learning research? *Michigan Journal of Community Service Learning*, 7(Special Issue), 28-34.
DePree, M. (2006). *Creative leadership*. Retrieved January 2, 2007, from http://www.missoulacultural.org/docs/DePree.doc
Dorado, S., & Giles, D. (2004). Service-learning partnerships: Paths of engagement. *Michigan Journal of Community Service Learning*, 11(1), 25-37.
Enos, S., & Morton, K. (2003). Developing a theory and practice of campus-community partnerships. In B. Jacoby & Associates (Eds.), *Building partnerships for service-learning* (pp. 20-41). San Francisco: Jossey-Bass.
Eyler, J., Giles, D., Stenson, C., & Gray, C., (2001). *At a glance: What we know about the effects of service-learning on college students, faculty, institutions, and communities, 1993-2000* (3rd ed.). Nashville, TN: Vanderbilt University: Corporation for National Service, Learn and Serve America, National Service-Learning Clearinghouse.
Fisher, R., Fabricant, M., & Simmons, L., (2004). Understanding contemporary university-community connections: Context, practice and challenges. In T. Soska & A. Butterfield (Eds.), *University-community partnerships: Universities in civic engagement* (pp. 13-32). Binghamton, NY: The Haworth Press.
Furco, A., & Holland, B. (2004). Institutionalizing service-learning in higher education: Issues and strategies for chief academic officers. In M. Langseth & W. Plater (Eds.), *Public work & the academy: An academic administrator's guide to civic engagement and service-learning* (pp. 23-40). Bolton, MA: Anker.
Gall, M. G., Gall, J. P., & Borg, W. R. (2003). *Educational research: An introduction* (7th ed.). Boston: Allyn & Bacon.
Harkavy, I. (2005). Higher education collaboratives for community engagement and improvement: faculty and researchers' perspectives. Partnerships for engagement futures. In P. A. Pasque, R. E. Smerek, B. Dwyer, N. Bowman & B. L. Mallory (Eds.), *Higher education collaboratives for community engagement and improvement* (pp. 22-27). Ann Arbor, MI: National Forum on Higher Education and the Public Good.
Harward, D. (2004). Bates College: Liberal education, community partnerships, and civic engagement. In M. Langseth & W. Plater (Eds.), *Public work & the academy: An academic administrator's guide to civic engagement and service-learning* (pp. 89-98). Bolton, MA: Anker.
Holland, B. A. (1999). From murky to meaningful: The role of mission in institutional change. In R. Bringle, R. Games, & E. Malloy, (Eds.), *Colleges and universities as citizens* (pp. 48-72). Needham Heights, MA: Allyn & Bacon.
Holland, B. A., & Gelmon, S. (2003). The state of the "engaged campus": What we have learned about building and sustaining university-community partnerships? In Campus Compact, *Introduction to service-learning toolkit* (2nd ed., pp. 193-194). Providence, RI: Campus Compact.
Howard, J. (2003). Academic service-learning: A counternormative pedagogy. In Campus Compact, *Introduction to service-learning toolkit* (2nd ed., pp. 253-256). Providence, RI: Campus Compact.
Jacoby, B. & Associates. (2003). *Building partnerships for service-learning*. San Francisco: Jossey-Bass.

Kretzmann, J., & McKnight, J. (1993). *Building communities from the inside out: A path towards finding and mobilizing a community's assets.* Chicago: ACTA.

Langseth, M., & Plater, W. (2004). *Public work and the academy: An academic administrator's guide to civic engagement and service-learning.* Bolton, MA: Anker.

Maurrasse, D. (2003). Higher education/community partnerships: Assessing progress in the field. In Campus Compact, *Introduction to service-learning toolkit* (2nd ed.) (pp. 199-204). Providence, RI: Campus Compact.

Percy, S., Zimpher, N., & Brukardt, M. (2006). *Creating a new kind of university: institutionalizing community-university engagement.* Bolton, MA: Anker.

Phillips, J. T. (2007). *Transformative campus/community service-learning partnerships.* Unpublished doctoral dissertation, Johnson & Wales University, Providence, RI.

Plater, W. (2004). Civic engagement, service-learning, and intentional leadership. In M. Langseth & W. Plater (Eds.), *Public work & the academy: An academic administrator's guide to civic engagement and service-learning* (pp. 1-22). Bolton, MA: Anker.

Reardon, K. (2005). *Straight A's? Evaluating the success of community/university development partnerships.* Retrieved April 10, 2009, from http://www.bos.frb.org/commdev/c&b/2005/Summer/University.pdf

Senge, P. (1996). The ecology of leadership. Retrieved January 2, 2007, from http://leadertoleader.org/leaderbooks/l2l/fall96/senge.html

Senge, P., Kleiner, A., Roberts, C., Ross, R., Roth, G., & Smith, B. (1999). *The dance of change.* New York: Doubleday.

Singleton, S., Hirsch, D., & Burack, C., (1999). Organizational structures for community engagement. In R. Bringle, R. Games, & E. Malloy (Eds.), *Colleges and universities as citizen* (pp. 121-140). Needham Heights, MA: Allyn & Bacon.

Strand, K., Marullo, S., Cutforth, N., Stoecker, R., & Donahue, P. (2003a). *Community-based research and higher education: Principles and practices.* San Francisco: Jossey-Bass.

Strand, K., Marullo, S., Cutforth, N., Stoecker, R., & Donohue, P. (2003b). Principles of best practice for community-based research. *Michigan Journal of Community Service Learning, 9*(3), 5-15.

Torres, J. (2002). *Benchmarks for campus/community partnerships.* Providence, RI: Campus Compact.

Winer, M., & Ray, K. (1994). *Collaboration handbook: Creating, sustaining, and enjoying the journey.* St. Paul, MN: Amherst H. Wilder Foundation.

Wolshok, M., (1999). Strategies for building the infrastructure that supports the engaged campus. In R. Bringle, R. Games, & E. Malloy (Eds.), *Colleges and universities as citizens* (pp. 74-95). Needham Heights, MA: Allyn & Bacon.

Zimpher, N., Percy, S., & Brukardt, M. (2002). *A time for boldness: A story of institutional change.* Bolton, MA: Anker.

Zlotkowski, E. (2003). Pedagogy and engagement. In Campus Compact, *Introduction to service- learning toolkit* (2nd ed., pp. 63-78). Providence, RI: Campus Compact.

PART III

SERVICE-LEARNING STUDENTS' ACADEMIC, PERSONAL, INTERPERSONAL, AND CIVIC OUTCOMES

CHAPTER 6

DOES QUALITY
REALLY MATTER?

Testing the New K-12 Service-Learning
Standards for Quality Practice

Shelley H. Billig

ABSTRACT

The K-12 Service-Learning Standards and Indicators for Quality Practice were published in 2008. These standards were created on the basis of an extensive review of the literature within the field of K-12 service-learning and the larger body of literature on effective practices in education. This chapter presents some of the literature on which the standards were based and an analysis of the extent to which the standards are associated with positive outcomes for middle and high school programs implemented in the School District of Philadelphia. Using a quasi-experimental design, researchers compared changes in various academic measures between students in high-quality service-learning programs and students in matched classrooms that did not implement service-learning. Students in high-quality programs, as defined by the standards, showed more statistically significant positive outcomes than their nonparticipating peers on measures of

Creating Our Identities in Service-Learning and Community Engagement
pp. 131–157

academic achievement, attendance, tardiness, and suspensions. Possible explanations and implications for future studies are discussed.

INTRODUCTION

For many years and across many studies, researchers who have studied K-12 service-learning approaches have found that "high quality" service-learning was associated with significant results in academic engagement and performance, civic engagement and acquisition of knowledge and skills, and social-emotional and personal development including increases in resilience, ability to manage conflict, and other skills and traits related to character development (Ammon, Furco, Chi & Middaugh, 2002; Billig, 2000; Billig, 2004; Billig, Jesse, & Grimley, 2008; Billig, Root & Jesse, 2005; Furco, 2002; Hecht, 2003; Laird & Black, 2002; Melchior, 1999; Meyer & Billig, 2003; Scales, Blythe, Berkas, & Kieslmeier, 2000; Yamauchi, Billig, Meyer, & Hofschire, 2007; and many others). In most of these studies, the definition of "high quality" was based on the Essential Elements of Service-Learning (National Service-Learning Cooperative, 1999).

Operationalization of these elements varied slightly in the research conducted, but most typically, they were used as a group for analysis purposes. While there were some articles identifying specific factors associated with the Essential Elements, several studies (Billig et al., 2005) showed that while the Essential Elements as a group continued to predict overall outcomes, many of the single Elements did not. These and other findings from the research literature spurred service-learning leaders, researchers, and practitioners to call for a revision of the Elements so that those practicing service-learning could have more assurance that their implementation would produce the outcomes desired.

A standards-setting process was then launched, as described in the last chapter of this volume. The research in the field from the past 20 years or so was summarized and synthesized, and studies that showed relationships between implementation variables and outcomes were identified. The service-learning research summaries were supplemented with summaries of larger studies from the more general educational reform literature from the past 20 years. The resulting literature review identified eight major categories of activity related to service-learning implementation that appeared to be most strongly associated with civic and academic outcomes. The eight categories were duration/intensity, link to academic or program curriculum or objectives, meaningful service, youth voice, community partnerships, diversity, reflection, and progress monitoring. A brief review of some of the research studies supporting these eight implementation variables is presented next.

Duration and Intensity

Duration and intensity was found in multiple studies to be strongly correlated with most of the impact areas measured by researchers. As defined by Billig and Northup (2008), "sufficient intensity and duration means that service-learning experiences include investigation, planning, action, reflection, demonstration, and celebration, and occur during concentrated blocks of time (intensity) and are long enough (duration) to meet community needs and learning goals" (p. 1). The effects of duration and intensity were found in multiple studies. For example, Eyler and Giles (1997) demonstrated that service-learning programs had stronger impacts when they had more depth in terms of concentrated hours of activity provided students with more challenging and varied tasks, a greater sense of ownership, more opportunities to make important decisions, stronger collegial relations with professionals in the field, more opportunities to apply content from the classroom to the community, and greater contributions to the community when they were compared to service-learning experiences that were less intense. Similarly, Melchior and Orr (1995) found that in their national study of Learn and Serve that program duration was correlated with multiple positive student outcomes.

In their quasi-experimental study of service-learning in high schools, Billig et al. (2005) reported that program duration of at least one semester was significantly related to all civic outcomes and enjoyment of subject matters. This same finding was shown in a national study by Spring, Dietz, and Grimm (2006), who found that middle and high school students that had service-learning experiences with a duration of at least one semester and who participated in reflection activities and decision making were "three times as likely to believe they can make a great deal of difference in their community than youth who participated in school-based service without any of the quality elements of service-learning" (p. 3). Students that participated in programs with these quality elements were also more likely to report that they talked about politics with friends and family more often, would likely volunteer in the future, and were more interested in world events.

Conrad and Hedin (1980) found that duration of high school service-learning programs was significantly related to multiple academic and civic outcomes, especially when the program was one semester or longer. Billig and Brodersen (2007) showed that duration of service-learning activities was positively related to valuing school, civic engagement, social responsibility, and locus of control. Many more studies could be cited (see Billig & Northup, 2008) but the trend is clear: Intensity and duration are strongly associated with outcomes. However, as Blyth, Saito and Berkas (1997) caution, the number of hours in which a program exists is not the best prediccator for intensity and quality since it is how the hours are used that matters. In their words, "the field should be very cautious in implementing service programs that require or mandate so many hours of service in the absence of teaching methods that allow students to interpret and learn from the experiences they encounter" (p. 52).

Link to Curriculum

Link to curriculum refers to teachers or facilitators making an explicit connection between content standards and/or program objectives and the content of service and reflection activities. This seems like an obvious predictor of academic outcomes and, not surprisingly, the service-learning research in K-12 settings repeatedly shows high correlations. For example, Billig et al. (2005) found that the more teachers linked their service-learning activities to academic standards or their school curriculum, the stronger all of the student academic engagement and performance outcomes that were measured. The same has been reported to be true of after-school programs that link service to program objectives (see, for example, Northup, 2007).

Hamilton and Zeldin (1987) demonstrated that high school students learned more and were more satisfied with their service experiences when the issues that were being discussed in the classroom were aligned with those being debated in legislative sessions they observed. Conrad and Hedin (1980) found higher increases in problem solving skills when students engaged in service had experiences that were linked to issues discussed in class.

The more general literature on how children learn strongly supports this concept. Studies summarized by the National Research Council (1999) showed that the ability to transfer or apply what students learn to multiple other contexts was enhanced when students used their knowledge in multiple contexts. "With multiple contexts, students are more likely to abstract the relevant features of concepts and develop a more flexible representation of knowledge" (p. 65).

Meaningful Service

The notion of meaningfulness refers to individuals feeling a sense of purpose and believing that the activities in which they engage are relevant and have intrinsic worth. Many definitions of meaningfulness include the four aspects of an experience that Dewey (1933) identified as necessary for an experience to result in learning, that is, that the experience must generate interest; have intrinsic worth; present problems that stimulate curiosity and create a demand for learning; and foster development over a considerable amount of time so that span.

The research literature that reflects the importance of meaningfulness is vast. For example, a synthesis of the factors related to students' academic engagement showed that engaging schools make teaching and learning relevant to the students' background cultures, experiences, and long-term goals (National Research Council, 2004). Catalano, Haggerty, Oesterle, Fleming, and Hawkins (2004) found that students who worked in communities developed a greater sense of efficacy and stronger connections to the community norms and values when they interacted with others, developed skills, and felt rewarded upon project completion, all of which are associated with operationalization of the term meaningfulness. Similarly, Root and Billig (2008), in their case studies of effective service-learning programs, reported that high school students were most likely to find meaning in their service-learning experiences when they interacted with individuals faced with personal difficulties or confronted examples of injustice. They concluded that meaningfulness was associated with emotional investment in an issue and a desire to make a difference through service.

In his study of high school students, Furco (2002) also demonstrated that the students that had the most positive civic outcomes were engaged in meaningful service activities in which they had responsibility and interest, and/or ones that challenged them to some degree. Other dimensions of meaningfulness that appeared to maximize outcomes were students feeling that they had some control over their activities, were committed to the cause associated with their efforts, thought that they were making a difference, and believed that they had strong, positive relationships with collaborating adults and peers.

In their high school study, Billig et al. (2005) found that perceived meaningfulness was associated with greater commitment to service-learning projects and greater acquisition of knowledge and skills. Meaningfulness was related to students' developing their own ideas and making important decisions about service projects, feeling efficacy in their work, and feeling challenged by the tasks in which they were engaged.

Youth Voice

Researchers typically operationalize youth voice as providing young people with the opportunity to make decisions about the content of the service-learning project and how the project is to be planned and implemented. Billig et al. (2005) demonstrated that giving young people the opportunity to engage in decision-making throughout the service-learning project was associated with more positive outcomes on measures of academic and civic engagement. Fredericks, Kaplan and Zeisler (2001) summarized the literature and found that young people who felt that they were not actively involved in making decisions often expressed dissatisfaction with their service-learning experiences, and were more likely to report that they lacked efficacy and felt alienated and disrespected. Blyth et al. (1997) showed that providing youth with more opportunities to plan and work together was associated with stronger impacts on social responsibility and the development of an ethic of service.

Spring et al. (2006) similarly reported that young people with more voice in planning projects (along with sufficient project duration and opportunities for reflection) were more likely to feel efficacious, were more interested in world events, and were more likely to report that they would volunteer in the future. Morgan and Streb (2003) also found that voice was associated with multiple positive outcomes, including greater gains in political knowledge, less cynicism about government, and a greater desire to be politically active. Finally, Oldfather (1995) demonstrated that giving disconnected youth more voice in their activities resulted in an increased sense of efficacy and a stronger awareness that they could make changes in their schools for themselves and others. Other researchers have found connections between youth voice and development of social agency, belongingness and competence (Mitra, 2004); identity and connectedness to the community (Zeldin, 2004); productivity (Wang & Stiles, 1976); and leadership and self-confidence (Larson, Walker, & Pearce, 2004).

Community Partnerships

Research has shown that service-learning performed in the context of a community partnership is associated with stronger participant outcomes, both for youth and for the adults involved in the partnerships. An effective community partnership features an ongoing reciprocal relationship, with mutual goals, regular two-way communication, examination of each partner's expectations, and a commitment to bridge the different cultures of schools and organizations (Fredericks & Billig, 2008).

Fredericks (2002) has documented the essential functions of community partners in service-learning projects, citing their ability to provide a site for projects, resources including funds and staff time, a "real-world" context for learning, and guidance so that youth can participate in structured, mutually beneficial activities. Wade (1997) identified multiple, substantial benefits of strong service-learning partnerships including participants' acquisition of skills, information, resources and technical assistance needed to meet a genuine community need; more effective services to clients; better understanding about community issues; and the pooling of information and resources.

Ammon et al. (2002), in their study of CalServe initiatives and institutionalization of service-learning, reported that program sustainability was associated with schools having reciprocal partnerships with community organizations. Their studies revealed that partnerships were strengthened by having a strong issue focus that served as a central organizing principle for partnership and curriculum development. In other studies, Billig (2002) and Kramer (2000) also demonstrated that long-term reciprocal partnerships were essential for sustainability.

Diversity

Diversity in service-learning has multiple dimensions and its relationship to outcomes is often hard to dissect. Researchers have explored the multiple benefits that derive when various racial and ethnic populations and/or those with various abilities and disabilities come together in service projects, and especially, when the diversity was apparent both among those providing the service and those being served (see, for example, the summary by Roehlepartain, 2007). Examples of strong outcomes for students from various subpopulations may be found in studies by Billig et al. (2005); Billig, Jesse, and Grimley. (2008); Hammond and Heredia (2002); Hobbs (2001); Lennon (2009); Gregory, Steinbring, and Sousa (2003); Vang (2004-2005); and many others.

Billig et al. (2005) found that academic engagement, valuing school, enjoyment of subject matters, civic dispositions, and civic engagement were all related to having greater diversity in the backgrounds of service-learning participants and programming. Hurtado, Milem, Clayton-Pederson, and Allen (1999) demonstrated that students who socialize with individuals from multiple cultural backgrounds are more likely to be tolerant of diverse ideas, accepting of people unlike themselves, and culturally aware.

Literature on the need for diverse experiences, the need to address multiple intelligences, and the need to differentiate instruction is abundant. Interested readers should review meta-analyses by the National Research Council (1999; 2004).

Reflection

Reflection is a key component of any service-learning experience. However, the quality of reflection varies tremendously within service-learning practice and therefore the nature and frequency of reflection activities were identified as aspects of quality practice.

In general, high quality reflection has been characterized as being frequent, occurring before, during, and after service experience, and being cognitively challenging. "Cognitive challenge is typically defined as presenting the learner with a problem or situation that the learner cannot tackle with his/her existing cognitive structure. In many of the studies on cognitive challenge, researchers also describe prompts that engage students in metacognition, defined as thinking about thinking or being conscious of one's own thinking and reasoning processes. Challenge within the service-learning context also involves "relating experiences to various social and civic issues in order to understand connections to public policy and civic life" (Billig & Fredericks, 2008, p. 1).

Andersen (1998), in her synthesis of the service-learning literature, found that high quality reflection activities helped students become more caring, develop closer relationships with others, build bonds with others from different ethnic or cultural backgrounds, and develop a better sense of connection and belonging. Billig et al. (2005) found that students were more likely to value school, feel more efficacious, engage in school and enjoy subject matters, and acquire more civic knowledge and more positive civic dispositions when they were presented with cognitively challenging reflection activities. Root and Billig (2008), in their case studies, showed that the strongest student outcomes were associated with teachers who asked students to delve more deeply into issues, prompting them to investigate root causes and solutions, weigh alternatives, engage in conflict resolution and persuasion, and manage complex tasks.

Eyler and Giles (1999) demonstrated that reflection helped students gain a deeper understanding of what they learned and develop both problem solving skills and the ability to transfer their learning to other situations. Students with better reflection opportunities also were more open to new ideas, better able to take multiple perspectives, and better able to analyze issues systemically. Conrad and Hedin (1987) similarly found that students that engaged in frequent reflection activities were more likely than their peers to be able to identify changes in their own attitudes and behaviors, develop a sense of community, and display internal locus of control. Blyth et al. (1997) wrote that youth that engaged in more reflection were more likely to be engaged in school and have greater social responsibility than those that did not. Finally, Waterman (1993) reported that students that reflected within their service-learning experiences more often had stronger self-confidence and social responsibility than those that did not.

Progress Monitoring

Progress monitoring refers both to the process of collecting information on the quality of the activities within the service-learning experience and the process of gathering data to determine whether movement has been made toward goal attainment. Typically, progress monitoring is not used for evaluation purposes, but rather to ensure that effective practices are in place and appropriate advancement is being made. However, in practice, many of the activities that take place as part of progress monitoring are also used for evaluative purposes.

In their study of high school service-learning, Billig et al. (2005) showed that assessments of service-learning process and progress, along with more formal evaluation, were associated with higher outcomes in the areas of student enjoyment of subject matter, civic knowledge, and efficacy. The assessments could be conducted by either teachers or students, and could be either formal or informal, but the key to success appeared to be in checking to see how well the project was progressing, primarily in terms of goal attainment. Greene and Diehm (1995) found that provision of frequent written feedback to students on their reflections was related to students' feeling more personally invested in the service.

Additional evidence of the effectiveness of progress monitoring may be found in the broader educational research literature. For example, Schunk and Pajares (2002) showed that students' sense of efficacy was related to receiving feedback and being given opportunities to improve. Safer and Fleischman (2005), in their review of the research of progress monitoring in educational settings, reported that students learn more and teacher decision making improves when there is more progress monitoring.

The New Standards and Indicators of Quality

The research literature cited here, along with dozens of other studies, was used as the foundation for the development of the new K-12 Standards and Indicators of Quality Practice (National Youth Leadership Council, 2008). As described in the final chapter of this book, reactor panels across the nation participated in tuning the standards, using a standardized standards-setting process. The final standards and indicators of quality are presented in Exhibit 6.1.

Testing the Standards

The standards represent an important step in helping the field of service-learning to progress, both in terms of motivating others to adopt service-learning as an important pedagogy and to implement it effectively, and in demonstrating the impact of participation in service-learning on K-12 youth. Now that the standards have been distilled and broadly disseminated, it is even more important that they be tested, both as a group and as single predicators of outcomes, to validate their existence as standards. For this reason, Billig and colleagues developed a set

Exhibit 6.1.   K-12 Standards and Indicators of Quality Practice (NYLC, 2008)

Duration and Intensity
Standard: Service-learning has sufficient duration and intensity to address community needs and meet specified outcomes.

Indicators:
1. Service-learning experiences include the processes of investigating community needs, preparing for service, action, reflection, demonstration of learning and impacts, and celebration.
2. Service-learning is conducted during concentrated blocks of time across a period of several weeks or months.
3. Service-learning experiences provide enough time to address identified community needs and achieve learning outcomes.

Link to Curriculum
Standard: Service-learning is intentionally used as an instructional strategy to meet learning goals and/or content standards.

Indicators:
1. Service-learning has clearly articulated learning goals.
2. Service-learning is aligned with the academic and/or programmatic curriculum.
3. Service-learning helps participants learn how to transfer knowledge and skills from one setting to another.
4. Service-learning that takes place in schools is formally recognized in school board policies and student records.

Meaningful Service
Standard: Service-learning actively engages participants in meaningful and personally relevant service activities.

Indicators:
1. Service-learning experiences are appropriate to participant ages and developmental abilities.
2. Service-learning addresses issues that are personally relevant to the participants.
3. Service-learning provides participants with interesting and engaging service activities.
4. Service-learning encourages participants to understand their service experiences in the context of the underlying societal issues being addressed.
5. Service-learning leads to attainable and visible outcomes that are valued by those being served.

Youth Voice
Standard: Service-learning provides youth with a strong voice in planning, implementing, and evaluating service-learning experiences with guidance from adults.

Indicators:
1. Service-learning engages youth in generating ideas during the planning, implementation, and evaluation processes.
2. Service-learning involves youth in the decision-making process throughout the service-learning experiences.

(Table continues on next page)

Exhibit 6.1. Continued

3. Service-learning involves youth and adults in creating an environment that supports trust and open expression of ideas.
4. Service-learning promotes acquisition of knowledge and skills to enhance youth leadership and decision-making.
5. Service-learning involves youth in evaluating the quality and effectiveness of the service-learning experience.

Community Partnerships
Standard: Service-learning partnerships are collaborative, mutually beneficial, and address community needs.

Indicators:
1. Service-learning involves a variety of partners, including youth, educators, families, community members, community-based organizations, and/or businesses.
2. Service-learning partnerships are characterized by frequent and regular communication to keep all partners well-informed about activities and progress.
3. Service-learning partners collaborate to establish a shared vision and set common goals to address community needs.
4. Service-learning partners collaboratively develop and implement action plans to meet specified goals.
5. Service-learning partners share knowledge and understanding of school and community assets and needs, and view each other as valued resources.

Diversity
Standard: Service-learning promotes understanding of diversity and mutual respect among all participants.

Indicators:
1. Service-learning helps participants identify and analyze different points of view to gain understanding of multiple perspectives.
2. Service-learning helps participants develop interpersonal skills in conflict resolution and group decision-making.
3. Service-learning helps participants actively seek to understand and value the diverse backgrounds and perspectives of those offering and receiving service.
4. Service-learning encourages participants to recognize and overcome stereotypes.

Reflection
Standard: Service-learning incorporates multiple challenging reflection activities that are ongoing and that prompt deep thinking and analysis about oneself and one's relationship to society.

Indicators:
1. Service-learning reflection includes a variety of verbal, written, artistic, and nonverbal activities to demonstrate understanding and changes in participants' knowledge, skills, and/or attitudes.
2. Service-learning reflection occurs before, during, and after the service experience.
3. Service-learning reflection prompts participants to think deeply about complex community problems and alternative solutions.
4. Service-learning reflection encourages participants to examine their preconceptions and assumptions in order to explore and understand their roles and responsibilities as citizens.

(Table continues on next page)

Exhibit 6.1. Continued

5. Service-learning reflection encourages participants to examine a variety of social and civic issues related to their service-learning experience so that participants understand connections to public policy and civic life.

Progress Monitoring
Standard: Service-learning engages participants in an ongoing process to assess the quality of implementation and progress toward meeting specified goals, and uses results for improvement and sustainability.

Indicators:
1. Service-learning participants collect evidence of progress toward meeting specific service goals and learning outcomes from multiple sources throughout the service-learning experience.
2. Service-learning participants collect evidence of the quality of service-learning implementation from multiple sources throughout the service-learning experience.
3. Service-learning participants use evidence to improve service-learning experiences.
4. Service-learning participants communicate evidence of progress toward goals and outcomes with the broader community, including policy-makers and education leaders, to deepen service-learning understanding and ensure that high quality practices are sustained.

---

of subscales to measure the extent to which the standards were being implemented in various programs and the degree to which they indeed predict desired outcomes for K-12 students.

The research presented here represents one of the many studies now in place to measure the extent to which the standards predict outcomes. The particular study that is being reported in this chapter is the third year of a character education evaluation project for the School District of Philadelphia. Service-learning is the strategy being used to promote character development and civic engagement. Background for the study and the overall research results from previous years of evaluation of the School District of Philadelphia's character education program were presented in last year's volume of the *Advances in Service-Learning Research* series (Billig et al., 2008) and in another journal (Billig, Jesse, Brodersen & Grimley, 2008). Overall results for the study that is discussed here are also presented elsewhere (Billig & Brodersen, 2008).

The overall results, comparing students participating in service-learning with those in classrooms not using service-learning, were moderately positive but did not confirm the larger, statistically significant effects of participation in service-learning seen in previous studies. The researchers wondered whether the overall modest effects of participating in service-learning were being statistically masked by variation in quality. It was hypothesized, then, that when quality was taken into account, outcomes would be significant and positive. Specifically, the hypothesis was students that participated in high quality service-learning experiences would be more likely to have increases in scores of academic proficiency as measured by standardized achievement tests and improvement in behavioral measures associated with academic success, than would students that did not participate in service-learning. Further, it was hypothesized that each of the separate standards for quality would be positively associated with academic outcomes.

To test these hypotheses, analyses were conducted in which comparison students' academic and behavioral achievement data were compared to data for those participating students from classes exhibiting high quality service-learning practice. High quality practice was measured by teacher responses to the portion of the survey measuring the K-12 standards of quality practice. Details of the study are presented next.

Research Questions

The questions guiding the research presented here were the following:

1. To what extent do students who participate in high quality service-learning experiences show differences relative to their nonparticipating peers on state assessments measuring academic achievement (test scores)?

2. To what extent do students who participate in high quality service-learning experiences show differences relative to their nonparticipating peers on measures of attendance, tardiness, and disciplinary referrals for suspension?

3. To what extent are each of the K-12 standards and indicators of quality practice associated with measures of academic achievement and behaviors and which have the strongest associations?

METHOD

This study employed a quasi-experimental design with matched comparison groups. In each school, participating classrooms were matched with nonparticipating classrooms at the same grade level and for the same subject matter. By matching classrooms from the same schools, grade levels, and subject matters, it was assumed that groups would be equivalent at the outset and this was borne out, as described below.

Sample

The sample for Grades 6-12 portion of the study reported here included 261 service-learning students and 272 matched comparison students. The sample included only those that completed both pre- and posttest surveys. Because of attrition, group equivalence was determined at the pre- and posttest. Groups were statistically equivalent with regard to demographic characteristics and test scores from the previous year's test administration. The characteristics of the entire sample (all students in the participating classrooms) can be found in Exhibit 6.2.

The exhibit shows that there were more females than males in this study, typical for an urban school district with high dropout rates that affect males more than females. The sample also had the largest percentage of children in the seventh and eighth grade, attending middle school.

Exhibit 6.2.   Student Sample Characteristics

	All Students	
	Frequency	*Percentage*
Gender*		
Male	240	45.6
Female	286	54.4
Grade Level		
6	84	15.9
7	118	22.4
8	194	36.8
9	36	6.8
10	52	9.9
11	36	6.8
12	7	1.3
Ethnicity**		
White	26	5.0
Asian	47	9.0
Black	276	52.9
American Indian	3	0.6
Hispanic	91	17.4
Other/Mixed	79	15.1

Note: *Seven students did not complete the question. **Respondents could choose more than one category.

Finally, more than half of the sample was either of African American or black heritage. Most of the rest of the sample also came from communities of color.

In addition to the student survey, the 35 teachers that offered service-learning in their classrooms completed a post-only survey.

Measures

Service-Learning Quality

The independent variable, quality, was determined by teacher responses to a series of items that closely paralleled the indicators of service-learning quality practice from the K-12 standards. Exhibit 6.3 shows the names of the subscales used to measure quality, a sample item, and the internal reliability of the overall scale and each subscale. Items were rated on a 4-point agreement scale where 1 = *strongly disagree* and 4 = *strongly agree*. Cronbach's *alpha* coefficient for the index of overall quality, using all items, was .948. Coefficients for all subscales and for the overall scale that included all of the subscales, showed high internal consistency. Correlations for student estimations of quality with teacher estimations were high, ranging from .89 to .96. An additional item, number of professional development sessions that were attended, was also included as a quality indicator, though it is not one of the K-12 standards or indicators, because other studies have shown that more training in service-learning was associated with stronger results (see, for example, Billig et al., 2005). Also, in addition to answering one item on the quality subscale, duration and intensity was measured by asking teachers how many hours per week and how many weeks per year were spent in service-learning activities. In the analysis, both measures were examined. Results were the same, but only the analysis based on the estimated hours and weeks provided by teachers are presented here.

Exhibit 6.4 presents the ways in which students were clustered for data analysis. Students were grouped by classroom based on estimation of quality provided by the teachers. For each subscale that measured quality, students were categorized based on the median value of each variable. Those students who were in the high quality service-learning group were then compared with those students from matched classrooms who did not participate in service-learning.

Academic Achievement and Behaviors

Academic achievement was measured by changes in test scores on the Pennsylvania State System of Accountability (PSSA). Scores from the spring 2007 test administration were compared with scores from the

Exhibit 6.3.   Teacher Survey Reliability Analysis: Service-Learning Quality Indicators (*N* = 35)

	Number of Items	Sample Item(s)	Cronbach's Alpha
Overall quality	33	(See items below)	.948
Duration and intensity	1	There was enough time devoted for service-learning activities to achieve the intended project outcomes.	—
Link to curriculum	3	Learning goals for service-learning activities were clearly articulated.	.794
Meaningful service	5	Service-learning activities addressed issues that were personally relevant to the youth.	.835
Youth voice	6	Youth generated ideas throughout the service-learning process.	.860
Community partnerships	5	Service-learning partners collaborated to set common project goals.	.899
Diversity	4	Service-learning activities helped youth recognize and overcome stereotypes	.834
Reflection	5	Reflection occurred before, during, and after the service experience.	.841
Progress monitoring	4	Evidence was used to improve the service-learning process.	.830

Exhibit 6.4.   Service-Learning Quality Variables Used to Group Participating Students

	Category Definitions for Service-Learning Quality Groupings	
	Low Quality	High Quality
Total number of hours class was engaged in service-learning	30 or fewer	More than 30
Link to curriculum	At or below median (3.33)	Above median
Meaningful service	At or below median (3.80)	Above median
Youth voice	At or below median (3.67)	Above median
Community partnerships	At or below median (3.20)	Above median
Diversity	At or below median (3.50)	Above median
Reflection	At or below median (3.40)	Above median
Progress monitoring	At or below median (3.00)	Above median
Overall service-learning quality	At or below median (3.45)	Above median
Number of professional development (PD) sessions attended by the teacher	4 or fewer	5 or more

spring 2008 test administration in mathematics and reading for all students with matched pre and post surveys. Scores from the science and writing portions of the test were also examined.

Behavioral measures included average daily attendance (score ranges from 0.00–1.00, with 1.00 indicating perfect attendance for the year), total number of serious behavioral incidents, and total number of suspensions (in-school and out-of-school).

Analyses

For the analysis of test scores and behavioral outcomes, ANCOVA were used that controlled for students' test scores from the previous school year, since those scores are consistently found to be the best predictors of future scores.

Because the PSSA science and writing tests were not administered in consecutive years, students' prior achievement scores could not be controlled, so for these data, t tests were used to compare the student groups. (These analyses should be viewed with greater caution.) All PSSA scaled scores were converted into normal curve equivalency scores (NCEs) so that the data could be aggregated across grade levels for the analyses.

RESULTS

The first research question addressed the relationship between high-quality service-learning and academic achievement. First, the ANCOVA for students' mathematics test scores revealed that students that participated in high quality reflection activities achieved significantly higher test scores than their peers ($F(1, 433) = 3.997$, $p < .05$, $d = .132$), as shown in Exhibit 6.5. Average differences in test scores were 2.64 NCEs.

Results of the ANCOVA analyses showed that PSSA Reading scores were significantly higher for service-learning students in classrooms that had several quality variables, specifically number of hours spent doing service-learning, reflection, links to the curriculum, and progress monitoring. These results are displayed in Exhibit 6.6.

Exhibit 6.7 shows that the PSSA science scores of participating students were significantly higher than those of comparison students when the following quality indicators were evident: Over 30 hours spent on service-learning, high numbers of professional development sessions attended by the teachers, better quality partnerships, and meaningful service.

Finally, results from t-tests showed that service-learning students had significantly higher PSSA writing scores than comparison students when

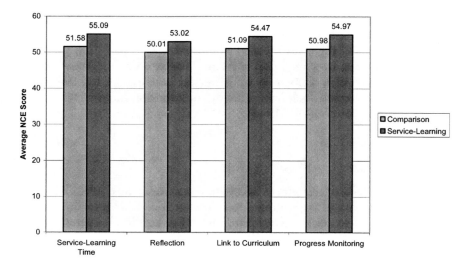

Note: Service-Learning Time: $F(1, 401) = 5.013, p < .05, d = .171$. Reflection: $F(1, 431) = 4.139, p < .05, d = .148$. Link to Curriculum: $F(1, 446) = 5.750, p < .05, d = .163$. Progress Monitoring: $F(1, 434) = 7.620, p < .01, d = .191$.

Exhibit 6.5.   Differences between comparison students and students from high quality service-learning classrooms on PSSA reading scores.

their projects were characterized by sufficient time spent on service-learning, overall high quality, strong links to the curriculum, good partnerships, meaningful service, and use of progress monitoring. Differences between the groups are presented graphically in Exhibit 6.8.

Behavioral Results

The second research question explored the impact of high-quality service-learning on students' school-related behaviors. Behavioral measures included attendance, tardiness, suspensions, and serious incidents. Results from the ANCOVA analyses showed that every quality indicator except reflection and student voice had a significant effect on students' average daily attendance. For each indicator, the students participating in higher quality service-learning activities attended school significantly more frequently than comparison students. As seen in Exhibit 6.9, overall service-learning quality and meaningful service had the strongest positive impact on student attendance.

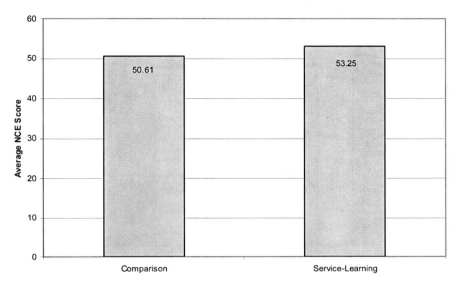

Note: $F(1, 433) = 3.997, p < .05, d = .132$. (The F statistic provides a basis to test for statistical significance when used in ANOVA).

Exhibit 6.6.   Differences between comparison students and students from service-learning classrooms utilizing high-quality reflection on PSSA mathematics scores.

Results for tardiness showed an association with one of the quality variables. After controlling for students' tardiness rated from the 2006-2007 school year, ANCOVA analyses showed that service-learning students had significantly fewer tardies than comparison students when their service-learning activities occupied more than 30 hours ($F(1, 618) = 4.358, p < .05, d = .162$.) Average differences were 2.11 tardies per year.

Several service-learning quality indicators were associated with the number of suspensions students received during the school year. Overall service-learning quality, partnership quality, meaningful service, and progress monitoring all had a significant positive effect. As demonstrated in Exhibit 6.10, students participating in high-quality service-learning received significantly fewer suspensions over the year.

Finally, the influence of high-quality service-learning on the frequency of serious incidents was examined. Participation in high-quality service-learning was not found to significantly affect the number of serious incidents in which students were involved during the school year.

The third research question addressed the extent to which each of the standards separately affected results. As can be seen in Exhibit 6.11, at least some associations were found between each of the standards of qual-

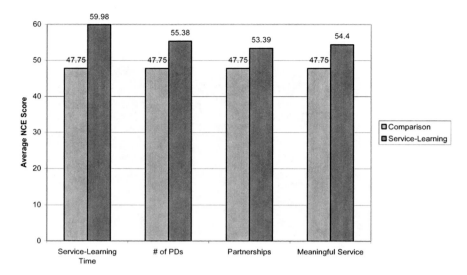

Note: Service-Learning Time: $t(175) = 4.041, p < .001, d = .608$. # of PDs: $t(211) = 2.692$, $p < .01, d = .372$. Partnerships: $t(234) = 2.088, p < .05, d = .278$. Meaningful Service: $t(201) = 2.332, p < .05, d = .328$.

Exhibit 6.7.   Differences between comparison students and students from high quality service-learning classrooms on PSSA science scores.

ity and the measures of academic performance and behaviors, with the exception of student voice.

DISCUSSION

From these data, it is clear that quality impacts various measures of student achievement. Interestingly but perhaps not surprisingly, duration, meaningful service, partnership quality, progress monitoring, and link to curriculum had the largest number of effects. In addition, the patterns of effects are revealing. For example, reading scores were more likely to be affected by duration, link to curriculum, reflection, and progress monitoring. This seems logical, particularly in the instances where the service being provided was also discussed in relationship to novels on the same topic or if reflection promoted comprehension or drawing inferences. More time spent in investigations would also seem to be potentially linked to higher reading scores and, presumably, progress monitoring meant

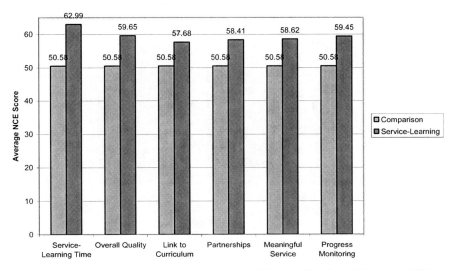

Note: Service-Learning Time: $t(349) = 3.860$, $p < .001$, $d = .430$. Overall Quality: $t(323) = 4.800$, $p < .001$, $d = .577$. Link to Curriculum: $t(339) = 2.862$, $p < .01$, $d = .325$. Partnerships: $t(369) = 3.473$, $p < .01$, $d = .369$. Meaningful Service: $t(337) = 3.274$, $p < .01$, $d = .377$. Progress Monitoring: $t(323) = 3.371$, $p < .01$, $d = .400$.

Exhibit 6.8.   Differences between comparison students and students from high quality service-learning classrooms on PSSA writing scores.

that teachers and students alike were assessing the extent to which they were reaching important goals, such as mastery of curricular objectives.

The relationship between duration and the academic outcome areas is consistent with other findings that show that students are more highly engaged in service-learning than other instructional strategies and therefore come to class more often (e.g., Billig et al., 2005) It also seems apparent that if students attend school more often, they are more likely to learn the curricular objectives they are expected to master. The relationship to partnership quality also seems rather easy to explain in that if the quality was high, students would be more motivated to engage in the activity than if the quality was low.

The influence of meaningfulness on a variety of outcome measures also appears to suggest that engaging in more meaningful activities may be related to efficacy, which in turn is often associated with gains in academic performance, as was discussed in the literature review provided at the beginning of this chapter.

The surprise in these findings is the lack of relationship between student voice and the academic and behavioral outcomes. The literature

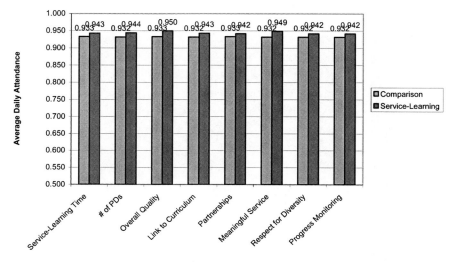

Note: Service-Learning Time: $F(1, 615) = 4.960, p < .05, d = .179.$# of PDs: $F(1, 642) = 7.727, p < .01, d = .214.$Overall Quality: $F(1, 640) = 15.826, p < .001, d = .303.$ Link to Curriculum: $F(1, 671) = 6.216, p < .05, d = .188.$ Partnerships: $F(1, 683) = 5.579, p < .05, d = .159.$ Meaningful Service: $F(1, 642) = 15.173, p < .001, d = .280.$ Respect for Diversity: $F(1, 642) = 5.295, p < .05, d = .177.$ Progress Monitoring: $F(1, 674) = 5.787, p < .05, d = .168.$

Exhibit 6.9.   Differences between comparison students and students from high quality service-learning classrooms on average daily attendance.

strongly suggests that students who have more control over their learning do better (e.g., Eccles, Early, Frasier, Belansky, & McCarthy, 1997). It is curious, then, why voice is not related to outcomes in this study. It is possible that more voice meant that students were not stretching themselves and learning new content. It is also possible that voice was not well-understood by teachers and that they rated their implementation higher than what it was, though their ratings were highly correlated with student ratings. It is also possible that the wrong dimensions of voice are being specified and thus measured as part of this standard. Much more research is needed to understand the lack of relationship found here.

While this study represents an important contribution to the body of literature, much more research is needed to test all of the standards and indicators so that practitioners can know with certainty that they represent the most effective practices. More studies are also needed to understand acceptable variation and the contexts in which the variables operate most effectively. Interactions with specific content matter need to be

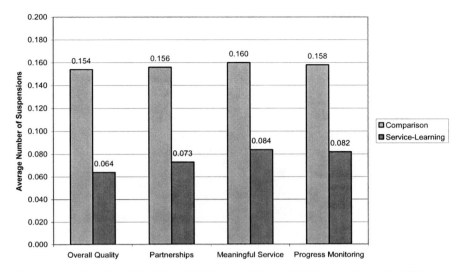

Note: Overall Quality: $F(1, 643) = 69.859, p < .001, d = .229$. Partnerships: $F(1, 683) = 6.635, p < .05, d = .203$. Meaningful Service: $F(1, 642) = 4.446, p < .05, d = .170$. Progress Monitoring: $F(1, 674) = 4.772, p < .05, d = .172$.

Exhibit 6.10.   Differences between comparison students and students from high quality service-learning classrooms on average number of suspensions.

investigated, along with questions about which of the standards appear to be most important for different types of students or schools.

This research represents the beginning of a fruitful line of inquiry. Studies such as these serve to illuminate the important factors of practice that will help service-learning to thrive and become more prevalent in K-12 schools. Clearly, the K-12 standards should also be used to inform teacher education programs. Finally, studies like this one also suggest promising avenues for research in higher education.

REFERENCES

Ammon, M. S., Furco, A., Chi, B., & Middaugh, E. (2002). *A profile of California's CalServe service-learning partnerships, 1997-2000.* Sacramento: California Department of Education.

Andersen, S. (1998, September). *Service learning: A national strategy for youth development.* Washington, DC: George Washington University. Retrieved June 1, 2007, from www.gwu.edu/~ccps/pop_svc.html

**Exhibit 6.11. Student Impact Areas by
Service-Learning Quality Standard**

Service-Learning Time • PSSA Reading • PSSA Science • PSSA Writing • Tardiness • Average daily attendance	Link to Curriculum • PSSA Reading • PSSA Writing • Average daily attendance
Meaningful Service • PSSA Science • PSSA Writing • Average daily attendance • Number of suspensions	Youth Voice • No effects
Community Partnerships • PSSA Science • PSSA Writing • Average daily attendance • Number of suspensions	Diversity • Average Daily Attendance
Reflection • PSSA Mathematics • PSSA Reading	Progress Monitoring • PSSA Reading • PSSA Writing • Average daily attendance • Number of suspensions

Billig, S. H. (2002). Adoption, implementation, and sustainability of K-12 service-learning. In A. Furco & S. H. Billig (Eds.), *Service-learning: The essence of the pedagogy.* Greenwich, CT: Information Age.

Billig, S. H. (2004). Heads, hearts, hands: The research on K–12 service-learning. In J. Kielsmeier, M. Neal, & M. McKinnon (Eds.), *Growing to greatness (G2G): The state of service-learning project* (pp. 12-25). St. Paul, MN: National Youth Leadership Council.

Billig, S. H., & Brodersen, R. M. (2007). *Case studies of effective practices in the partnership in character education project: Evaluation for the School District of Philadelphia.* Denver, CO: RMC Research Corporation.

Billig, S. H. & Brodersen, R. M. (2008). *Evaluation of the Philadelphia Partnerships in Character Education Grant.* Denver, CO:RMC Research Corporation

Billig, S. H., & Fredericks, L. (2008). *Community partnerships.* St. Paul, MN: National Youth Leadership Council. Retrieved April 30, 2009 from www.nylc.org/standards/research/communitypartnerships

Billig, S. H., Jesse, D., & Grimley, M. (2008). *The Philadelphia story.* In M. Bowden, S. H. Billig, & B. A. Holland (Eds.), *Scholarship for sustaining service-learning and civic engagement.* Greenwich, CT: Information Age.

Billig, S. H., Jesse, D., Brodersen, M., & Grimley, M. (2008). Using service-learning to promote character education in a large urban district. *Journal of Research in Character Education, 6*(1), 21-34.

Billig, S. H,. & Northup, J. (2008) *Intensity and duration.* St. Paul, MN: National Youth Leadership Council. Retrieved April 30, 2009 from www.nylc.org /standards/research/duration

Billig, S. H., Root, S., & Jesse, D. (2005). The relationship between quality indicators of service-learning and student outcomes: Testing professional wisdom. In S. Root, J. Callahan, & S. H. Billig (Eds.), *Advances in service-learning research: Improving service-learning practice: Research on models to enhance impacts* (pp. 97-115). Greenwich, CT: Information Age.

Blyth, D., Saito, R., & Berkas, T. (1997). A quantitative study of the impact of service-learning programs. In A. Waterman (Ed.), *Service-learning: Applications from the research* (pp. 39-55). Mahwah, NJ: Erlbaum.

Catalano, R. F., Haggerty, K. P., Oesterle, S., Fleming, C. B., & Hawkins, J. D. (2004). The importance of bonding to school for healthy development: Findings from the Social Development Research Group. *Journal of School Health, 74*(7), 252-261.

Conrad, D., & Hedin, D. (1980). *Executive summary of the final report of the experiential education evaluation project.* Minneapolis: University of Minnesota, Center for Youth Development.

Conrad, D., & Hedin, D. (1987). *Youth service: A guidebook for developing and operating effective programs.* Washington DC: Independent Sector.

Dewey, J. (1933). *School and society* (2nd ed.). Chicago: University of Chicago Press.

Eccles, J., Early, D., Frasier, K, Belansky, E., & McCarthy, K. (1997). The relation of connection, regulation, and support for autonomy to adolescents' functioning. *Journal of Adolescent Research, 12*(2), 263-286.

Eyler, J., & Giles, D., Jr. (1997). The importance of program quality in service-learning. In A. Waterman (Ed.), *Service-learning: Applications from the research* (pp. 57-76). Mahwah, NJ: Erlbaum.

Eyler, J., & Giles, D., Jr. (1999). *Where's the learning in service-learning?* San Francisco: Jossey-Bass.

Fredericks, L. (2002). *Learning that lasts: How service-learning can become an integral part of schools, states and communities.* Denver, CO: Education Commission of the States.

Fredericks, L., & Billig, S. H. (2008). *Meaningful service.* St. Paul, MN: National Youth Leadership Council retrieved April 30, 2009 from www.nylc.org /standards/research/meaningfulservice

Fredericks, L., Kaplan, E., & Zeisler, J. (2001). *Integrating youth voice in service-learning.* Denver, CO: Education Commission of the States.

Furco, A. (2002). Is service-learning really better than community service? A study of high school service program outcomes. In A. Furco & S. H. Billig (Eds.), *Service-learning: The essence of the pedagogy.* Greenwich, CT: Information Age.

Greene, D., & Diehm, G. (1995). Educational and service outcomes of a service integration effort. *Michigan Journal of Community Service Learning, 2,* 54-62.

Gregory, P., Steinbring, Y. J., & Sousa, C. M. (2003, April). *Voluntary community involvement of Latinos: A literature review.* Davis: University of California. Retrieved May 31, 2009, from http://ucce.ucdavis.edu/files/filelibrary/5433/ 8114.pdf

Hamilton, S. F., & Zeldin, R. S. (1987, Winter). Learning civics in the community. *Curriculum Inquiry, 17*(4), 407-420.

Hammond, L., & Heredia, S. (2002, Spring). Fostering diversity through community service learning. *Service-Learning Network, 9*(1), 2-5.

Hecht, D. (2003). The missing link: Exploring the context of learning in service-learning. In S.H. Billig & J. Eyler (Eds.), *Deconstructing service-learning: Research exploring context, participation, and impacts* (pp. 25-49). Greenwich, CT: Information Age.

Hobbs, B. B. (2001, August). Diversifying the volunteer base: Latinos and volunteerism. *Journal of Extension, 39*(4), 1-7. Retrieved May 31, 2009, from http://www.joe.org/joe/2001august/a1.html

Hurtado, S., Milem, J. F., Clayton-Pedersen, A. R., & Allen, W. R. (1999). Enacting diverse learning environments: Improving the climate for racial/ethnic diversity in higher education. *ASHE-ERIC Higher Education Report, 26*(8). San Francisco: Jossey Bass. (ERIC Document Reproduction Service No. ED430514)

Kramer, M. (2000). *Make it last forever: The institutionalization of service learning in America.* Washington, DC: Corporation for National Service.

Laird, M., & Black, S. (2002). *Report for U.S. Department of Education Expert Panel on Safe, Disciplined, and Drug-Free Schools.* Annapolis Junction, MD: Lions-Quest. Retrieved May 31, 2009 from http://www.lions-quest.org/content/whatsnew/SFG_EvaluationReport.pdf

Larson, R., Walker, K., & Pearce, N. (2004). A comparison of youth-driven and adult-driven youth programs: Balancing inputs from youth and adults. *Journal of Community Psychology, 33*(1), 57–74.

Lennon, T. (2009) *Service-learning and Hispanic students: What works in the field.* Denver, CO: Education Commission of the States.

Melchior, A. (1999). *National Evaluation of Learn and Serve America School and Community-Based Programs: Final report.* Washington, DC: Corporation for National and Community Service.

Melchior, A., & Orr, L. (1995). *Evaluation of National and Community Service Programs* (Report prepared for the Corporation for National Service). Cambridge, MA: Abt Associates.

Meyer, S., & Billig, S. H. (2003). *Evaluation of need in deed.* Denver, CO: RMC Research Corporation.

Mitra, D. (2004). The significance of students: Can increasing "student voice" in schools lead to gains in youth development? *Teachers College Record, 106*(4), 651–688.

Morgan, W., & Streb, M. (2003). First do no harm: The importance of student ownership in service-learning. *Metropolitan Universities, 13*(3), 321–345.

National Research Council. (1999). *How people learn.* Washington, DC: National Academies Press.

National Research Council. (2004). *Engaging schools, engaging students.* Washington, DC: National Academies Press.

National Service-Learning Cooperative. (1999). *Essential elements of service-learning.* St. Paul, MN: National Youth Leadership Council.

National Youth Leadership Council. (2008). *K-12 Service-learning standards for quality practice*. Retrieved May 31, 2009 from www.nylc.org/standards

Northup, J. (2007, September). *Evaluation of the CampFire USA community preparedness initiative*. Denver, CO: RMC Research Corporation.

Oldfather, P. (1995). Songs "come back most to them": Students' experiences as researchers. *Theory into Practice, 34*(2), 131.

Roehlkepartain, E. C. (2007). Service-learning with disadvantaged youth (fact sheet). Scotts Valley, CA: National Service-Learning Clearinghouse. Retrieved from www.servicelearning.org

Root, S., & Billig, S. H. (2008). Service-learning as a promising approach to high school civic engagement. In J. Bixby & J. Pace (Eds.), *Educating democratic citizens in troubled times: Qualitative studies of current efforts*. Albany: SUNY Press.

Safer, N., & Fleischman, S. (2005, February). Research matters: How student progress monitoring improves instruction. *Educational Leadership, 62*(4), 81-83.

Scales, P. C., Blyth, D. A., Berkas, T. H., & Kielsmeier, J. C. (2000, August).The effects of service-learning on middle school students' social responsibility and academic success. *Journal of Early Adolescence, 20*(3), 332-358.

Schunk, D., & Pajares, F. (2002). The development of academic self-efficacy. In A. Wigfield & J. Eccles (Eds.), *Development of achievement motivation* (pp. 16–32). San Diego, CA: Academic Press.

Spring, K, Dietz, N., & Grimm, R. (2006, March). *Youth helping America: Service-learning, school-based service and youth civic engagement*. Washington, DC: Corporation for National & Community Service.

Vang, K. (2004-2005, Winter). Engaging the voices from the rim: Refugees, immigrants, migrants, and service-learning in urban communities. *The Generator*, 21-23.

Wade, R. C. (1997). *Community service-learning: A guide to including service in the public school curriculum*. Albany: State University of New York.

Wang, M., & Stiles, B. (1976). An investigation of children's concept of self-responsibility for their school learning. *American Educational Research Journal, 13*, 159.

Waterman, A. (1993). Conducting research on reflective activities in service-learning. In H. Silcox (Ed.), *A how-to guide to reflection: Adding cognitive learning to community service programs* (pp. 90-99). Philadelphia: Brighton Press.

Yamauchi, L., Billig, S. H., Meyer, S., & Hofshire, L. (2007). *Student outcomes associated with service-learning in a culturally relevant high school program.*

Zeldin, S. (2004). Youth as agents of adult and community development: Mapping the processes and outcomes of youth engaged in organizational governance. *Applied Developmental Science, 8*(2), 75–90.

CHAPTER 7

RECIPROCAL BENEFITS OF MENTORING

Results of a Middle School-University Collaboration

Angela M. Harwood and Sara A. Radoff

ABSTRACT

We report on a 2-year investigation of an after-school mentoring project collaboratively designed through a middle school-university partnership. The program was developed to meet the middle school's need to support moderately at-risk youth, while also providing a powerful experiential learning opportunity for preservice teachers. Participants engaged in self-exploration and relationship-building activities, in addition to working together to design and implement community action projects. Outcomes for both service-learners and recipients of service are presented. Middle school youth gained social and emotional skills, improved academic attitudes, and heightened community engagement. Mentors developed knowledge of middle school youth, teaching, and interpersonal skills, increased understanding of the community and changed attitudes about teaching. Differential findings from year 1 and year 2 of implementation are interpreted based on changes in program design.

Creating Our Identities in Service-Learning and Community Engagement
pp. 159–188
Copyright © 2009 by Information Age Publishing

INTRODUCTION

Designing mutually beneficial partnerships is a key cornerstone of service-learning pedagogy. Our research helps to address a gap in the literature about how service-learning experiences benefit both the recipients and the service providers. This paper includes data from a two-year investigation of an after-school group mentoring program collaboratively designed through a middle school-university partnership. Teams of middle school youth and preservice teacher mentors participated in activities designed to lead both youth and adults through self-exploration, relationship building, and social skill development, as they took part in community engagement projects.

Group Mentoring and Community-Based Learning Outcomes for Youth

Our mentoring programs were designed to increase youth engagement and improve behaviors in school by employing school connectedness theories. School connectedness is the belief by students that they are supported academically and emotionally by adults in their school (Blum, 2005). Connectedness literature suggests when youth are confident in themselves, have positive relationships with peers, school staff, and administrators, feel physical and emotional safety at school, and are active in their schools or communities, they may become more "connected" to school (Blum, 2005; Karcher, 2005). Connectedness increases educational motivation, classroom engagement, academic performance and school completion rates, in addition to decreasing absenteeism, fighting, bullying and vandalism (Blum, 2005).

We also considered social and emotional learning (SEL) approaches in creating and evaluating our programs. SEL programs guide youth to explore themselves, appreciate the perspectives of others, develop positive attitudes and goals, make responsible decisions, and handle interpersonal situations effectively (Greenberg, Weissberg, O'Brian, Zins, Fredricks, Resnick, et al., 2003). Durlak and Weissberg (2007) found that as a result of SEL approaches, youth improved self-confidence and self-esteem, demonstrated positive feelings about school, exhibited positive social behaviors, and improved school grades. Program participants also showed reductions in problem behaviors including aggression, noncompliance and misconduct.

A well-developed body of research on traditional one-on-one mentoring indicates positive effects on the social development of youth (DuBois, Holloway, Valentine, & Cooper, 2002; Grossman & Tierney, 1998;

Hamilton, Hamilton, Hirsch, Hughes, King, & Maton, 2006; Rhodes, Spencer, Keller, Liang, & Noam, 2006). Traditional mentoring also improves academic performance and behaviors (Herrera, Grossman, Kauh, Feldman, McMaken, & Jucovy, 2006). However, despite common assumptions that traditional one-on-one mentoring would improve self-esteem, DuBois et al. (2002) found that it actually had only a marginal effect on emotional development.

Group mentoring may yield outcomes not typically obtained through traditional one-on-one mentoring by increasing healthy peer relationships and fostering emotional development. Herrera, Vang, and Gale (2002) reported that group mentoring helps youth develop peer social skills and form relationships with adults. Specifically, group mentoring promoted youths' ability to work with peers and increased their communication skills. It helps youth extend their social circles and problem-solve relationships. The researchers found that group mentoring also influenced emotional development by providing a safe place for self-exploration where youth became less shy and inhibited.

In our program, youth and mentors complete a community-based action project together. Pittman and Wright (1991) suggested that community service programs have the capacity to meet adolescents' needs for belonging, self-worth, contribution, independence and personal confidence by creating a sense of group cohesion, and presenting achievable and challenging goals while establishing meaningful outlets for creative contribution to the community. Engaging youth in community action projects strengthens their connection to society, leading to personal and relational outcomes (Damon, 2004). Lerner, Fisher, and Weinberg (2000) indicated that such engagement opportunities increased not only a young person's connection to society, but also their personal confidence and efficacy, in addition to establishing positive bonds based on care and compassion for others.

Although youth participation in our program does not meet the pure definition of service-learning because the program was organized as an extra-curricular rather than a classroom-based academic activity, the service-learning literature does inform our understanding of potential youth outcomes. Fertman (2000) asserts that during this period of cognitive development, early adolescents are forming identities, becoming more independent, and solidifying perceptions of morality and belonging, all of which are enhanced through service-learning. Billig (2006) noted that service-learning can contribute to school engagement, helping students to develop a sense of belonging and connectedness to school. Service-learning contributes to enjoyment of school, particularly when the service-learning experience includes cognitive challenge, meets genuine needs, values diversity and features student-chosen topics (Billig,

Root, & Jesse, 2005). Melchoir and Balis (2002) also reported that service-learning increases school engagement; others report improved motivation (RMC Corporation, 2002).

Researchers examining service-learning have reported gains in youth social or emotional development, academics, or community awareness. Social and emotional gains include helping youth relate to adults (Fertman, White & White, 1996), facilitating the development of self-efficacy (Fertman et al., 1996; RMC Corporation, 2002), and developing empathy and a sense of group belonging (Billig, Jesse, Brodersen, & Grimley, 2008). It can also lead to skill development such as improved communication or interpersonal skills (Billig et al., 2008; Melchior & Balis, 2002; RMC Corporation, 2002) or teamwork and leadership skills (Billig et al., 2008; RMC Corporation, 2002.) Reported academic outcomes include reduced absenteeism, grade or grade point average improvement (Melchoir & Balis, 2002) and developing skills in project organization (Billig et al., 2008). Finally, participating in service-learning may change youths' perceptions of their community. Community outcomes include finding realistic solutions to problems (Fertman et al., 1996), increased involvement in service (Melchoir & Balis, 2002), gaining knowledge of community issues (Billig et al., 2008) and developing a sense of personal and social responsibility, (RMC Corporation, 2002).

Preservice Teacher Service-Learning Outcomes

In designing and evaluating this program we reviewed research on the outcomes of mentoring for mentors, mentoring as a service-learning approach in teacher education, and intersections between service-learning outcomes and national standards in teacher education. Benefits for mentors who have participated in traditional one-on-one mentoring experiences include developing listening and communication skills that value youth perspectives (Libby, Rosen, & Sedonaen, 2005; Russ, 1993) and a commitment to and appreciation for others (Cameron & Manju, 1997). Mentors also develop teaching strategies and motivational techniques (Russ 1993). Personal benefits from mentoring include increased confidence and affirmation of personal identity (Good, Halpin, & Halpin, 2000) or improved academic attitudes and performance (Good et al., 2000; Russ, 1993). Group mentoring, in particular, provides mentors insight into youth behaviors, social skills, interests and needs (Herrera et al., 2002).

While much of the existing literature on service-learning in teacher education focuses specifically on tutoring or academic classroom placements, there is also an emerging literature on the impact of mentoring placements specifically. Mentoring enabled preservice teachers to develop critical instructional skills (Murray, 1996) such as a better understanding of English language learners and their families (Crawford & Post, 2007; Hale, 2007) and an increased understanding of cross-cultural communication and relationship building (Crawford & Post, 2007). In addition, involving preservice teachers in facilitating service-learning projects with K-12 students—a form of service-learning mentoring—results in their increased understanding of students, service-learning and general pedagogy, the community, and themselves (Harwood, Fliss, & Gaulding, 2006). Other researchers report that assisting P-12 teachers in implementing service-learning in their classrooms leads to more positive attitudes toward the pedagogy (Wade, 1995) or the intent to use it in their future classrooms (Root, Callahan & Sepanski, 2002).

Previous researchers have drawn connections between service-learning experiences and the competencies established by the Interstate New Teacher and Support Consortium (INTASC, 1992) and the National Council for the Accreditation of Teacher Education (NCATE, 2002) (Callahan, Diez, & Ryan, 2001; Harwood & Salzman, 2007; Ryan & Callahan, 1999, 2002). Harwood and Salzman (2007) reported that these outcomes directly related to the standards include increased understanding of diverse learners, practice collaborating with community organizations, social services, and community members, and communicating with parents.

The Present Study

Our study explores the social, emotional and skill-based outcomes for the recipients of service—in this case, the middle school youth. We also explore how mentoring placements develop compassionate and skilled educators equipped to reach even the most challenging populations. Specifically, we explore the following questions:

1. What are outcomes for mentored youth following experiential activities focused on self-exploration, relating to others, and community engagement?

2. What are the outcomes for preservice teachers participating in a service-learning mentoring program?

3. How do changes in program structure affect outcomes for all participants?

METHOD

Program Description

The data reported here were collected during year-end evaluations of programs offered during the 2006-07 and 2007-08 school years. Both years the program sought to enhance youth connectedness to their peers, caring adults, and their community by engaging them in group mentoring and positive youth development methods. It was also designed to offer preservice teachers the opportunity to get to know youth on an individualized basis while practicing essential teaching skills.

The program design evolved substantially between Year 1 and Year 2. In both years, mentors and youth met together during after school hours once per week and engaged in community exploration activities and large group field trips, including visits to the university campus. Each year mentors and youth worked in teams to identify problematic community issues and implement projects to address them. From Year 1 to Year 2 of implementation, however, many elements of the program changed. Changes included moving from a one-on-one to a small-group mentoring format, from a 6- to 9-month delivery, and from a focus solely on community projects to an emphasis on personal self-exploration and relationship development components. Details for each program year follow.

The Year 1 program, named CLIMB (Community Leadership Investment and Mentor Building), ran for a 6-month period and featured one-to-one mentoring for an hour each week. The program loosely followed a 4-H civics curriculum called Public Adventures (National 4-H, 2005). Weekly meetings consisted of a one-on-one check-in between mentors and youth, followed by a short opening activity with the entire group. The majority of the time during these meetings was spent in community action project teams consisting of 2-3 youth/mentor pairs. In Year 1, there were three community project teams, each of which independently chose to do projects benefiting animals. Projects included a movie night fundraiser for the Alternative Humane Society, a dog biscuit bake sale to benefit the Whatcom Humane Society, and the filming of a public service announcement on the importance of properly disposing of pet waste.

The Year 2 program, "Youth4R.E.A.L.," (Relationships, Exploration, Action and Leadership) ran for a 9-month period and employed group mentoring techniques. The program focus expanded in the second year to include personal exploration and relationship-building in addition to community action projects. The 2-hour meeting schedule included time for "home team" groups of two mentors and 4-6 middle school students to check in, followed by a mentor-led opening activity, a large group activity, and a wrap-up in home teams. During fall, participants engaged in personal introduction activities and trust-building games; in addition, mentors led enrichment workshops based on a skill, talent or interest they wanted to share with middle schoolers. During winter quarter, they looked outward into the community by doing a community mapping activity, listening to a guest panel of community activists, and participating in a day of direct service. Spring quarter was devoted to taking action and focused on the design and implementation of community-based projects. Several large-group activities helped participants identify potential topics for projects; four action teams were then formed around those interests. Two of these teams focused on issues they identified within their school community—one group created an antihate speech Web site and the other planned an antigang rally. The two remaining teams implemented projects for the wider community. One created an animal adoption information campaign while the other collected dessert donations for a local homeless organization.

Participants

The youth who participated each year were chosen by teachers and staff at the school and were identified as "moderately at-risk." Students may have any number of the following characteristics: challenging socioeconomic environments; potential first-generation college attendees; single-parent homes; poor school attendance; low self-esteem or confidence; poor interpersonal relationship skills; or they were identified as students who would benefit from adult interaction and guidance. During Year 1, a total of 17 middle school youth participated in the program, including eight sixth graders and 11 seventh graders. Of those, we interviewed 10 youth, 5 female and 5 male. In Year 2, the program involved 20 youth, five of whom returned from the first year. They included 10 sixth graders, seven seventh graders and three eighth graders. We interviewed 15 youth, 8 female and 7 male. We interviewed every student possible each year—based on availability and our having obtained permission for the youth's research participation.

The 550 students in the sixth through eighth grades of this middle school comprise a 53% free and reduced lunch enrollment; 38% are students of color. Among our program participants both years, 50% were students of color, including 11 Latina/os, two Asians, two Native Americans and one African American. Students in the interview sample did not differ from the total program group in either gender or racial representation.

The preservice teachers participating in this program were students in the department of secondary education pursuing either postbaccalaureate or master's in teaching degrees. In total, 11 preservice teachers served as CLIMB mentors during winter and spring quarters of 2007. In that group there were 5 postbaccalaureate and 6 MIT students; eight female and three male. During Year 2, there were again 11 mentors, comprised of 2 postbaccalaureate and 9 MIT students, 8 female and 3 male. Two mentors returned from Year 1.

All preservice teacher-mentors completed service-learning components connected to teacher education courses in adolescent development, introduction to middle schools, curriculum and instruction, and management, motivation and discipline. Instructors in these courses employed reflective writing assignments to assist the preservice teachers in connecting their field experiences with course content. In addition to the connections made by instructors in these courses, the preservice teacher-mentors engaged in reflective on-site debriefing discussions at the end of each weekly mentoring session. The mentors were prepared for their work through training sessions at the outset of the program in both years, and during the second year, in two additional trainings at the beginning of winter and spring quarters.

Procedure

We conducted end-of-the-program interviews with both middle school youth and preservice teacher-mentors. A standardized interview protocol was used for each interview and was designed to elicit participants' perspectives on the structure and outcomes of the program. Year 1 youth were asked to describe their community projects and mentors' and youths' roles in them. They were then asked to describe the relationships that developed between mentors, youth and within groups. Finally, they were asked what impacts the program had on them and program evaluation questions. Based on findings from Year 1, and on the changes in program structure, Year 2 youth interviews were changed substantially. Year 2 youth interviews focused primarily on outcomes, including prompts about skill development, peer and adult relationships, academic outcomes, and community action projects.

Each year the mentors were asked to address three main topics during the interviews. They were first asked several questions prompting them to describe the program, they were then asked to assess program impacts on both themselves and on the youth, and finally, they were prompted to evaluate program strengths and weaknesses, suggesting changes for the future. Mentors were asked to consider personal outcomes related to teaching skills, community, and understanding young people. Excerpts from the interview protocols used with youth and mentors, including the question prompts used to elicit information about program outcomes, are included in the Appendix.

In analyzing participant interviews, the authors employed the analytic induction method (Bogden & Bicklen, 1992; Glasser & Strauss, 1999; Patton, 1990). In this approach, themes emerge from the data and are constantly tested and re-tested as additional data are analyzed. Over the span of two years, the authors worked with graduate students on this project. To initiate the analytical process, emergent themes were noted as the interviews were transcribed. Researchers then read all of the mentor and youth interviews, again noting emergent themes. Each team member was then assigned one segment of the data to read and for which to develop a coding schema; teammates then re-read and coded data. Researchers then participated in a series of meetings during which data were reviewed and consensus coding was reached on each data point. Researchers created data arrays of the mentor and youth outcomes in which the data were arranged by code. After rereading each of these segments of data some coding categories were combined with others, and in some instances codes were eliminated and the data sets were re-arrayed. We present program impact findings from mentors for those categories in which at least one third of the mentors over the 2 years reported outcomes. Regarding youth data, since we have outcomes reported by both youth and mentors, we report those findings separately, and indicate whether results: (1) were either consistent across or varied between mentor and youth data; (2) varied for either group substantially from Year 1 to Year 2, or (3) showed what we considered promising outcomes for future program development.

In results section below, we present both the numbers of participants whose responses fit in each category and the total number of data points. In some cases the number of data points includes multiple mentions by the same participant. We counted repeat mentions as separate data points only when participants made similar responses to different interview questions or, in some cases, when they contributed new thoughts that were coded in the same category. Reiterations or elaborations of the same thought were not counted as new data points.

RESULTS

Youth Outcomes

During interviews each year, both mentors and youth identified youth growth in four major categories including: (1) social development;

(2) emotional development; (3) community understanding; and (4) academic changes. Exhibit 7.1 summarizes youth reports and Exhibit 7.2 summarizes mentor reports of youth outcomes.

Social Development

Social development was the most frequently stated outcome by both groups, with reports from all 25 youth (194 data points) and all 22 mentors (108 data points). This category showed striking consistency across youth and mentors, over both years, with a few notable exceptions. Subcategories included the development of adult and peer relationships,

Exhibit 7.1.   Youth Reports of Youth Outcomes
(N of Youth = 25; N of Data Points = 358)

Youth Outcomes	Year 1		Year 2		Y1 + Y2
	n of Youth (n = 10)	n of Data Points (n = 56)	n of Youth (n = 15)	n of Data Points (n = 302)	Total N of Data Points (N = 358)
Social Development	10	29	15	165	194
Adult relationships	5	7	15	69	76
Peer relationships	8	15	15	34	49
Communication	3	5	9	17	22
Teamwork	1	1	11	15	16
Sensitivity to others	0	0	6	14	14
Social self-understanding	0	0	7	8	8
Diversity awareness	0	0	5	5	5
Safe environment	1	1	2	3	4
Emotional Development	9	8	15	59	67
New interests	3	3	11	17	20
Leadership	2	2	9	12	14
Self-esteem/confidence	0	0	8	13	13
Voicing ideas	3	3	6	9	12
Heightened engagement	0	0	3	5	5
Self-efficacy	0	0	2	3	3
Community Understanding	7	10	12	46	56
Involvement	6	6	12	27	33
Issue awareness	0	0	9	13	13
Community awareness	4	4	4	6	10
Academic Changes	7	9	13	32	41
Improved school attitudes	5	6	9	13	19
Academic skills	1	2	8	11	13
Project skills	1	1	8	8	9

improved communication and teamwork skills, and access to a safe environment. The second year data also revealed outcomes regarding increased sensitivity to others, social self-understanding, and diversity awareness.

The development of at least one relationship with an adult was mentioned by half of the youth in the first year and by every youth in the second year. Youth spoke about "connecting," "bonding," and "becoming friends" with the mentors. Mentors also identified adult relationships as an important outcome for youth, labeling those relationships as "stable," "respectful" and "supportive." One said, "Week in and week out, we are

Exhibit 7.2. Mentor Reports of Youth Outcomes
(N of Mentors = 22; N of Data Points = 255)

Outcome	Year 1		Year 2		Y1 + Y2
	n of Mentors (n = 11)	n of Data Points (n = 124)	n of Mentors (n = 11)	n of Data Points (n = 131)	Total N of Data Points (N = 255)
Social Development	11	64	11	44	108
Adult relationships	8	25	8	11	36
Peer relationships	8	15	6	11	26
Safe environment	3	4	7	13	17
Communication	9	14	2	2	16
Teamwork	5	6	1	1	7
Sensitivity to others	0	0	3	4	4
Social self-understanding	0	0	2	2	2
Diversity awareness	0	0	0	0	0
Emotional Development	8	38	11	64	102
Self-esteem/confidence	4	10	11	23	33
Self-efficacy	4	10	7	12	22
Voicing ideas	4	7	9	12	19
Leadership	5	9	3	3	12
Heightened engagement	0	0	7	12	12
New interests	2	2	2	2	4
Community Understanding	4	12	8	18	30
Involvement	4	9	5	6	15
Community awareness	2	3	4	7	10
Issue awareness	0	0	3	5	5
Academic Changes	4	10	4	5	15
Project skills	2	8	4	5	13
Improved school attitudes	1	1	0	0	1
Academic skills	1	1	0	0	1

going to be there for you no matter what ... so providing them that stable adult, is such a huge thing."

Participants also reported increased numbers of youth peer relationships. Youth spoke about connecting with existing friends, making new friends, and recognizing common interests. One sixth grader explains her new found admiration of her eighth grade peers:

> I thought that eighth graders were always so rude and like "arggg." Like really mean and aggressive and stuff. But they're not. They're really nice and they're always there to help you and they're role models to everybody.

Mentors also noted how youth expanded their circle of friends, learned more about one another, and that youth "got to see a different side of their peers." As one mentor noted:

> There's like a bond that develops. Whether or not the kids get along, they share this experience.... It's kind of like a way of connecting different students in ways in which otherwise they wouldn't have been connected.

Communication skills were the third most frequently cited social development outcome by youth and the fourth most frequently cited outcome by mentors. Communication skills included talking to different audiences, presenting to groups, and listening. One youth declared, "I got comfortable talking to new people," and another explained learning how to call organizations, "And talking appropriate with them. Not all slang words, but like, business kind of talk." A mentor comments:

> I know that at first, just speaking, like making phone calls or something like that would have freaked her out ... but then like you saw at the movie night, there weren't tons of people there, but there was a crowd, and it was her idea to introduce the woman.

Other subcategories within social development were identified differentially by youth and mentors. Although mentors infrequently identified teamwork skills as an outcome for youth, in the second year, 11 of the 15 youth claim they learned to work better with others. More than half of the mentors felt youth benefited from a safe environment in which students felt it was okay to be themselves, take risks, and engage in open conversation.

In Year 2 only, participants reported social outcomes of heightened sensitivity to others, social self-understanding and diversity awareness. Heightened sensitivity to others related to developing respect, trust, and empathy. Social self-understanding included comments where youth articulated refinements in social behavior or interpersonal relationship skills. One student remarked, "I was really mean to people. And I just like, stopped because of this program." Youth also discussed gaining awareness about issues related to race and class, although mentors did not identify this outcome.

Emotional Development

Emotional development was the second most frequently reported outcome, mentioned by 24 youth (64 data points) and 19 mentors (102 data points), and included the subcategories new interests, leadership, self-esteem/confidence, voicing ideas, heightened engagement, and self-efficacy. Whereas mentors identified emotional development outcomes in the first year more often than youth did, both youth and mentors recognized growth in this area in Year 2. A notable increase in emotional outcomes occurred between Year 1 and Year 2.

Youth most often reported discovering new interests. Youth developed new extracurricular interests in a broad range of activities from art to sports and literary pursuits. A youth discovered, "I did not realize I could actually garden that well ... and I like beading necklaces and stuff now." Another commented, "I didn't realize that I was a good photographer and this year I got to mess around with a camera and I had a lot of fun." Youth also identified leadership skill development. As a youth explicitly described, "I've always wanted to be a leader, and I found here that I can be." Another youth proclaimed:

> It [the program] changed um, mostly like my leadership, because I have never really been a leader of that kind of thing, like until CLIMB. So leadership was the one thing I learned.

Mentors most frequently mentioned self-esteem development, and in Year 2, youth cite this outcome as well. Mentors reported that youth developed a willingness to take risks, "step outside their normal boundaries" and "get out of their comfort zones," through program activities. They claimed that youth became more confident in expressing themselves, and sharing themselves with others. Youth discussed building confidence and becoming "less shy." One youth said she learned, "just be yourself skills" and another reiterates the idea, stating "I'm just a little bit more me." Some youth also became more confident about expressing themselves.

In addition, mentors commented that youth showed increases in self-efficacy, although only two youth in Year 2 mention this outcome. Mentors reported that youth discovered a newfound belief that they can make a difference in their own lives and the community. Both youth and mentors also felt youth found a place to voice their ideas. In addition, Year 2 mentors indicated that youth became more engaged throughout the year in program activities.

Community Understanding

Community understanding was the third most frequently reported outcome, mentioned by 19 youth (65 data points) and 12 mentors (36 data points). In both years, subcategories included community involvement and general community awareness; in Year 2, community issue awareness emerged as well.

Community involvement was cited most frequently by both groups. This category incorporated learning how to contribute to the community or expressing a desire to do so. One youth explained his new philosophy, "I actually have a part in the community. Everybody has a part in the community if you live in a community." Another youth stated, "At first I wasn't really into helping out with the Humane Society or the community at all. But after I joined CLIMB, all of the sudden I was enjoying helping out." Mentors also cite community involvement; one states: "I was really impressed about how into their communities they were ... they were just so passionate about what they were doing and it was really exciting to see that." Youth gained general community awareness. One states, "When I came here and found all these things that you can do in the community, and what is happening out in the community, I really thought that I could really be a lot interested." Mentors indicated that youth developed an awareness of local community needs, issues and nonprofit organizations.

In Year 2, youth also identified learning about specific community issues, for example, "I just kind of learned they [homeless] are just like us, but without a home." Another explains, "We learned from it, don't litter.... We took pictures, we learned from the pictures."

Academic Changes

The final category of youth outcomes is academic change, mentioned by 20 youth (41 data points) and 8 mentors (15 data points). This category includes improved attitudes about school, improved academic skills and project skill development. Youth cite this outcome significantly more than mentors, particularly the subcategories of improved school attitudes and academic skills.

Each year about half of the youth stated that their attitudes about school had improved as a result of the program, often connecting improved social relationships to that change. They gained an understanding of the purpose of school, increased investment, and heightened confidence in their academic abilities. Youth (especially in the second year) also reported gaining in academic skills. They specified learning to speak in class discussions and participate in activities. They also mentioned acquiring study skills such as learning how to ask questions or practicing persistence to see an assignment to its completion. Three youth specified gains in writing or math skills. Both youth and mentors state that youth gained project skills such as planning, organization, decision making and presentation.

Mentor Outcomes

Mentors participating in both programs reported three primary categories of outcomes for themselves: (1) development of teaching skills; (2) knowledge of youth; and (3) community understanding. In addition, Year 2 data revealed a new category, shifts in attitudes about teaching. Exhibit 7.3 gives an overview of the data from both years and illustrates how the relative frequency of outcomes varied across years.

Exhibit 7.3.   Mentor Outcomes
(N of Mentors = 22; N of Data Points = 258)

Outcome	Year 1 – CLIMB Results		Year 2 – Y4R Results		Y1 + Y2
	n of Mentors (n = 11)	n of Data Points (n = 122)	n of Mentors (n = 11)	n of Data Points (n = 136)	n of Mentions (N = 258)
Teaching Skills	11	72	10	23	95
Instruction	8	19	3	5	24
Management	5	11	8	12	23
Relating to students	8	19	3	3	22
Planning	8	15	0	0	15
Working with middle schoolers	5	8	2	3	11
Knowledge of Youth	11	22	10	52	74
Understanding individuality	5	6	10	13	19
Complexity of youths' lives	4	4	8	11	15
Challenging prejudgments	0	0	10	14	14
Capability of youth	4	5	5	5	10
General/youth perspectives	6	7	7	9	16
Community Understanding	10	28	10	35	63
Working with students in community	9	15	10	17	32
	3	13	4	5	18
Personal change Issue/resource awareness	0	0	7	13	13
Attitudinal Shifts	0	0	9	26	26
Importance of relationships	0	0	7	15	15
Efficacy	0	0	9	11	11

Teaching Skills

Twenty-one of the 22 mentors indicated gaining teaching skills (95 data points) including instruction, management of students, developing relationship skills, planning, and gaining ability to work with middle schoolers. Of these outcomes, the development of instructional and management skills was most frequently and consistently mentioned both years. Instructional skills varied widely, ranging from learning how to ask better questions to how to facilitate project-based teaching approaches. Those who said they gained instructional skills commented on the importance of taking individual learners into account, and on becoming a facilitator, not driver of the learning process. One labeled it learning to "give the kids the steering wheel." Another elaborates:

> You know, direct kids without doing it for them ... getting her to say, "Okay, well did you check your email, did you write the woman from the Alternative Humane Society, did she write you back?' Just kinda probing questions without taking over ... I guess my tendency is just to do it for them.

Management outcomes included learning how to motivate students, as well as how to shape their behaviors. Mentors consistently described how they learned to engage youth in activities, defuse negative behavior and promote positive behavior. They often drew a connection between management and developing relationships with youth.

Mentors from both program years noted growth in their ability to relate with students, although those from Year 1 reported this outcome much more frequently. Mentors improved their ability to talk to middle school students; as one said, "it showed me how to be able to reach so many different personalities, because I know I am going to have all of these different personalities in my classroom." Other mentors noted the importance of developing better strategies to get youth to open up to them, or how to get them involved in conversations, as this mentor describes: "I learned to ask a lot more questions than I was used to ... if I got one word answers I would draw more out." Mentors from both years also reported that they had become more comfortable working with middle schoolers and explained how experiences in the program would inform their actions in the classroom.

Knowledge of Youth

Twenty-one mentors achieved a deeper understanding of youth and the many facets of their lives (74 data points). Outcomes included understanding youths' individuality, the complexity of their lives, their capability, interests and perspectives, and the need to challenge prejudgments about youth.

Mentors most frequently mentioned developing an understanding of youths' individuality. These comments typically addressed the importance of remembering how each youth is unique and brings different characteristics to the learning context:

> They are all completely different, even though they are all chosen based on … the same criteria to get into this program, but they are all completely different and have different beliefs and obviously different personalities, and different ways of interacting with each other.

Mentors developed a more informed understanding of the characteristics of middle schoolers, describing them as "funny, great, amazing kids" who have unique perspectives on life and who are engaged in a plethora of interesting activities. "It definitely gave me a better sense of what they are like as people," one remarked.

Mentors also discovered how complex the lives of adolescents can be. The opportunity to interact one-on-one provided mentors insight into the multifaceted dynamics affecting youth. As one mentor explained "I learned a lot about the kids' home lives and how so much of how they perform academically and how they interact socially is determined by their family/home situation." In addition, mentors developed knowledge of how intellectually and emotionally capable youth are, and they gained insight into youth perspectives on life and school.

Another outcome, reported from mentors in Year 2 only, was their newfound ability to challenge prejudgments and their resolve to look past "good kid, bad kid" labels. Ten of the eleven mentors reported this outcome. "I think if you see the label, you suddenly see that in the classroom," one explained. Another elaborated:

> And no matter what it is, there's always more going on than what you first see. I think that's the biggest lesson.… I guess just that every student has their own individual story and every student has their own, that they come with their own bags, and I need to figure out what that is and not judge them when they walk in because there is always another side to it.

Community Outcomes

The third most frequent outcome, reported by twenty mentors, relates to community understanding (63 data points) and included learning about working with students in the community or experiencing a personal change in community attitudes. In addition, mentors in Year 2 gained awareness of issues or resources in the community.

Of all the community outcomes, increased knowledge about how to work with students, and the intent to do so were the most frequently mentioned. Some discussed optimism about their ability to engage students in community learning. Others, like this quote illustrates, reconsidered the importance of doing so:

> Well, before this program ... I'd never really looked all that much in the community beyond the school. Once I saw how excited the kids could be when they were doing things like going to the Humane Society or, like planning projects, or just even walking around and taking pictures of the community, it definitely showed me that service-learning would be good for them.

Some mentors reported personal changes in their attitudes toward or involvement in the community. While some mentors had already had experience working in the community, most reported enhanced community knowledge and increased likelihood of future work in the community. Mentors from Year 2 also gained deeper awareness of the issues and resources within their community and how to draw from them as a future teacher. One explained, "I think that the one thing I learned from the experience ... was the variety of opportunities that there are in Bellingham to serve and just seeing all the ways that are out there that you can get involved in the community."

Attitudinal Shifts

Finally, a total of nine mentors from Year 2 reported changing attitudes towards teaching (26 data points). These shifts included recognition of the importance of developing relationships with students and heightened feelings of efficacy as teachers. They reported how developing relationships with students might impact their teaching. As two commented, "it makes learning so much easier when they trust you," and "I think what I learned from them, is that I really need to get to know my students before I try to start teaching them." Mentors also expressed a heightened sense of their ability to have a positive impact on youths' lives as a result of the program. As one put it, "I think it made me more of a hopeful teacher, that I have the ability to make a difference."

DISCUSSION

With the goal of fostering connectedness as a backdrop, CLIMB and Youth 4 R.E.A.L. were designed to guide youth through identity exploration, enhance youth relationships with their peers and caring adults, and involve youth in community projects. Participating in group mentoring and community-based projects are two methods our programs utilized to accomplish these objectives.

From the information we obtained from both youth and mentors, across both years, we conclude that group mentoring plays a key factor in youth outcomes, most explicitly evident in social development. Both years, the group format allowed youth to develop relationships with multiple supportive adults. It also provided opportunities for youth to interact with peers from different grades and social circles. Youth were able to witness their peer's talents and interests, make more friends, and "connect" with other youth. Our findings confirm Herrera et al.'s (2002) report that group mentoring is a productive format for supporting social development.

In contrast to previous studies of traditional one-on-one mentoring research, which showed only a marginal effect on youth emotional development (DuBois et al., 2002; Grossman & Tierney, 1998), our research suggests that *group* mentoring may enhance emotional development. In our study, mentors reported emotional development as the second largest set of outcomes for youth, particularly in the areas of self-esteem, confidence, self-efficacy and the propensity to voice ideas. Additionally, Year 2 youth identified developing new interests, leadership skills, self-esteem and confidence.

Involvement in community-based projects may have played a significant role in youth social and emotional outcomes as well. The mentors provided scaffolding and structure to enable youth to address social issues in meaningful ways. In our program, the community-based projects provided opportunities for youth to develop communication and teamwork skills, in addition to allowing them to step into leadership roles and increase self-efficacy. In Year 2, community projects provided some youth a constructive space to address race and class issues, stereotyping or intolerance. Although this outcome was reported only by five students, we believe it is an area for promising future program development.

Changes in program structure likely influenced the differing youth outcomes between Year 1 and Year 2. Although social and emotional development outcomes were consistent both years, the increase in these reports for Year 2 is striking and may be attributed to the increased session duration and program length. In Year 2 all fifteen youth identified gaining positive adult relationships, as opposed to Year 1 where only half of the youth claimed this outcome. Researchers suggest that duration and length play an important role in youth outcomes in mentoring relationships (DuBois et al., 2002).

The integration of social and emotional learning strategies in Year 2 may have also contributed to the increased reports of social and emotional development. In Year 2, early introspective and relational activities provided a foundation for self-affirmation and supportive group dynamics. Subsequently, in the second year of interviews, among social development outcomes, teamwork skills became more prevalent and social self-understanding emerged. Youth also reported significant gains in leadership skills, increased self-esteem and new interests. In addition, findings from the second year included youth developing sensitivity to others, social self-understanding and expanding diversity awareness. Previous research indicates these as potential social and emotional learning outcomes (Durlak & Weissberg, 2007; Greenberg et al., 2003).

Community understanding remained fairly consistent between the two years. In Year 2, however, community project topics demonstrated deeper significance, and youth remained engaged and motivated throughout their projects. Whereas projects in the first year all related to animal advocacy, during Year 2 youth tackled issues such as hate speech, gangs and homelessness. During the second year there were more activities designed to prepare youth to address issues, including arts and brainstorming activities that tapped into real and relevant concerns in their lives. These activities may have contributed to a supportive environment where youth felt comfortable voicing ideas and addressing personally sensitive issues. In addition, in Year 2 a more general awareness of community issues emerged. Youth were exposed to the community and its issues through guest speakers, community field trips, and direct service projects, which gave them opportunities to more widely explore a range of pertinent topics.

Youth in both years of the mentoring program developed improved attitudes toward school, reporting that they valued and cared about it. The reported attitudes of heightened engagement and caring may be reflecting an increased connectedness to school (Karcher, 2008). Connectedness literature indicates that positive social relationships with peers and adults and participation in extracurricular activities improve youths' attitudes about school (Blum, 2005). In the second year of interviews, youth also specified academic and project skill outcomes. They articulated a sense of "how to do school" by increasing their participation in classes and assignments, and improving their communication with teachers and school staff. The increase in findings for academic and project skills reported in Year 2 may reflect changes in our interview protocol; given reports by Year 1 youth about academic gains, we specifically asked youth in Year 2 about academics.

Mentor outcomes as a result of participating each year were quite consistent, and are congruent with findings of other researchers. Data in our study corroborate findings that mentoring provides preservice teachers with an opportunity to improve their teaching and interpersonal skills (Crawford & Post, 2007; Hale, 2007; Harwood, McClanahan, & Nicholas, 2007; Middleton, 2003; Murray, 1996) as well as increasing their knowledge of both the community (Harwood et al., 2007; Root, 2005; Wade,

1995) and the youth with whom they will be working (Harwood et al., 2007; Murray, 1996). We also corroborate Crawford and Post's (2007) finding that mentoring placements facilitated preservice teachers' development of relationship building skills with youth.

Although the large categories of outcomes were consistent both years, the outcomes varied in terms of frequency across the two. CLIMB mentors most frequently reported teaching skills as an outcome, followed by community understanding and knowledge of youth. Youth4R.E.A.L. mentors most frequently reported knowledge of youth, followed by community understanding, shifts in attitudes about teaching, and teaching skills. Changes in the structure of the mentoring program, as well as curricular elements of the teacher education courses, may have contributed to these changes. With the single focus during Year 1 on project-based learning, which may be viewed by mentors as a more academic teaching task, it seems reasonable that they would report greater gains in the area of teaching skills. In addition, the Year 1 mentors were enrolled in curriculum and instruction and then management courses during their mentoring experience, and they were given more direct responsibility for the planning and implementation of the community projects, which were the primary focus of the mentoring program for that year. That may explain why mentors in Year 1 reported "planning" as a teaching skill they gained, while no mentors in Year 2 reported it.

In Year 2, the number of mentor reports of gaining knowledge about youth increased overall, which probably reflects the fact that the focus of the program expanded to include multiple activities to build relationships and get to know youth better. The increased focus on relationship building during the second year gave mentors more insight into how youths' home lives connect to schooling. These more complex understandings of youth pushed mentors to look beyond labels given to youth to the contextual causes behind them. In turn, mentors expressed a desire to reject labels and see each youth from a fresh perspective. In addition, mentors in the second year of programming were enrolled in courses that addressed both adolescent development and management techniques during their mentoring experience, and those courses included a high level of integration with the service-learning experience.

While community understanding was reported by mentors during both years of the program, Year 2 mentors gained more insight into community issues and resources. Like the youth, mentors in the second year of the program were exposed to more community exploration activities, which probably contributed to this result. Finally, mentors in Year 2 reported two types of attitudinal shifts that were not present in the Year 1 data. The first of these was an acknowledgment of how important it is to build relationships with students in order to be effective teachers, and specifically how it would contribute to classroom management. Again, the focus on relationship building and the integration of the classroom management course during the second year are probably contributors to this outcome.

Overall, the mentoring placements resulted in outcomes closely related to those articulated in national teaching standards, confirming the potential to do so mentioned by previous researchers (Callahan et al., 2001; Harwood & Salzman, 2007; Ryan & Callahan, 1999, 2002). Mentors both years gained a deeper understanding of youth and developed teaching and interpersonal skills in addition to learning about the community. The after-school program in which our preservice teachers participated afforded a context in which they could develop capabilities related to standards that may be difficult to address without time interacting closely with students. The mentoring placement enabled preservice teachers to get to know youth on a more intimate basis than do classroom placements, primarily because the nature of their interactions are quite different from those that typically occur in a classroom. The types of close relationships developed in the program also yielded a deep knowledge of families and community, two standards-based requirements that are especially challenging to address in college coursework without experiential components.

National standards also require that preservice teachers demonstrate competency in students' social, emotional, and moral development; mentoring may provide a means for practicing that. In addition, mentoring programs may help preservice teachers develop SEL capabilities. Although research has indicated that SEL is a valuable preventative technique for reducing risk factors at school, Greenberg et al. (2003) claim it has not yet significantly made its way into teacher education programs.

In summary, this collaboratively designed approach to supporting middle school students and enhancing preservice teacher's education resulted in benefits for all participants. Our study is limited, however, by a focus on a single site and type of mentoring placement and by a reliance on interview data only. To strengthen our understanding of how program components affect outcomes for preservice teachers, we will conduct a multisite study that includes assessment of students placed in other service-learning mentoring placements. Given the potential for preservice teachers to develop diversity awareness and connections with youths' families suggested by other researchers, we also intend to give more focus on those elements in our future programming and research. To more fully assess youth outcomes, we will access the school's administrative information about youth, enabling us to measure changes in behavior referrals, attendance records and academic gains as reflected in grades.

We are also reflecting upon the most accurate assessment of youth outcomes. Our analysis was complicated by deciding how to consider both youth and mentor perceptions of youth outcomes. On one hand, we believed youth were the best compass for describing their own experiences and determining personal outcomes. On the other hand, we felt that mentors provided interesting insight into youths' emotional and social development, because they could identify growth in areas such as self-esteem, upon which youth may not have the maturity to reflect. Although the agreement between youth and mentor reports of youth outcomes indicates validity for our interview procedure, we still question whether research on youth development should honor youth perceptions as most accurate and valid, or whether it is appropriate to consider adult, parent, teacher or mentor perceptions on their development. Further research will enable us to more fully understand and address these issues.

ACKNOWLEDGMENTS

The authors would like to thank Jessica Nicholas, Thomas Baltzell, and Ashley Rolph for their assistance in collecting and analyzing data.

APPENDIX:
INTERVIEW QUESTIONS RELATED TO PROGRAM IMPACTS

Youth Interview PromptsCLIMB Youth, Year 1 (June 2007)

Mentor Relationship

1. Tell us about your relationship with your mentor
   - Can you please describe your relationship with your mentor?
   - How often did you meet with your mentor outside of the Friday meeting times?
   - How close did you feel to your mentor?
   - Did your mentor help you develop any skills?
2. What words would you use to describe the role of the adults in this program?
3. Would you describe the adults in your group to be most like teachers, councilors, friends or parents? Why?

Impacts of the Program

Now we are wondering what you got out of the program.

1. How would you describe your feelings about participating in the program?
2. Did you feel motivated to do the project? Why or why not?
3. Can you tell me something you gained from this experience?
4. Do you think this program helped you develop any skills?
   - Leadership
   - Communication (Did you talk with any new people?)
   - Social Skills (Did you make any new friends?)
   - Attitude changes (Did being a part of CLIMB help you feel good about going to school? Doing something in the community?)

Youth4R.E.A.L. Youth, Year 2 (June 2008)

What do you think you got out of being in the program?

Themselves

1. Did you learn about yourself through the program?
   - Skills
   - Interests
   - Qualities

Peers

1. Did you make any new friends? Tell me more about that.
2. How did you get to know them?
3. Would you have these friendships without Youth for REAL?

Mentor

1. Tell us about your relationship with the mentors in your home team.
2. Did you connect with any other mentors in the program?

School

1. Before you participated in Youth 4 REAL, were your attitudes about school any different than they are today? How so?
2. Do you think you developed any skills in Youth 4 REAL that you can use in the classroom?

Community

1. Tell us about your community action project.
2. What kind of impact did your project have?
3. What did you learn from doing the project?
4. Do you see yourself participating in community projects again?

Other Skills

1. Do you think this program helped you develop any skills?
   - Leadership
   - Communication (speak with new people or got comfortable speaking to groups)
   - Team work?
   - Working on projects?
   - Building friendships or relationships?
2. Is there anything else you want to tell us about your experience?

MENTOR INTERVIEW PROMPTS

CLIMB Mentors, Year 1 (June 2007)

Impacts of the Program

1. First let's discuss the impacts on your mentee(s)
   - What do you think your mentee got out of his/her relationship with you?
   - What do you think your mentee got out of working on the group project?
   - What changes or growth did you observe in your mentee – and can you give some specific examples?
     o Communication
     o Leadership

- o Social skills
- o Attitude changes
- o Any negative outcomes observed?
- What role do you think you personally played in facilitating this growth?

2. Now we'd like to explore the impacts on you as a mentor
    - What would you say are the most important things you learned from being part of this project?
    - Do you think this project helped you develop any skills – if so, what types of skills did it help you develop?
      - o Leadership
      - o Communication
      - o Teaching skills
      - o Other?
    - How might your participation in this project shape what you do as a teacher in the future?
    - Did doing the project change any of your ideas about the community or being involved in the community?
      - o About involving youth in community projects?

Also, from section A (Program Description)

- What were the outcomes of your group project?

Youth4R.E.A.L. Mentors, Year 2 (June 2008)

From Section A (program description) What types of things did you learn about the youth you worked with?

B. Impacts of the Program

1. First let's discuss the impacts on the youth.
    - What do you think the youth got out of Youth 4 REAL?
    - What changes or growth did you observe in any of the Y4R youth, and can you give some specific examples?
      - o Why do you think this growth occurred?
    - What activities do you think the youth most benefited from?
      - o Can you explain what you believe the youth got out of these activities and why that benefited them?

- Tell us more about your community action project
  - What was your group project?
  - What do you think the youth got out of working on their projects?
  - Did you feel your project was successful? Why or why not?

2. Now we'd like to explore the impacts on you as a mentor

- What would you say are the most important things you learned from being part of Y4R?
- What would you say are the most important things you learned from being a mentor?
- Do you think this program helped you develop any skills that will help you as a teacher? If so, what types of skills did it help you develop?
- Did participating in Youth 4 REAL change any of your ideas about the community or being involved in the community?
  - How about involving youth in the community?

REFERENCES

Billig, S. H. (2006). Lessons from research on teaching and learning: Service-learning as effective instruction. In J. C. Kielsmeier, M. Neal, & A. Crossley (Eds.), *Growing to greatness: The state of service-learning project* (pp. 25-32). St. Paul, MN: National Youth Leadership Council.

Billig, S. H., Jesse, D., Brodersen, R. M., & Grimley, M. (2008). Promoting secondary students' character development in schools. In M. A. Bowdon, S. H. Billig, & B. A. Holland (Eds.), *Scholarship for sustaining service-learning and civic engagement* (pp. 57-84). Greenwich, CT: Information Age.

Billig, S. H., Root, S., & Jesse, D. (2005). The relationship between the quality indicators of service-learning and student outcomes. In S. Root, J. Callahan, & S. H. Billig (Eds.), *Improving service-learning practice: Research on models to enhance impacts* (pp. 97-115). Greenwich, CT: Information Age.

Blum, R. (2005). *School connectedness: Improving the lives of students.* Baltimore: John Hopkins Bloomberg School of Public Health.

Bogden, R., & Bicklen, S. (1992). *Qualitative research for education: An introduction to theory and methods.* Boston: Allyn & Bacon.

Callahan, J. P., Diez, M. E., & Ryan, L. B. (2001). Service-learning and standards-based teacher education. In J. Anderson, K. Swick, & J. Yff (Eds.), *Service-learning in teacher education: Enhancing the growth of new teachers, their students, and communities* (pp. 53-68). New York: AACTE Publications.

Cameron, L., & Manju, V. (1997). Citizens for a new century: Project Harmonie. *Canadian Ethnic Studies, 29*(2), 121-132.

Crawford, G., & Post, A. (2007, October). *Transforming students through reciprocal learning experiences: Cross-disciplinary academic service-learning.* Paper presented at the 7th International Research Conference on Service-Learning and Community Engagement, Tampa, FL.

Damon, W. (2004) What is positive youth development? *The ANNALS of the American Academy of Political and Social Science, 591(1)*, 13-24.

DuBois, D. L., Holloway, B. E., Valentine, J. C., & Cooper, H. (2002). Effectiveness of mentoring programs for youth: A meta-analytic review. *American Journal of Community Psychology 30*(2), 157-97.

Durlak, J. A., & Weissberg, R. P. (2007). *The impact of after-school programs that promote personal and social skills*. Chicago: Collaborative for Academic, Social and Emotional Learning.

Fertman, C. I. (2000). *Contributions of adolescent development research to service learning research*. Paper presented at the annual meeting of the American Educational Research Association, New Orleans, LA.

Fertman, C. I., G. P. White, & L. J. White. (1996). *Service-Learning in the middle school: Building a culture of service*. Westerville, OH: National Middle School Association.

Glasser, B. G., & Strauss, A. L. (1999). *The discovery of grounded theory: Strategies for qualitative research*. New York: Aldine de Gruyter.

Good, J., Halpin, G., & Halpin, G. (2000). A promising prospect for minority retention: Students becoming peer mentors. *The Journal of Negro Education, 4*(69), 375-384.

Greenberg, M. T., Weissberg, R. P., O'Brien, M. U., Zins, J. E., Fredericks, L., Resnick, H., et al. (2003). Enhancing school-based prevention and youth development through coordinated social, emotional and academic learning. *American Psychologist, 59*(6/7), 466-474.

Grossman, J. B., & Tierney, J. P. (1998). Does mentoring work? An impact study of the Big Brothers Big Sisters program. *Evaluation Review 22*(3), 403-426.

Hale, A. (2007, October). *Assessing the effects of service-learning on bilingual/ESL teacher development*. Paper presented at the 7th International Research Conference on Service-Learning and Community Engagement, Tampa, FL.

Hamilton, S., Hamilton, M., Hirsch, B., Hughes, J., King, J., & Maton, K. (2006). Community contexts for mentoring. *Journal of Community Psychology, 34*(6), 727-746.

Harwood, A. M., Fliss, D., & Gaulding, E. (2006). Impacts of a service-learning seminar and practicum on pre-service teachers' understanding of pedagogy, community and themselves. In K. M. Casey, G. Davidson, S. H. Billig, & N. C. Springer (Eds.), *Advancing knowledge in service-learning: Research to transform the field* (pp. 137-158). Greenwich, CT: Information Age.

Harwood, A. M., McClanahan, L., & Nicholas, T. (2007). Making "mythical creatures" real: Developing an awareness of adolescent needs through service-learning. In S. B. Gelmon, & S. H. Billig (Eds.), *From passion to objectivity: International and cross-disciplinary perspectives on service-learning research* (pp. 217-237). Charlotte, NC: Information Age.

Harwood, A. M., & Salzman, S. (2007, February). *Service-learning in teacher education: Proof, promise and possibility*. Paper presented at the Annual Conference of the Association of Colleges of Teacher Education, New York

Herrera, C., Grossman, J. B., Kauh, T. J., Feldman, A. F., McMaken, J., & Jucovy, L. (2006). *Making a difference in schools: The Big Brothers Big Sisters school-based mentoring impact study.* Philadelphia: Public/Private Ventures.

Herrera, C., Vang, Z., & Gale, L. (2002). *Group mentoring: A study of mentoring groups in three programs.* Philadelphia: Public/Private Ventures.

Interstate New Teacher Assessment and Support Consortium. (1992). *Model standards for beginning teacher licensing, assessment and development: A resource for state dialogue.* Retrieved March 16, 2005, from http://www.ccsso.org/content/pdfs/corestrd.pdf

Karcher, M. (2005). *The Hemingway measure of adolescent connectedness: A manual for scoring and interpretation.* Retrieved March 25, 2008, from http://www.adolescentconnectedness.com/survey.php

Karcher, M. (2008) *Hemingway: Measure of adolescent connectedness.* Retrieved March 25, 2008, from http://www.adolescentconnectedness.com/research.php

Lerner, R. M, Fisher, C. B., & Weinberg, R. A. (2000). Toward a science for and of the people: Promoting civil society through the application of developmental science. *Child Development, 71*(1), 11-20.

Libby, M., Rosen, M., & Sedonaen, M. (2005). Building youth-adult partnerships for community change: Lessons from the youth leadership institute. *Journal of Community Psychology, 34*(1), 111-120.

Melchior, A., & Balis, L. N. (2002). Impact of service-learning on civic attitudes and behaviors of middle and high school youth: Findings from three national evaluations. In A. Furco & S. H. Billig (Eds.), *Service-learning: The essence of the pedagogy* (pp. 202-222). Greenwich, CT: Information Age.

Middleton, V. A. (2003). A diversity-based, service learning PDS partnership. *Equity and Excellence in Education, 36*, 231-237.

Murray, D. R. (1996, November). *Charting a new course and facilitating college and school collaboration through service learning and service leadership development.* Paper presented at the meeting of the International Council for Innovation in Higher Education, Vancouver, British Columbia, Canada.

National Council for the Accreditation of Teacher Education. (2002*). NCATE unit standards, 2002 edition.* Retrieved 3/23/06 from http://www.ncate.org/public/unitStandardsRubrics.asp?ch=4#1

National 4-H Cooperative Curriculum Systems Inc. (2005) *Public adventures: An active citizenship curriculum for youth.* Chevy Chase, MD: Author

Patton, M. Q. (1990). *Qualitative evaluation and research methods.* Newbury Park, CA: SAGE.

Pittman, K., & Wright, M. (1991) *Bridging the gap: A rational for enhancing the role of community organizations in promoting youth development.* Washington, DC: Carnegie Council on Adolescent Development.

Rhodes, J., Spencer, R., Keller, T., Liang, B., & Noam, G. (2006). A model for the influence of mentoring relationships on youth development. *Journal of Community Psychology, 34*(6), 691-707.

RMC Research Corporation. (2002). *Evaluation of W.K. Kellogg Foundation retrospective of K-12 service-learning projects, 1990-2000.* Retrieved march 24, 2008 from http://www.service-learningpartnership.org/site/DocServer/RetrospectiveStudy.pdf?docID=1061

Root. S. (2005). The national service-learning in teacher education partnership: A research retrospective. In S. Root, J. Callahan, & S. H. Billig (Eds.), *Improving service-learning practice: Research on models to enhance impacts* (pp. 13-16). Greenwich, CT: Information Age.

Root, S., Callahan, J., & Sepanski, J. (2002). Building teaching dispositions and service-learning practice: A multi-site study. *Michigan Journal of Community Service-Learning, 8*(2), 50-60.

Russ, P. (1993). Partners in education: A university-middle school mentorship program. *The Clearing House 66*(5), 285-287.

Ryan, L. B., & Callahan, J. P. (1999, February). *Making connections: Service-learning competencies and beginning and expert teacher standards.* Paper presented at the annual meeting of the American Association of Colleges of Teacher Education, Washington, DC.

Ryan, L. B., & Callahan, J. P. (2002). Making connections: Service-learning competencies and beginning teacher standards. *The Teacher Educator, 38*(2), 126-140.

Wade, R. (1995). Developing active citizens: Community service-learning in social studies teacher education. *Social Studies, 86*(3), 122-128.

CHAPTER 8

AN EXPLORATION OF THE VALUE OF CULTURAL-BASED SERVICE-LEARNING FOR STUDENT AND COMMUNITY PARTICIPANTS

Lori Simons, Brittany Russell, Nancy Hirschinger-Blank, Elizabeth Williams, and Kimyette Willis

ABSTRACT

A triangulation mixed-methods design was used to demonstrate that cultural-based service-learners in a high diversity condition ($N = 51$) increased more from the beginning to the end of the semester in their social justice awareness and academic engagement skills than did cultural-based service-learners in a low diversity condition ($N = 33$). Cultural-based service-learners showed positive changes over the semester in problem-solving skills, awareness of racial privilege and blatant racial issues, ethnic identity, and racial attitudes, regardless of whether they were exposed to high or low diversity content. Cultural-based service-learners acquired culture competence as they moved through 5 stages of racial identity develop-

Creating Our Identities in Service-Learning and Community Engagement
pp. 189–214

ment before, during, and after service. Implications for developing culturally based service-learning courses are discussed.

INTRODUCTION

There has been a dramatic increase during the past decade in published research on the impact of cultural-based service-learning for college students and a modest increase in studies that focus on the impact of this pedagogical approach on service recipients (Boyle-Baise, 2002; Eyler & Giles, 2001). Cultural-based service-learning, also known as multicultural or diversity service-learning, is a pedagogical approach that intentionally integrates race- or diversity-related content with community service by providing students with opportunities to learn about social disparities associated with diverse communities (Boyle-Baise, 2005; Waldstein & Reiher, 2001). It also serves as a vehicle through which students examine their personal biases, gain a better understanding of diversity, and critically analyze the perceived realities of social injustices that affect the community (Baldwin, Buchanan, & Rudisill, 2007). Research in this area has been criticized for lacking rigorous evaluations of the influence of cultural-based service-learning on student development and the perceived impacts of students on community recipients (Eyler, 2002). The goals of the present study were threefold: First, to determine whether attitudes change for students in high and low diversity conditions from the beginning to the end of the semester; second, to explain the possible change of attitudes through multicultural theories; and third, to add to earlier studies by including a sample of community recipients (i.e., supervising teachers from participating schools).

Cultural-Based Service-Learning

Intergroup Contact Theory

Allport (1979) proposed that prejudice will be reduced and favorable attitudes will develop when members of two groups who differ in race are brought together. Erickson and O'Connor (2000) suggest that contact between ingroup and outgroup members in a service-learning context serves as a prejudice-reduction method, because students forge relationships with service recipients and acquire personal evidence that contradicts their stereotypes. Myers-Lipton (1996) compared two waves of students randomly assigned to service-learning, service no learning, and non-service-learning conditions. Students in the service-learning condition demonstrated a greater reduction from pretest to posttest in modern racism scores than did those in the service no learning and non-service-learning conditions. Fitch (2004) compared 92 students assigned to one of four groups and measured attitude change from the beginning to the end of service-learning. Although mean scores did not significantly differ, students in the cultural service-learning group had higher posttest intercultural sensitivity scores compared to those in the cultural, service-learning, and noncultural/non-service-learning groups. Fitch (2005) also measured intercultural sensitivity before and after service and found that students who engaged in cultural service-learning improved their postservice diversity attitudes, civic awareness, and social responsibility.

In contrast, Hess, Lanig, and Vaughan (2007) propose that service-learning is a "deficit model" where students view themselves as the advantaged providing a service for the disadvantaged, thus further reinforcing students' stereotypes (p. 32). Schofield's (1986) groundbreaking work at Wexler Middle School revealed that the majority of teachers adopt color-blind attitudes, ignoring possible cultural differences. Baldwin et al. (2007) interviewed 41 preservice teachers and similarly found that some of them changed their preconceived notions while others maintained their negative assumptions about the children they tutored. Boyle-Baise and Langford (2004) conducted a case study with eight students enrolled in a social justice seminar and observed that service-learners acquired limited information about their own privilege or oppression from the beginning to the end of service. Thus, there appear to be conflicting research conclusions regarding intergroup contact theory.

Racial Identity Theories

Cross (1991) developed a five-stage model that describes the psychological process associated with Black racial identity development. Each stage is characterized by racial identity attitudes toward Black/White reference groups, self-concept issues, and cognitive-affective processes. The five stages are preencounter, encounter, immersion-emersion, internalization, and internalization-commitment (Cross, 1991; Parham & Helms, 1985). In the preencounter stage, the person has a salient view of race and behaves in ways that idealize Whiteness. For example, Black and White service-learners adopt colorblind views of service recipients (i.e., *I treat everyone the same*). In the encounter stage, the person begins to abandon this racial view and recognizes the social implications of Black or White reference groups. Service-learners recognize racial and social disparities at a placement site (i.e., *My school did not have bars on the windows, because it was located in a White, upper-class neighborhood*). In the immersion-emersion stage, the person immerses him/herself in Black experiences, may denigrate Whites, and forms a new racial identity. Black service-learners acknowledge how White privilege contributes to racism, while

White service-learners are resistant to acknowledging how racial privilege contributes to social problems (i.e., *If service recipients work hard they could go to college and break the poverty cycle*). In the internalization stage, the person achieves inner security with his/her Blackness and develops a positive racial identity. Service-learners develop a deeper understanding of oppression, privilege and racism, and incorporate these elements into their racial identity (i.e., *Service recipients have struggles beyond my hardships*). In the internalization-commitment stage, the person continues to express his/her racial identity by engaging in groups, activities, and organizations that promote social change. Service-learners engage in activities that combat racism and work towards the elimination of sociopolitical oppression (i.e., *I have confronted and corrected my peers after they made a derogatory remark about service recipients*).

Helms (1990) amended Cross's model to suggest each stage be considered a cognitive template that individuals use to organize racial information. Helms' proposed White racial identity development occurs through six stages in which Whites move from a colorblind view of race to a nonracist identity. The six stages are contact, disintegration, reintegration, pseudo-independence, immersion-emersion, and autonomy. In the contact stage, the person is oblivious to racial issues and adopts a colorblind view. Service-learners have a naïve view of race and are resistant to think of themselves in racial terms (i.e., *I am part of the human race*). In the disintegration stage, the person becomes aware of the social implications of race on a personal level. Service-learners begin to think of themselves in racial terms and recognize their racial privilege. For instance, White service-learners gain an awareness of White privilege, while Black service-learners acquire an awareness of class privilege (i.e., *The images of squalor and decay that I saw in this neighborhood are prohibited in my middle-class neighborhood*). In the reintegration stage, the person idealizes everything perceived to be White and denigrates everything perceived to Black. The person understands, but is resistant to accept that Whites are responsible for racism. Service-learners are resistant to acknowledge how White or class privilege contributes to racism (i.e., *Although opportunities available to White students from middle-class neighborhoods exceed those given to minority students from the inner city, I am not responsible for racial, educational, or social disparities*). In the pseudo-independence stage, the person understands the unfair advantages of growing up White and the disadvantages of growing up Black in the United States. Service-learners adopt liberal views in which they perceive programs such as affirmative action or special education as ways to improve racial or educational disparities (i.e., *I think the tutoring program is a great way to help children who are academically behind in an underfunded school. However, I wonder if a White school would embrace Black tutors the same way this Black school accepts White tutors*). In the immersion-emersion stage, the person assumes personal responsibility to combat racism. Service-learners participate in activities, groups, or other service projects that promote social change (i.e., *I have continued to work with the community through my involvement in the multicultural club*). In the autonomy stage, the person values cultural similarities and differences, feels a kinship with people regardless of race, and acknowledges racial oppression. The person develops a positive, nonracist self-concept. Service-learners develop relationships with service recipients and gain an appreciation of cultural similarities and differences (i.e., *I have maintained relationships with others who differ from me even though it contradicts my parents' values*). These two racial identity development models may be useful in describing students' attitudes before, during, and after service.

The Present Study

The cultural-based service-learning course objectives were to contribute to students' personal and interpersonal development (i.e., civic action, problem solving, leadership, social justice, diversity, and political awareness), cultural competence (i.e., colorblind, ethnic identity, racial attitudes), and engagement skills (i.e., community, academic, and interpersonal engagement). Students were required to tutor or mentor children who differ from them in race, ethnicity, and socioeconomic status at an elementary public school in a district that consistently ranks low on state performance indicators (Pennsylvania Department of Education, 2007). In fact, all public schools in the district qualify for Federal Title funding for basic academic programming, because standardized test scores reveal that in the third grade less than 40% of the children score at a proficient level in mathematics and only 46% score at a proficient level in reading (Pennsylvania Department of Education, 2007). The school district serves children from one of the most racially segregated and economically distressed cities in the United States (United States Census Bureau, 2000).

Students were also required to watch a film that was either high or low in diversity content. Films ranked high in diversity content foster students understanding of different cultures by allowing them to vicariously experience racial, economic, and educational issues within these cultures (Pinterits & Atkinson, 1998, cited in Gladding, 2000). More than half of the students chose to watch a film that was high in diversity content and the remaining group of students watched a film that was low in diversity content. Specifically, this study sought to answer four questions:

1. Did students who participated in high-diversity cultural-based service-learning show greater attitude change over a semester than those who experienced low-diversity cultural-based service-learning?
2. What and how did students learn while engaged in a cultural-based service-learning program?
3. What were the supervising teachers' views of the cultural-based service-learning program?
4. How closely do findings for the quantitative and qualitative measures correspond in helping us understand the impact of cultural-based service-learning?

METHOD

Participants

College Students

College students from a private teaching university in a northern metropolitan area completed a survey in their educational psychology course. Data were gathered from 90 students at the beginning and at the end of the semester during two academic years (2006-2007, 2007-2008). Ninety-three percent ($N = 84$) of the students provided complete pretests and posttests. Cultural-based service learners in Sample 1 (2006-2007) did not differ from those in Sample 2 (2007-2008), in terms of gender, race, age, and service activities, according to independent t and chi-square tests used to measure possible differences between the two groups. Most students identified themselves as White (80%) and female (80%). Students worked as tutors (53%), mentors (25%), or teacher assistants (22%) at one of two public elementary schools.

Community Recipients

Teachers from two public schools located in an urban area were interviewed about their views of the cultural-based service-learning program. Data were gathered from 22 of the 30 teachers who were eligible to participate in the interview (response rate = 73%). Most teachers identified themselves as either White (54%) or Black (45%) and female (86%). Thirty-two percent of them reported that they had taught at another school in the district prior to their current place of employment. Teachers' average length of teaching in the district was 17 years and their average length of teaching in their current position was 11 years.

Course Content

The educational psychology course is a three-credit course intended to prepare students to work with children in public schools. This course requires a field placement (i.e., cultural-based service-learning) and is a prerequisite for upper-level education courses. In-class time (50 minutes, 3 times per week, 15 weeks) began with a lecture on cultural-based service-learning. The next two classes consisted of a two-hour orientation on mentoring and tutoring by guest speakers representing two placement sites. The rest of the course was devoted to lecture, activities and discussion. Students were required to complete three examinations, a cultural competence paper, and a journal assignment.

The cultural competence assignment required students to watch one movie that was either high (i.e., *Stand & Deliver, Dangerous Minds, the Ron Clark Story, to Sir with Love, Lean on Me*) or low (i.e., *Mr. Holland's Opus, Music of the Heart, Good Will Hunting, Dead Poets Society, Homeless to Harvard, A Beautiful Mind*) in diversity content. Students were invited to watch a movie as an out-of-class activity in the middle of the semester. They were unaware of whether the film was high or low in diversity content; this information was recorded by the researcher. More than half of the students ($N = 51$, 56% of the sample) self-selected to watch a film that was high in diversity content and the remaining students ($N = 33$, 36% of the sample) self-selected to watch a film that was low in diversity content. Students watched the movie with their peers and answered structured questions based on the movie as part of their culture competence paper. (See below.)

Measures

A *demographic questionnaire*, developed by the researchers, was used to gather information on gender, race, age, grade point average (GPA), area of study, and year in school.

The Civic Attitudes and Skills Questionnaire (CASQ), developed by Moely, Mercer, Ilustre, Miron, and McFarland (2002), assessed civic attitudes and skills. The CASQ, an 84-item self-report questionnaire, yields scores on six scales: (1) civic action (respondents evaluate their intentions to become involved in the future in some community service); (2) interpersonal and problem-solving skills (respondents evaluate their ability to listen, work cooperatively, communicate, make friends, take the role of the other, think logically and analytically, and solve problems); (3) political awareness (respondents evaluate their awareness of local and national events and political issues); (4) leadership skills (respondents evaluate their ability to lead); (5) social justice attitudes (respondents rate their agreement with items expressing attitudes concerning the causes of poverty and misfortune and how social problems can be solved); and (6) diversity attitudes (respondents describe their attitudes toward diversity and their interest in relating to culturally different people. Internal consistencies for each scale reported by Moely et al. (2002) ranged from .69 to .88, and test-retest reliabilities for each scale ranged from .56 to .81

Aspects of Engagement, developed by Gallini and Moely (2003), assessed students' views of their engagement. This 27-item self-report questionnaire yields scores on three scales: (1) community engagement (respondents evaluate the extent to which their attitudes changed as a result of course participation, working with people of different backgrounds, and feeling connected to the community); (2) academic engagement (respondents describe their satisfaction with the academic course and university, and their connectedness to their studies and field of interest); and (3) interpersonal engagement (respondents evaluate the course's influence on their ability to effectively work with others, communicate with other students, and make friends). Items are added together to produce three subscale scores. Cronbach's coefficient alpha for each scale ranged from .85 to .98.

The *Color-Blind Racial Attitude Scale* (CoBRAS), developed by Neville, Lilly, Duran, Lee, and Browne (2000), assessed contemporary racial issues. The CoBRAS, a 20-item self-report measure, yields scores on three scales: (1) unawareness of racial privilege (respondents evaluate their lack of awareness of White racial privilege): (2) unawareness of institutional discrimination (respondents evaluate their lack of awareness of social policies, affirmative action, and discrimination); and (3) unawareness of blatant racial issues (respondents evaluate their awareness of racial problems in the United States). Item scores are added together to produce three subscale scores. Cronbach's coefficient alpha for each scale ranged from .86 to .88.

The *Multigroup Ethnic Identity Measure* (MEIM), developed by Phinney (1992), measured two aspects of students' ethnic identity: (1) ethnic identity achievement based on exploration and commitment; and (2) sense of belonging to and attitudes toward, one's ethnic group. Mean scores were calculated to produce two subscale scores. Reliability for this scale is strong ($\alpha = .80$).

The *Modern Racism Scale (MRS)*, developed by McConahay (1986), assessed the extent to which individuals have negative attitudes toward

Blacks. Seven items were added together to produce a full-scale score. Reliability for this scale is strong ($\alpha = .81$). The MRS scale was modified to measure prejudice toward minorities by changing the term "Blacks" to "Minorities" in the questions.

The *Pro-Black Scale and Anti-Black Scale*, developed by Katz and Hass (1988), measured positive and negative components of people's contemporary racial attitudes. The Pro-/Anti-Black scale is a 20-item self-report measure, yielding two subscales scores: (1) the Anti-Black Scale (respondents indicate higher prejudicial attitudes toward Blacks); and (2) the Pro-Black Scale (respondents indicate less prejudicial attitudes toward Blacks). Items are added together to produce two separate subscale scores. Cronbach's coefficient α is .75 for the Pro-Black scale and .84 for the Anti-Black scale. This scale was modified to measure attitudes toward minorities by replacing the term "Blacks" with "Minorities" in the questions.

The *Service Journals* developed by Simons (2007) required students to answer structured reflection questions before, during and after their service experiences. The structured reflection questions required them to apply their service experiences to the course content, integrate textbook and supplemental reading material to support their perspectives, and reflect on their thoughts and feelings about both the service context and the course content.

The *Culture Competence Paper* developed by Simons (2007) required students to summarize the movie, describe the main character, and compare and contrast the demographic characteristics of this character to the child with whom they were paired at the placement. Students were also required to apply one theoretical concept from the diversity chapter in the text, Cross/Helms, Bruner, Erikson, Marcia, Piaget, Vygotsky, and Werner to explain the development of the main character. Students summarized the value of this assignment by describing what they did or did not learn about multicultural education.

Design and Procedures

A triangulation mixed-methods design was used to evaluate differences in interpersonal and personal development, cultural competence, and engagement skills for students in high and low conditions from the beginning to the end of the semester. Creswell (2005) wrote that a triangulation mixed-methods design refers to simultaneously collecting quantitative and qualitative data and merging the results to understand the problem under investigation. All of the respondents completed an informed consent form and a survey with six embedded measures that assess personal and interpersonal development, cultural competence, and engagement skills. Students completed the survey, placed it in a coded, confidential envelope and gave it directly to the researcher. Surveys took about 45 minutes to complete. Students were required to complete the survey again postservice (i.e., after completing 15 hours of service) and to write one journal entry before, for each day of, and after service.

A research assistant conducted an interview with each teacher at the placement site. The interview technique developed by Miron and Moely (2006) was used and qualitative analyses were made of the teachers' interview responses. Interviews took about 30 minutes to complete.

RESULTS

Quantitative Analyses

Repeated measures analyses of variance with planned orthogonal contrasts were conducted to evaluate attitude change between cultural-based service-learners in high ($N = 51$) and low ($N = 33$) diversity conditions from the beginning to the end of the semester. The pretest and posttest scores for CASQ, Aspects of Engagement, cobras, MEIM, MRS, and Pro-Black/Anti-Black were used as dependent variables, and high and low diversity condition was the independent variable. The significant effects for these measures are shown in Exhibit 8.1. Orthogonal contrasts were significant for Group × Time interaction effects for two scales, indicating that students in the high diversity condition increased their social justice attitude and academic engagement more than students in the low diversity condition from the beginning to the end of the semester. Main effects for Group indicate that cultural-based service-learners in the high diversity condition had lower modern racism and higher pro-Black/anti-Black attitudes compared to cultural-based service-learners in the low diversity condition. Finally, main effects for Time indicate that cultural-based service-learners improved their problem-solving skills, awareness of racial privilege and blatant racial issues, and ethnic identity achievement and pro-Black/anti-Black attitudes by the end of semester, regardless of whether they were in high or low diversity conditions.

Qualitative Analyses

Two sources of information (i.e., student journals, cultural competence papers) underwent an item analysis through which thematic patterns were identified and coded using grounded theory techniques (Creswell, 2005).

Exhibit 8.1.   Mean Scores, Standard Deviations, and *F* Ratios for Pre- and Posttest Scores for Personal Development, Cultural Competence and Engagement, as a Function of High and Low Diversity Conditions

	Time Points				F ratios		
	Pretest		Posttest				Time ×
Measure	M	SD	M	SD	Group	Time	Group
Civic Attitudes and Skills Questionnaire (CASQ)							
Civic Action	**30.90**	**4.76**	**31.53**	**4.47**	**.89**	**.99**	**1.17**
Low condition	31.91	4.76	31.87	4.47			
High condition	30.33	4.89	31.33	4.78			
Problem solving[3]	**41.40**	**3.84**	**42.32**	**3.74**	**.35**	**6.31***	**.31**
Low condition	41.60	2.90	42.82	2.69			
High condition	41.29	4.28	42.06	4.15			
Political awareness	**17.22**	**3.89**	**17.68**	**3.75**	**.74**	**1.39**	**.16**
Low condition	17.29	4.40	17.96	3.92			
High condition	17.18	3.59	14.51	3.68			
Leadership skills	**15.21**	**2.38**	**15.33**	**1.96**	**.72**	**.24**	**.01**
Low condition	15.30	2.41	15.46	1.98			
High condition	15.16	2.54	15.25	1.97			
Social justice[1,3]	**28.50**	**3.84**	**29.79**	**4.41**	**2.54**	**5.71***	**6.74***
Low condition	28.26	3.44	28.17	4.03			
High condition	28.64	3.84	30.74	3.95			
Diversity	**18.31**	**2.16**	**18.41**	**2.94**	**.18**	**.14**	**.02**
Low condition	18.11	2.16	18.26	2.40			
High condition	18.43	2.88	18.50	3.24			
Aspects of Engagement							
Academic[1]	**47.96**	**11.87**	**43.96**	**7.60**	**.07**	**2.62**	**7.88****
Low condition	44.88	6.69	43.96	7.60			
High condition	44.83	8.69	46.09	5.68			
Community	**41.19**	**5.77**	**42.04**	**5.72**	**.08**	**1.13**	**.07**
Low condition	41.08	6.36	41.66	6.08			
High condition	41.25	5.49	42.25	5.58			
Interpersonal	**24.94**	**3.36**	**25.07**	**3.39**	**2.59**	**.05**	**.05**
Low condition	25.77	3.50	25.77	3.36			
High condition	24.41	3.20	24.62	4.10			
Color-Blind Racial Attitude Scale (CoBRAS)							
Racial privilege[3]	**28.05**	**5.83**	**26.25**	**4.47**	**.87**	**4.16***	**.00**
Low condition	28.81	4.95	27.06	4.78			
High condition	27.42	6.55	25.57	4.20			
Institutional discrimination	**23.58**	**4.14**	**23.86**	**4.49**	**.32**	**.22**	**1.10**
Low condition	22.69	3.83	23.84	5.36			
High condition	24.31	4.36	23.87	3.82			

(Table continues on next page)

Exhibit 8.1.   (Continued)

Measure	Time Points				F ratios		
	Pretest		Posttest				Time ×
	M	SD	M	SD	Group	Time	Group
Color-Blind Racial Attitude Scale (CoBRAS) (Continued)							
Blatant racial issues[3]	**17.31**	**4.72**	**15.88**	**4.26**	**.56**	**6.88***	**.10**
Low condition	18.00	4.63	16.37	4.71			
High condition	16.73	4.84	15.47	4.26			
Multigroup Ethnic Identity Measure (MEIM)							
Identity achievement[3]	**15.13**	**4.34**	**16.32**	**4.10**	**1.76**	**5.63***	**1.76**
Low condition	16.00	4.12	16.46	3.92			
High condition	14.60	4.43	16.24	4.24			
Sense of belonging	**28.33**	**5.58**	**27.54**	**5.54**	**.63**	**2.72**	**.01**
Low condition	29.00	5.22	28.14	4.86			
High condition	27.93	5.85	27.18	5.95			
Modern Racism Scale (MRS)							
MRS[2]	**16.95**	**2.77**	**17.24**	**3.37**	**12.48***	**1.00**	**1.61**
Low condition	17.89	2.26	18.82	2.73			
High condition	16.37	2.91	16.26	3.39			
Pro-Black/Anti-Black Attitudes							
Pro-Black[2, 3]	**4.22**	**7.96**	**17.16**	**14.70**	**4.40***	**50.82***	**1.28**
Low condition	2.36	7.45	12.84	14.97			
High condition	5.36	8.13	19.80	14.06			
Anti-Black[2, 3]	**-0.61**	**7.15**	**13.03**	**16.46**	**5.86***	**34.70***	**3.55**
Low condition	-2.04	7.25	6.61	11.94			
High condition	.30	7.05	17.13	17.75			

Notes: [1]Differential change by service-learners, reflected in an interaction of Group by Time, at ***$p < .000$, **$p < .01$, *$p < .05$. ANOVA F ratios are Wilk's approximation for Group × Time interactions. [2]Differential change as a function of group, $p < .05$. [3]Differential change as a function of time. CoBRAS rating scales 1 = *strongly disagree*; 6 = *strongly agree*. Lower posttest scores indicate an increase in awareness of racial privilege, institutional discrimination, and blatant racial issues. MEIM rating scales: 1 = *strongly disagree*; 5 = *strongly agree*. Higher posttest scores indicate greater ethnic identity achievement and sense of belonging to one's ethnic group. MRS rating scale: 1 = *strongly disagree*; 5 = *strongly agree*. Lower posttest scores indicate a reduction in negative racial attitudes. Pro-Black/Anti-Black rating scales: +3 = *strongly agree*; -3 = *strongly disagree*. Higher posttest scores indicate increases in positive and negative racial attitudes.

Data from 90 journals (including entries made at three points during the semester) and 90 papers from service-learners were compared and analyzed using open, axial, and selective coding procedures to construct a conceptual framework. Open coding consisted of categorizing and naming the data according to theoretical concepts of service-learning (Eyler & Giles, 1999) and cultural competence (i.e., awareness, knowledge, and skills) (Howard-Hamilton, 2000), while axial coding consisted of systematically analyzing the data using topical codes based on racial identity development models (Cross, 1991; Helms, 1990), as shown in Exhibit 8.2. Coders counted the number of responses for each category and divided the responses by the total number of student journals and papers to obtain the percentage for each category. Selective coding consisted of analyzing student responses across preservice, during-service, and post-service. Coders counted the number of responses for racial identity stages and time patterns and divided the responses by the total number of student journals in order to obtain the percentage for each stage over time as shown in Exhibit 8.3.

Students acquired cultural competence through five-stages of cultural-ethnic identity development from pre- to postservice. Cross (1991) and Helms (1990) describe the preencounter/contact stage of racial identity development as an individual's colorblind view of race. In the preencounter stage, many students (83%) described preconceived notions about working in an ethnically-diverse and lower-income community. In fact, most students (87%) described their early visits at the school as a cultural-shock or an eye-opening experience. However, few (24%) students conveyed colorblind attitudes in their preservice journal entries.

Cross and Helms propose that continual contact between Blacks and Whites influences their perceptions of their racial identity. In the encounter/disintegration stages, individuals recognize the social implications of their race on outgroup members. Most students acquired awareness (89%) and understanding (74%) of racial differences between themselves and service recipients, and 86% of them provided examples illustrating White or class privilege.

Cross and Helms describe the immersion-emersion stage as a process in which individuals become interested in their ethnic heritage and develop racial identity attitudes in light of historical and contemporary racism. In the immersion-emersion stage, individuals develop a new racial identity predicated on their ability to attribute social problems to racial privilege. White individuals are resistant to acknowledge that race is an underlying cause of social and educational inequities. In our student sample, very few (23%) were resistant to attributing social problems to race. More than half of the students described reduced stereotyping (73%), tolerance (63%), and the development of new attitudes about service recipients (69%) and social inequities in the community (72%) in the middle of their journal entries.

Cross asserts that the internalization stage is a process in which individuals develop a positive racial identity and assume personal responsibility

Exhibit 8.2. The Five Stages of Racial Identity Development

Time	Stage	Categories	Typical Expressions
Preservice	Preencounter	Culture shock	I was immediately shocked once I entered the school because it did not resemble my elementary school. A fight broke out between two third graders. The classroom was crowded, there were not enough books or supplies, and two children left the classroom to wonder the halls. This behavior would not have been tolerated in a middle-class, suburban school.
		Preconceived notions	I was really annoyed that I had to take time out of my hectic schedule to observe students. On the first day I dreaded going to the school to meet the teacher and the students. The entire way to the school I wanted to turn around and drive back to campus and drop this course. This sentiment was reinforced after the school security guard asked me if I had bullet proof vest on.
		Colorblind attitudes	After my first day at the school, I could see the eagerness of the children to learn. I did not notice anything different between this school and my elementary school. All children want to learn.
During-service	Encounter	Racial awareness	Today was an eye opener! I never acknowledged racial differences, but after working in a predominantly black classroom, I realized what it was like to be a minority. I felt uncomfortable and questioned if the students would treat me differently because I am white.
		White or social privilege	Service-learning clearly illustrates the concept of white privilege. To be honest, I never new this privilege existed and it was hard for me to comprehend. After working at this school and discussing this concept in class, I have learned that I am privileged because I am White. I now realize how my life has been a walk in the park compared to these children.
		Racial understanding	I feel that a person can not truly understand how poverty affects education until they go into the public schools in the Chester-Upland district. This experience helped me to understand the importance of government funding for both the school and the district. I learned that segregation still exists in the form of de facto segregation. By witnessing this township struggle to provide the best education for the children with limited resources, I gained a new respect for minorities.

Immersion-emersion	Reduced stereotyping	I honestly feel that before the service-learning I had stereotyped African Americans. This sounds terrible but I never was challenged to deal with these stereotypes until now. I learned to completely change my schema after working in a predominantly Black school.
During-service	Immersion-emersion	New racial attitudes about social inequities	I noticed one day a girl who was usually well-behaved was lethargic and inattentive during the lesson. I asked her what was wrong, and she said that "she didn't have breakfast and was very hungry." Although I marveled how Maslow's self-actualization theory could be applied to this situation, I learned something more valuable—racial and social oppression. This situation would never have occurred where I am from —the opportunities available to White, middle-class students are far above those given to the children of Chester.
	New racial attitudes about service recipients	I am very angry with myself for accepting beliefs I was fed through the media and other people. I can see the affect of low income problems in the school, but I can also see the eagerness of the children to learn. Although I love this experience, I can not help but feel hurt, because I know if a black woman came and did service-learning at my school, she would not be viewed the same as a white women going into a predominantly black school.
	Tolerance	I was told not to "go over the bridge." But after this service experience, I have gained a new perspective on social issues facing this community. I have developed an open-mind about urban education, underprivileged communities, and the people that I worked with. I am no longer afraid to cross the bridge!
	Resistance to attribute social problems to race	One student told me that I didn't know anything about his struggles because he was Black and I was White. I took him aside and explained that I could relate to him because I have had my own struggles. There are many Whites who equally struggle.
Internalization	Community connections	The moment I realized that I made a connection was when a student who I worked with asked me to his big brother through the Big Brother/Big Sister program.
	Self-knowledge	Although I think it is ironic that privileged college students are sent to an inner city, impoverished school district, I believe this experience forced me to evaluate my attitudes toward people who are racially and economically different.

(Table continues on next page)

Exhibit 8.2. (Continued)

Time	Stage	Categories	Typical Expressions
		Reward for helping	My service-learning experience was really rewarding. I really enjoyed working with the kids and actually completed almost 40 hours—more than double the time that was required for this course. I plan to go back and help the teacher once a week next year and have volunteered to be a Big Sister through the Big Brother/Big Sister program.
		Self-esteem	As a prospective teacher, I gained confidence in my ability to work with children who have different racial, economic, and social backgrounds.
		Community responsibility	The service-learning experience helped me to become apart of the Chester community. I continued to work with the children after my hours, because I felt it was my responsibility as a member of this community.
Postservice	Internalization-commitment	Diversity understanding	I learned that diversity is something that must be understood and accepted. If someone is not willing to accept differences in race or culture, he/she should not be involved in education. Being involved in a multicultural environment allowed me to better understand my own culture. Once I was able to understand my own culture then I was able to understand, appreciate, and respect the cultures of the students. If it were not for this service-learning experience, I may not have been able to acquire multicultural skills
		Diversity knowledge	Service-learning opened my eyes to diversity. I learned that to be a successful teacher and make a difference, I need to understand my own and others' culture.
		Diversity awareness	I have always thought of myself as open to new experiences, but it turns out that I was very narrow-minded. Service-learning challenged me to open my eyes to cultural differences. I have learned to feel more comfortable in my own skin as a minority at the placement site.
		Diversity skills	I learned to work with children who are racially and economically different from me. This is a benefit because it prepares you to work in a world that is becoming increasingly more diverse.
		Prejudice reduction	This course forced me to step out of my comfort zone and acknowledge things about my family that I did not want to. My father taught me to be prejudice. I have learned to disagree with my father and have developed my own thoughts about others who are different from me.

Exhibit 8.3.   Student Journal Reflections

Time Period	n	Stage	%	Concepts	%
Preservice	90	Preencounter	83	Culture shock	87
				Preconceived notions	83
				Colorblind attitudes	24
During-service	90	Encounter	91	Racial awareness	89
				White or social privilege	86
				Racial understanding	74
		Immersion-emersion	72	Reduced stereotyping	73
				New racial attitudes about social inequities	73
				New racial attitudes about service recipients	69
				Tolerance	63
				Resistance to attribute social problems to race	23
		Internalization	75	Community connections	83
				Self-knowledge	80
				Reward for helping	80
				Self-esteem	65
				Community responsibility	51
Postservice	90	Internalization-commitment	86	Diversity understanding	100
				Diversity knowledge	95
				Diversity awareness	92
				Diversity skills	84
				Prejudice reduction	63

Note: [1]The percentages for racial identity development stages are based on the total number of student journals. [2]The percentages for concepts are based on the number of student journals.

for racism. In the internalization stage, more than half of the students describe self-knowledge (80%) and self-esteem (65%) in their journal entries. Most students (83%) felt a part of the Chester community, and 80% of them also felt rewarded because their work had assisted the children and teachers. Half of the students (51%) demonstrated community responsibility by continuing to participate in service activities beyond their required hours.

Cross and Helms describe the internalization-commitment/autonomy stage as an individual's commitment towards social change and social justice. In the internalization-commitment stage, most students demonstrated cultural competence-diversity awareness (92%), knowledge (95%), and skills (84%). All (100%) students reported a deeper understanding of diversity, but only 63% of them provided examples illustrating prejudice reduction. Eighty percent of students reported that they plan to take another service-learning course as a way to demonstrate their commitment to the community.

Teacher Interviews

A content analysis of 22 teacher interviews described cultural-based service-learning views. Each teacher's response underwent an item-level analysis that resulted in 22 broad categories and three major themes as shown in Exhibit 8.4. The first theme that emerged from the data focuses on the impact of the placements on the college students' development. Almost all (95%) of the teachers felt that the placement had contributed to students' understanding of diversity, and 98% of them thought students were sensitive to the cultural and developmental needs of the children. The second theme captured the influence of cultural-based service-learners on service recipients. All (100%) of the teachers thought that students assisted the children, and 71% of them felt that the individual instruction helped the children improve their academic skills. More than half (84%) of the teachers also felt that having students in their classrooms allowed them to utilize cooperative education methods that would have been inappropriate for large classes. A final theme described methods for sustaining university-community partnerships. Few (22%) teachers made comments regarding program improvement, but slightly more than half (54%) of them did request that the same student assist them for a full year instead of one semester.

DISCUSSION

The current study expands research on cultural-based service-learning and student development. The first objective of this study was to measure differences in interpersonal and personal development, cultural competence, and engagement skills between cultural-based service-learners in high and low diversity conditions from the beginning to the end of the semester. Students who watched a film that was high in diversity content made improvements in their ratings of social justice attitudes and academic engagement skills. A second group of students, who watched a film that was low in diversity content, showed a slight drop in their ratings of

Exhibit 8.4.   Teachers' Views of
Multicultural Education and Service-Learning

Major Themes	Categories	%
The impact of placements on college student development	Students were aware and sensitive to the children's cultural and developmental characteristics	98
	Diversity knowledge	95
	Community connection: Relationships with teacher and children	88
	Real-world experience	84
	Knowledge about teacher/Education profession	65
	Students appeared to be in a cultural shock and lacked the skills to deal with the children's cultural and developmental characteristics	2
The impact of college students on service recipients (children)	Students helped the teachers by providing individual instruction to the students	100
	Students reduced the stress associated with teaching for teachers	100
	Individual attention enhanced the children's self-esteem, confidence, and prosocial skill development	100
	Students assisted the teachers by allowing them to use cooperative learning methods, and assisting with the overcrowded classrooms	84
	Individual attention helped the children master the course content; helped them improve their grades	71
University-community partnerships	Teachers did not feel that any changes were necessary to improve the service-learning program	78
	Teachers felt that the service-learning program should be improved	22
	Teachers requested students work with them for a year instead of the semester	54
	Teachers requested more than one student in each class	36
	Teachers requested students come more often - more than one or two hours per week	13
	Teachers requested the development of the service-learning handbook and/or the utilization of course syllabi at the placement	10
	Teachers requested faculty involvement at the site	9
	Teachers requested feedback from the students about the program	5
	Teachers requested copies of scholarly articles on cultural-based service-learning student development	4
	Teachers thought students should be more prepared to deal with diversity in the schools	2

social justice attitudes and academic engagement skills over the semester. Students in the high diversity condition had lower modern racism and higher pro-Black/anti-Black attitude scores compared to students in the low diversity condition. Both groups of students also made improvements in their ratings of problem-solving skills, awareness of racial privilege and blatant racial issues, ethnic identity achievement, and pro-Black/anti-Black attitudes by the end of semester, regardless if they were in high or low diversity conditions. These findings are partially consistent with those of previous studies showing service-learning enhances students' personal and interpersonal development (Moely, McFarland, Miron, Mercer, & Ilustre, 2002), cultural competence (Fitch, 2004), and academic, community, interpersonal engagement (Gallini & Moely, 2003).

A second objective of this study was to detect "what" and "how" the students learned while engaged in a cultural-based service-learning program. Students acquired cultural competence through five stages from pre- to postservice. In preservice, students' exhibited preconceived notions about working in a culturally-diverse and lower-income community. Students describe their early visits at the placement as a cultural-shock or an eye-opening experience, and their racial attitudes represent the preencounter stage.

Students moved through three stages while engaged in service during the program. First, in the encounter stage, students acquired awareness of racial differences and understanding of white privilege. Second, in the immersion-emersion stage, students acquired tolerance and developed new diversity attitudes about social inequities in the community. Cross-cultural interactions appear to have contributed to students' cognitive dissonance, which, in turn, further influenced them to change their preconceptions. Third, in the internalization stage, students made positive appraisals of their roles at the placement site, gained a deeper understanding of social disparities in the community, and felt more connected to service recipients. Placements that provided guidance and support may have enhanced students' value of diversity (Dunlap, 1998; Eyler & Giles, 1999).

In postservice, students demonstrated cultural competence: Their acquisition of awareness, knowledge, and skills represents the internalization stage. Students acquired a deeper understanding of diversity and prejudice reduction techniques. As a way to show their commitment to overcoming racial and social disparities in the community, students demonstrated both social and community responsibility.

A third objective was to describe the teachers' views of the cultural-based service-learning program. Three themes emerged from the coded data including: (1) the impact of placements on student development, (2) the influence of cultural-based service-learning on service recipients, and

(3) methods for sustaining university-community partnerships. Teachers made positive appraisals about the impact of the service-learning placement on student development and the impact from students on service recipients. Their evaluations revealed that students benefited both teachers and children by providing support in over-crowded classrooms. Few teachers made comments regarding student or program improvement; they did request that the same student assist them for a full year rather than a single semester. Teachers also asked for an increase in the number of students placed with them, required service hours and faculty involvement at the school. A small number of teachers desired course materials such as syllabi, handbooks, and scholarly articles to improve their ability to guide cultural-based service-learners.

A final objective was to compare the qualitative data with quantitative data to detect similarities and differences. Similarities between the qualitative and quantitative findings were observed in cultural competence between students' reports (i.e., journals, surveys) and teachers' interviews. Students developed their cultural competence through their community work. Teachers' reports confirm that students acquired a deeper understanding of racial, social, and educational disparities through their interactions with the children, and they demonstrated cultural sensitivity to the children with whom they worked. This consistency of data contributes to the confidence in our claims that cultural-based service-learning is an effective and innovative pedagogical method.

In contrast to racial identity development models, students did not exhibit colorblindness or resistance associated with the preencounter/contact and immersion-emersion stages. These aspects of the preencounter/contact and immersion-emersion stages may not have been observed among our sample of students because they demonstrated a greater level of cultural awareness than expected. Consistent with this view, teachers rarely described the students as exhibiting "culture shock" or lacking skills to deal with cultural differences. It is plausible that students' greater understanding how race, ethnicity, and class intersect, as well as their disconnection from incidents of historical racism, may explain why colorblindness and resistance were not observed in this sample. Moreover, the observed data illustrate Cross' (1991) model of Black rather than Helms' (1990) model of White racial identity development even though the sample was 80% White. Students in this sample did not demonstrate features of the reintegration and pseudo-independent stages of White racial identity development which are critical elements of Helms' model. This finding is consistent with previous research on White college students (Mercer & Cunningham, (2003). Mercer and Cunningham challenge the conceptualization of the White racial identity model and suggest that a multifaceted approach be taken to understand the development of White racial identity among students. For this reason, a culture-ethic identity development (CEID) model may be a more accurate paradigm for explaining how students development their ethnic identity in a service-learning context (Cross & Cross, 2006).

Differences between qualitative and quantitative data were also noted for community engagement. Cultural-based service-learners did not report increases in their community engagement skills over the semester, although slightly more than half of them continued to tutor and mentor students after they had completed their required hours. A possible explanation for this inconsistent finding may be attributed to ceiling effects associated with the community engagement subscale (Heppner, Kivlighan, Wampold, 1999). For instance, students may have rated their responses too high at pretest which would limit the amount of change that could be measured at posttest, thus contributing to the lack of observed difference in community engagement scores.

While this study adds to the literature on cultural-based service-learning, the results should be viewed in light of a few limitations. First, the student population is demographically homogenous. Student participants were predominantly White, came from middle-class backgrounds, and usually were the first-generation to attend a four-year college. Second, the two groups of students, self-selected to high and low diversity conditions, showed unexpected differences in their pretest ratings of modern racism and pro-black/anti-black attitudes. Students in the low diversity condition had higher modern racism and lower pro-black/anti-black pretest scores compared to students in the high diversity condition. Initial attitudes about race may have influenced students in their choice of film. Third, content specific to the cultural competence assignment may have influenced students' views. Students did not improve their awareness of white privilege, institutional discrimination, or blatant racism, but they did form both positive and negative racial attitudes after exposure to the enhanced diversity content. Students exposed to the high diversity condition completed a culture competence assignment based upon a movie ranked high in diversity content (e.g., *Stand and Deliver, Dangerous Minds*). It is possible that the cultural competence assignment, with the enhanced diversity content, forces students to think about how economic disparities and educational injustices affect the teaching of students of a different race and class in a public school system. However, this assignment did not require students to analyze how the public school system reinforces colorblind attitudes and maintains group inequities which may have been necessary for them to increase their awareness of power, privilege, and racism (Neville, Worthington, & Spanierman, 2001; Schofield, 1986). Finally, the sample of students in high and low diversity conditions was not as large as those in previous studies, especially since a number of participants were Non-White and may have reacted differently to the experience than the White students did (Neville et al., 2001). Future research should address these research limitations by replicating this study with equivalent groups of students randomly assigned to high and low diversity conditions.

Despite these limitations, the findings of this study have a few important implications. First, students exposed to enhanced diversity content in a cultural-based service-learning course improve their social justice awareness and academic engagement skills from the beginning to the end of the semester. This may be of value for faculty who are developing a culturally-based service-learning course for the first time. For instance, students should be required to systematically analyze class and race concepts within the context of their service experiences. Students could watch a diversity film, compare and contrast the main character in this movie to the service recipient with whom they are paired, and apply diversity and racial identity concepts to describe and explain the development of the main character. Students could also provide service examples to demonstrate their understanding of diversity concepts and racial identity theories through reflection activities, class discussions, and course examinations. Second, the service context influences students' racial attitudes. Students should engage in service activities with recipients who differ from them in class and race, compare and contrast the similarities and differences between themselves and recipients, and participate in experiential activities (i.e., crossing-the-line) that require them to think about race and class differences. Faculty will need to forge partnerships with community organizations and implement activities that foster cross-cultural interactions between students and service recipients. Third, reflection is an influence on students' attitudes and skills. Structured reflection assignments that require students to integrate service experiences with the diversity content are necessary for them to think critically about how race and class influence their interactions with service recipients. For example, students should answer structured reflection questions that require them to connect the course content to their service experiences and describe their thoughts and feelings about service activities before, during, and after service experiences. Students could also compare and contrast their reflections over time and explain why their thoughts and feelings did or did not change throughout the semester. Finally, the use of both qualitative and quantitative data expand previous research in this area in two important ways: First, it provides a conceptual model that describes how students develop cultural competence through five stages of cultural-ethnic development from preservice to postservice, and secondly, it provides a framework that describes how cultural-based service-learning assists teachers and children in overcrowded classrooms in an urban context.

ACKNOWLEDGMENTS

The authors would like to thank Ms. Jane Nyiri and the administration, teachers, and children in the Chester-Upland School District for their invaluable contributions to this research.

REFERENCES

Allport, G. W. (1979). *The nature of prejudice*. Cambridge, MA: Perseus.

Baldwin, S. C., Buchanan, A. M., & Rudisill, M.E. (2007). What teacher candidates learned about diversity, social justice, and themselves from service-learning experiences. *Journal of Teacher Education, 58*(4), 315-327.

Boyle-Baise. M. (2002). *Multicultural service learning: Educating teachers in diverse communities*. New York: Teachers College Press.

Boyle-Baise, M. (2005). Preparing community-oriented teachers: Reflections from a multicultural service-learning project. *Journal of Teacher Education, 56*(5), 446-458.

Boyle-Baise, M., & Langford, J. (2004). There are children here: Service-learning for social justice. *Equity and Excellence in Education, 37*, 55-66.

Creswell, J. W. (2005). *Educational research, 2nd edition*. Upper Saddle River, NJ: Pearson Prentice Hall.

Cross, W. J. (1991). *Shades of Black: Diversity in African-American identity*. Philadelphia: Temple University Press.

Cross, W. E, & Cross, T. B. (2006, February). *Self-concept structure and the overlap between racial and ethnic identity*. Paper presented at the meeting of the Winter Roundtable Conference, New York.

Dunlap, M. R. (1998). Voices of students in multicultural service learning settings. *Michigan Journal of Community Service Learning, 5*, 58-67.

Erickson, J. A., & O'Connor, S. E. (2000). Service-learning: Does it promote or reduce prejudice? In C. R. O'Grady (Ed.), *Integrating service learning and multicultural education in colleges and universities* (pp. 59-70). Mahwah, NJ: Erlbaum.

Eyler, J. (2002). Stretching to meet the challenge: Improving the quality of service learning. In S.H. Billig & A. Furco (Eds.), *Service-learning: Through a multidisciplinary lens* (pp. 3-13). Greenwich, CT: Information Age.

Eyler, J. S., & Giles, D. E. (1999). *Where's the learning in service-learning?* San Francisco: Jossey-Bass.

Eyler, J., & Giles, D.E. (2001). Beyond surveys: Using the problem solving interview to assess the impact of service-learning on understanding and critical thinking. In A. Furco & S.H. Billig (Eds.), *Service-learning: The essence of the pedagogy* (pp. 147-160). Greenwich, CT: Information Age.

Fitch, P. (2004). Effects of intercultural service-learning experiences on intellectual development and intercultural sensitivity. In N. Welch & S. H. Billig (Eds.), *New perspectives in service-learning research to advance the field* (pp. 107-126). Greenwich, CT: Information Age.

Fitch, P. (2005). A mixed methods approach to studying outcomes of intercultural service-learning with college students. In S. Root, J. Callahan, & S. H. Billig (Eds.), *Improving service-learning practice: Research on models to enhance impacts* (pp. 187-211). Greenwich, CT: Information Age.

Gallini, S. M., & Moely, B. E. (2003). Service-learning and engagement, academic challenge, and retention. *Michigan Journal of Community Service-Learning, 10*(1), 5-14.

Gladding, S. T. (2000). *Counseling: A comprehensive profession.* Upper Saddle River, NJ: Merrill.

Helms, J. E. (1990). *Black and white racial identity: Theory, research, and practice.* Westport, CT: Greenwood Press.

Heppner, P. O., Kivlighan, D. M., & Wampold, B. E. (1999). *Research design in counseling* (2nd ed.). Belmont, CA: Wadsworth.

Hess, D. J., Lanig, H., & Vaughan, W. (2007). Educating for equity and social justice: A conceptual model for cultural engagement. *Multicultural Perspectives, 9*(1), 32-39.

Howard-Hamilton, M. (2000). Programming for multicultural competencies. *New Directions for Student Services, 90,* 67-78.

Katz, I., & Hass, R. G. (1988). Racial ambivalence and American value conflict: Correlational and priming studies of dual cognitive structures. *Journal of Personality and Social Psychology, 55*(6), 893-905.

Mercer, S. H., & Cunningham, M. (2003). Racial identity in White American college students: Issues of conceptualization and measurement. *Journal of College Student Development, 44*(2), 217-230.

McConahay, J. B. (1986). Modern racism, ambivalence, and the modern racism scale. In J. F. Dovidio & S. L. Gaertner (Eds.), *Prejudice, discrimination, and racism* (pp. 91-126). San Diego, CA: Academic Press.

Miron, D., & Moely, B. E. (2006). Community agency voice and benefit in service learning. *Michigan Journal of Community Service, 12*(2), 27-37.

Moely, B. E., McFarland, M. Miron, D., Mercer, S., & Ilustre, V. (2002). Changes in college students' attitudes and intentions for civic involvement as a function of service-learning experiences. *Michigan Journal of Community Service Learning, 9*(1), 18-26.

Moely, B. E., Mercer, S. H., Ilustre, V., Miron, D., & McFarland, M. (2002). Psychometric properties and correlates of the civic attitudes and skills questionnaire (CASQ): A measure of student's attitudes related to service-learning. *Michigan Journal of Community Service Learning, 8*(2), 15-26.

Myers-Lipton, S. J. (1996). Effect of a comprehensive service-learning program on college students' level of modern racism. *Michigan Journal of Community Service Learning, 3,* 44-54.

Neville, H. A., Lilly, R. L., Duran, G., Lee, R. M., & Browne, L. (2000). Construction and initial validation of the Color-Blind Racial Attitude Scale (CoBRAS). *Journal of Counseling Psychology, 47,* 59-70.

Neville, H. A., Worthington, R. L., & Spanierman, L. B. (2001). Race, power, and multicultural counseling psychology. In J. G. Ponterotto, J. M Casas, L.A., Suzuki, & C. M. Alexander (Eds.), *Handbook of multicultural counseling* (2nd ed., pp. 257-288). Thousand Oaks, CA: SAGE.

Parham, T. A., & Helms, J. E. (1985). Relation of racial identity attitudes to self actualization and affective states of black students. *Journal of Counseling Psychology, 32*(3), 431-440.

Pennsylvania Department of Education. (2007). *Pennsylvania System of School Assessment (PSSA)*. Retrieved March 23, 2008. http://www.pde.state.pa.usa

Phinney, J. (1992). The multigroup ethnic identity measure: A new scale for use with adolescents and young adults from diverse groups. *Journal of Adolescent Research, 7*, 156-176.

Schofield, J. W. (1986). Causes and consequences of the colorblind perspective. In J. F. Dovidio & S. L. Gaertner (Eds.), *Prejudice, discrimination, and racism* (pp. 231- 253). San Diego, CA: Academic Press.

Simons, L. (2007). *Educational psychology syllabus*. Retrieved September 1, 2007, from the American Psychological Association, Office of Teaching Resources in Psychology Project Syllabus Web site: http://www.teachpsych.org/otrp/syllabi/ls06edpsych.pdf

United States Census Bureau. (2000). *US Census Data*. Retrieved March 23, 2008, from http://www.census.gov/main/www/cen2000.html

Waldstein, F. A., & Reiher, T. C. (2001). Service-learning and students' personal and civic development. *The Journal of Experiential Education, 24*(1), 7-13.

CHAPTER 9

SERVICE-LEARNING AND INTERDISCIPLINARITY

A Library Science Perspective

Liberty Smith, Heather J. Martin, Jason Burrage, Megan E. Standridge, Sarah Ragland, and Martina Bailey

ABSTRACT

Much of service-learning research is interdisciplinary, however the degree and implications of this interdisciplinarity have not been as of yet adequately analyzed. This chapter uses the library and information science research method of citation analysis, a form of bibliometrics, in order to assess the degree of interdisciplinarity of the service-learning literature as represented in articles in the *Michigan Journal of Community Service Learning* (*MJCSL*), in the *Advances in Service-Learning Research* (*ASLR*) series, and in masters theses and dissertations on service-learning and related topics published between 2004-2006. The results show a wide range of disciplinarity both in the departmental affiliation of service-learning scholars and in the research from which they draw.

Creating Our Identities in Service-Learning and Community Engagement
pp. 215–235
Copyright © 2009 by Information Age Publishing
All rights of reproduction in any form reserved.

215

INTRODUCTION

Service-learning scholars face significant day-to-day challenges to conduct literature reviews in this interdisciplinary area. This study attempts to assist them by providing a framework for understanding and developing strategies for working within this research context. Also providing an impetus to this work is the fact that the service-learning movement is at a crucial stage in its development, with its leaders paying increasing attention to the needs of the field as a field. To recognize an individual scholar's or an entire field's interdisciplinary nature can be an important aid for thriving under these challenging conditions. For the service-learning field, which is still facing significant struggles both to gain institutional footing in the K-12 and higher education sectors and to establish a rigorous evidence base, recognizing the extent of the field's interdisciplinary nature may be especially valuable for developing strategies for supporting and conducting research in this context and for further field-building efforts more generally. To date, however, the degree and implications of the field's interdisciplinary approach have not been adequately analyzed.

This chapter seeks to do that by using the library and information science research method of bibliometrics (specifically, citation analysis) to assess the degree to which the research published in articles in the *Michigan Journal of Community Service Learning* (*MJCSL*), in the *Advances in Service-Learning Research* (*ASLR*) series, and in masters theses and dissertations on service-learning and related topics, all published between 2004-2006 is interdisciplinary. This analysis serves as an entry point to a larger discussion of the implications of this broad interdisciplinarity, its meaning for the service-learning field, and strategies for individual scholars pursuing research within it.

REVIEW OF THE LITERATURE

Despite the importance of the topic for interdisciplinary scholars, academic leaders, and researchers in the field of library science, the notion of interdisciplinary research itself has no universally accepted definition and the multivariant viewpoints on the subject increase with each scholar who defines her own position across fields and spaces of research (Lau & Pasquini, 2004, p. 59). That said, the library science literature has been trying to define and measure interdisciplinarity for some time. Klein (1996) has identified interdisciplinarity as a practice in which "Borrowed tools and methods stimulate cross-fertilization. New concepts and theories transform the ways that objects are treated in traditional disciplines. New subjects generate interlanguages and hybrid knowledge communities" (p. 134). More prosaically, according to White (1996), interdisciplinarity

> might use concepts from one field to describe or explain things of central importance in another. Or it might unite parallel but hitherto separate concepts within a new superordinate scheme. At its best, it might blend concepts from different disciplines so subtly that no mechanistic formula could describe it. (p. 240).

Even with the disagreements about the definition of interdisciplinarity, as has been observed in the library science literature of at least the last decade (Dilevko & Dali, 2004; Frost & Jean, 2003; Hickey & Arlen, 2002; Klein, 1996; Lau & Pasquini, 2004; Spanner, 2001) and as has more recently been recognized in literature about the cultures and structures of academia (Committee on Facilitating Interdisciplinary Research, 2004; Domino, Smith, & Johnson, 2007; Feller, 2007; Pfirman, Collins, Lowes, & Michaels, 2005; Redden, 2007, 2008), interdisciplinary research, as it is variously defined, is increasingly common. Yet the borders between academia's traditional disciplines have, for the most part, stayed distinct and policed. Feller (2007) argues, in fact, that while an emphasis on interdisciplinary research has appeared more frequently in university strategic plans over the last decade, the actual commitment to supporting this work has been quite inconsistent. Why, then, do so many scholars risk the 'border crossings' between disciplines? Drawing on Boyer and others, Frost and Jean (2003) argue that such interdisciplinary work and interactions seem to "improve the ability of scholars to address societal problems, the caliber of solutions they pose, and the quality of academic life in general" (p. 120). With its practitioner's attention focused on providing real-world solutions to complex social problems, it should not be surprising to find that service-learning scholarship tends to have an interdisciplinary nature.

While interdisciplinarity holds great promise for those scholars who believe maintaining the rigid boundaries of traditional disciplines "reduces the richness of local interaction and dilutes the coherence of academic culture" (Frost & Jean, 2003, p. 120), there are also myriad challenges to conducting such scholarship. The vocabularies, methods, attitudes, and behaviors—in other words, the cultures—of scholars are largely defined by their disciplines (Dilevko & Dali, 2004; Spanner, 2001). Thus, interdisciplinary work demands significant effort to acculturate to new, complex, and often conflicting disciplinary norms and to find strategies for being intellectually bi- or multicultural. In addition, the tools and infrastructures that define and support academic disciplines themselves often resist interdisciplinary scholarship. As Hickey and Arlen (2002) have argued, for example, "the very organizational structure of libraries

eschews the cross-disciplinary framework in favor of one based on the traditional 'pure' disciplines" (p. 98).

At the same time, a related and intersecting, but not identical, conversation is taking place among interdisciplinary scholars and academic
leaders who are calling for recognition of the challenges of and support
needed for interdisciplinary research and careers writ large. Domino,
Smith, and Johnson (2007) discussed both the practical and institutional
challenges to interdisciplinary research, stating, "Academic tradition
organizes research by disciplinary departments, creating barriers to promotion for those who have interdisciplinary careers by disagreement over
what constitutes high-quality research, significant teaching effort, and
appropriate service" (p. 257). These discussions around interdisciplinary
research often focus on the barriers to achieving tenure for interdisciplinary scholars, with Gilligan claiming that "'interdisciplinary work is death
to tenure prospects' because such scholarship is tougher to evaluate than
work that is more narrowly conceived" (Gilligan, as quoted in Leatherman, 1996, p. 22).

However hyperbolic this claim, the general idea that interdisciplinary
scholars face special challenges in hiring, developing tenure dossiers,
having tenure cases reviewed against fair and appropriate criteria rather
than against all of the often-conflicting criteria from each of the fields
that make up their interdisciplinary area, et cetera, is echoed elsewhere in
the literature (Committee on Facilitating Interdisciplinary Research,
2004; Domino et al., 2007; Feller, 2007; Pfirman et al., 2005; Redden,
2007, 2008). With these challenges in mind, a group of research universities responded in 2007 by forming a consortium to study ways to foster
interdisciplinary research (Redden, 2007, 2008).

In much the same way that higher education leaders are paying
increasing attention to the need for systemic changes in order to foster
interdisciplinary work, both higher education and K-12 leaders are working to identify the structures and strategies needed to support quality and
growth in service-learning practice and research. This effort is largely taking place within the field-building framework first laid out within service-
learning in 1998 by Fine for the Academy for Educational Development
and supported by the W. K. Kellogg Foundation's *Learning In Deed* Initiative (Fine, 2001). Billig and Eyler (2003), drawing on Fine's work, identified seven essential elements that comprise a field:

- distinct identity,
- standard practice,
- knowledge base,
- leadership and membership,

- information exchange,
- resources, and
- committed stakeholders and advocates (p. 254).

This research into the essential elements of a field has informed strategic decision-making of field leaders. Although not based directly on this work, the Investment Prospectus (W. K. Kellogg Foundation Service-Learning Consortium, 2005) similarly emphasizes the development of a practice and research base as central investments for strengthening service-learning's position as a field. The current project intersects with these efforts to critically reflect on the state and needs of the field, its practitioners, and its scholars effort in two ways. First, it uses a similar macro lens to consider the contours and needs of the field as a field. Second, because it seems likely that interdisciplinarity may affect each of the essential elements of a field, the project uses the field-building framework as one entry point for exploring the implications of the field's interdisciplinarity.

As a first effort in this vein, the authors recently conducted a bibliometric analysis of several aspects of service-learning graduate theses and dissertations, including their home departments, topics, and research methods (Smith & Martin, 2007). The present study builds on that investigation, extending the analysis from graduate research to professional scholarly output in the field and expanding the research questions. Like the earlier work, the present project analyzes the home departments, topics, and research methods of each text considered. To gain a sense of the contours of the field as a whole, in addition to the patterns and commonalities between individual researchers and texts, the present project also analyzes entire bodies of research using citation analysis (the analysis of the citation patterns within given texts or an entire body of research). Using this combined approach of narrowly defined bibliometric analysis and citation analysis, the present study attempts to answer five research questions:

1. In which disciplines are service-learning scholars working?

2. To what degree is the community of service-learning scholars' research interdisciplinary?

3. From what type of resources are scholars drawing for their research?

4. From what disciplines do service-learning scholars draw for their research?

5. To what degree is the research base on which service-learning scholars draw interdisciplinary?

METHOD

The first measurable indicator of interdisciplinarity was established by Porter and Chubin in 1985. Here, the authors argued that in a given piece of research, the diversity of subject categories of a work's citations is one indicator of its interdisciplinarity. Hurd (1992) describes this work and subsequent research using similar indicators as based on the assumption that citing is a behavior that reflects "the utility of the cited material" (p. 286). However, citing also has numerous other motivations (including demonstrating breadth and/or depth of reading, indebtedness, relationship, etc.) (Hurd, 1992). To measure the interdisciplinarity of an entire field, it is valuable to look both at the citation patterns within its publications and to look at the disciplinary identifications of the authors themselves.

To assess the interdisciplinarity of the research base of service-learning scholarship, the authors used a citation analysis bibliographic method to look in detail at the works cited within a distinct period of time. Disciplinarity was assessed using the Library of Congress (LC) Classification System, the authoritative source for bibliographic classification.

For the initial sample, the authors selected 41 articles, excluding book reviews, from the *MJCSL* and 32 articles, excluding book reviews, from *ASLR* series, both for the years 2004-2006. This time period was selected for its currency and because it maps to the authors' recent bibliometric study of service-learning theses and dissertations for the same time period. These two peer-reviewed publications were selected because they focus exclusively on service-learning research. *MJCSL* focuses on research service-learning in the higher education context and *ASLR* addresses all service-learning research selected from papers presented at the annual International Research Conference on Service-Learning and Community Engagement.

To assess the disciplinary composition of the service-learning research field as represented in these publications, information about the authors published within each of the articles was studied. Professional departmental affiliation or the graduate departmental affiliation of the first four authors of each article were determined. For those whose affiliation was not indicated, online investigation of faculty pages on institutional Web sites was conducted to determine the disciplinary association. Because the authors were not sampled, the results of these two data sets were combined to provide a broader overview of author disciplinary distribution.

Of the 56 authors considered from the *ASLR* series and 80 authors from the *MJCSL* series, 17 and 4, respectively, were not affiliated with a particular department, but rather were associated with a research organization or a center for service-learning, civic engagement, or student life.

Because these settings are themselves interdisciplinary, but are not affiliated with a particular interdisciplinary department, these authors were combined into one group. After entering author affiliation into a spreadsheet, these data were sorted to determine the distribution of the contributing authors for each series both at the departmental level and at the level of the larger academic divisions of business, education, humanities, interdisciplinary, physical sciences, social sciences, and the research/service-learning center category discussed above. In addition to analyzing the departmental affiliation of the articles' authors within the two datasets, their citations were sampled and analyzed according to several factors. As neither publication is indexed, bibliographical information for all articles and citations was manually entered into an Excel spreadsheet. Citations for all of the articles in each dataset were given a unique number. For the years studied there were 1,549 citations in the 41 *MJCSL* articles and 1,006 citations in the 32 *ASLR* articles. A sample of 465 citations from *MJCSL* and 402 from *ASLR* was randomly selected from the total population using a table of random numbers. Individual data points were selected at random from the sample. As these are two separate datasets, a different percentage of items was sampled from each dataset in to ensure representativeness.

Bibliographic information for the sampled citations was entered into a spreadsheet which contained the following fields in addition to a unique identification number: resource type (the type of monograph or other source that is cited, such as academic journal, book, conference proceedings/proceedings, etc.), author(s), LC class, and LC subclass.[1]

Resource type categories were adapted from the work of Dilevko and Dali (2004). Resource type was either assigned according to the LC record or determined after examination of the item record in OCLC WorldCat (a global network of library catalog records from over 9,000 institutions and selected for its comprehensiveness and authority), or other institutional online public access library catalogs (OPACs).

If none of these sources contained information about a given citation, the authors assigned resource type themselves by examining the source document. Each citation was further determined to be either commercially published or noncommercially published (or grey) literature. Grey literature is considered to be that which falls under the definition of the Grey Literature International Steering Committee (GLISC) as, "Information produced on all levels of government, academics, business and industry in electronic and print formats not controlled by commercial publishing, i.e. where publishing is not the primary activity of the producing body" (GLISC, 2007, p. 1). For the purposes of this analysis, the category of grey literature was further divided into conference papers/proceedings, reports/statistics, and other.

The general subject matter of each citation in the samples, in other words, the discipline represented by each sampled citation, was determined by again consulting the Library of Congress Online Catalog to determine the LC class and subclass assigned to each work by LC catalogers. LC classes and subclasses were only assigned, however, at the level of journal, monograph, or resource title. In other words, citations to articles appearing in a journal or edited collection were classified according to the class and subclass of the journal or collection itself, not according to the specific article. For items not in the Library of Congress, OCLC WorldCat was consulted and classifications were determined accordingly. For very obscure items not appearing in either primary cataloging database, classification was assigned by the authors using the LC classification guidelines (the LC Schedules) (Library of Congress, n.d.).

The resulting data were filtered and analyzed to determine three factors: distribution of disciplinary affiliation of author contributors to the population, the most commonly cited resource type, and the level of interdisciplinarity according to LC classes and subclasses.

RESULTS

Disciplinary Identification of Service-Learning Scholars

A large portion of service-learning research is being written by authors who have an affiliation with a social sciences department, as illustrated in Exhibit 9.1. Over 40% of *MJCSL* authors and 36% of *ASLR* authors come from the social sciences. For combined total of both datasets, 38% of authors had an affiliation with a social sciences department. Within the *ASLR* series, the remainder of the authors came fairly evenly from education departments (27%) and research institutes or service-learning/civic engagement centers (30%), with a much smaller representation from the physical sciences (5%) and business departments (2%). The authors of the *MJCSL* series had a slightly different composition, with 21% from education, 18% from the humanities, 8% from the physical sciences, 7% from business schools, 5% from research institutes or service-learning/civic engagement centers, and authors from interdisciplinary departments making up the last 1%.

A further analysis of academic divisions into specific departments showed a greater part of articles in the combined datasets emerging from education departments (28%). This was also the case for the individual datasets with authors affiliated with education departments contributing to 38% of the *ASLR* collection and 28% of the *MJCSL*. The next most fre-

**Exhibit 9.1.   Author Academic Division Affiliation
(Combined Datasets)**

Academic Division	Number of Authors (n = 136)	
Business	7	5%
Education	32	24%
Humanities	14	10%
Interdisciplinary	1	1%
Physical sciences	9	7%
Research institutes/service-learning centers	21	15%
Social sciences	52	38%

quent affilations were in the fields of psychology (17%), anthropology (10%), sociology (7%), business (6%), and health sciences (6%). All of the other departments were represented by less than 5% of the sample.

As noted previously, these preliminary results are limited by the amount of information available on the authors and the complexity of affiliation status of researchers associated with interdisciplinary departments. However, these results do suggest the service-learning research field is an interdisciplinary one.

Type of Resource Cited

Examination of the type of resources that scholars are drawing from for their research indicates that published materials were the most often cited sources in both samples; grey literature of all types made up 20% of the *ASLR* sample, but only 8% of the *MJCSL* sample. While comprising a much smaller percentage of the sampled citations than published materials, the incidence of citations to grey literature is still quite significant. Information retrieval of grey literature tends to be more difficult and more dependent on being passed hand to hand via informal networks of scholars than commercially published literature.

In both samples academic/scholarly journals and books/edited books comprised the greatest number or cited materials: however the distribution among *MJCSL* and *ASLR* was slightly different. Books/edited books were the most commonly cited resource type in the *MJCSL* sample, with 51% of the total citations, followed by academic/scholarly journals (38%), grey literature—conference papers/proceedings (3%), grey literature—

reports/statistics(2.4%), grey literature—other (2.4%), Web sites/electronic resources (1.3%), dissertations/theses (0.7%), newspapers/broadcasts (0.2%), and magazines/trade publications (0.2%). Academic/scholarly journals made up 41% of the total number of cited materials in the *ASLR* sample as the most commonly cited resource type. Books/edited books followed with 37%, then grey literature—reports/statistics (11.7%), grey literature—conference papers/proceedings (4.2%), Web sites/electronic resources (2%), grey literature—other (4.2%), dissertations/theses (0.5%), newspapers/broadcasts (0.5%), and no citations of magazines/trade publications.

While not necessarily indicative of the extent of interdisciplinarity of the research base on which the service-learning field draws, these findings do suggest the field draws on a fairly diverse base of publication types, perhaps reflecting, to some extent, the differing evidentiary norms between the disciplines that make up the field. This relative diversity also suggests an increased challenge for conducting—and, especially, for supporting—service-learning research, since it may be necessary for a service-learning researcher to consult a greater range of source types for service-learning scholarship.

Disciplinarity of Research Sources

The disciplines from which service-learning scholars draw their research and the degree with which the research base on which service-learning scholars draw their research is interdisciplinary can be seen through an analysis of the Library of Congress classes and subclasses. Analyses of both the LC classes and, in more depth, the LC subclasses show a wide distribution of classification, illustrating the striking level of interdisciplinarity of service-learning research. That said, the majority of citations from both data sets come, not surprisingly, from the field of education (LC class L). This is especially the case for the sample of *ASLR* citations, where 73.6% fall into the L class compared to 58.5% in the *MJCSL* citations. Those citations from noneducation disciplines comprise 26.4% (*ASLR*), and 41.5% (*MJCSL*) of the samples. The range of these noneducation disciplines is wide, and between the two data sets citations can be found that are classed in all but 4 of the 21 LC classes. The only classes not represented were auxiliary sciences of history; music and books on music; naval science; and bibliography, library science, and information resources. In both datasets, the second most common classification of citations was from H-social science, with 21.1% of the *MJCSL* sample and 13.4% of the *ASLR* sample. The rest of the citations were widely distributed, with no other LC class having more than 5% of the total sampled citations for either of the data sets. It should be noted that despite having no LC classes predominating beyond L and H, the citations in these samples come from diverse and interdisciplinary fields, including 49 separate LC subclasses in the *MJCSL* sample and 39 separate subclasses in the *ASLR* sample.

Even the dominant field of education reflects a significant degree of interdisciplinarity. As with the other classes, Education is considered by the Library of Congress to be an interdisciplinary field, and is divided into subclasses. Within education, there is a wide distribution among differentiated subfields. As can be seen in Exhibits 9.2 and 9.3, many of the citations came from the LC subclass, which refers to "Special Aspects of Education" and includes "Community and the School." 39.1% of the *MJCSL* citations from the L class were classified as LC subclass, and similarly 42.0% of the L class citations from *ASLR* were classified as LC subclass. The remainder of the L class citations came from subclasses including, "history of education," "theory and practice of education," "individual institutions," "college and school magazines and papers," and "student fraternities and societies."

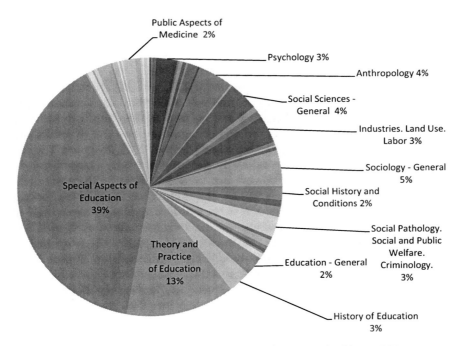

Exhibit 9.2.   LC subclasses of randomly selected sources cited in *MJCSL*.

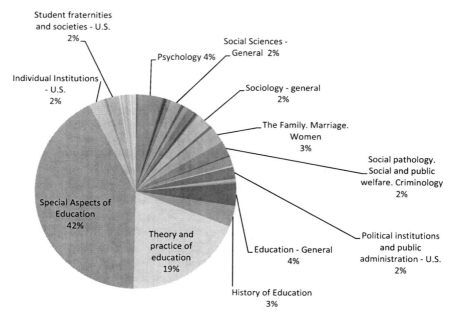

Exhibit 9.3.   LC subclasses or randomly selected sources cited in *ASLR*.

Dissertations and Theses Comparison

The findings from the analysis of the *MJCSL* and *ASLR* are fairly consistent with those from the authors' analysis of doctoral dissertations and masters theses on service-learning and related topics (Smith & Martin, 2007). In that study, abstracts from 144 dissertations and theses published from 2004-2006 were gathered by searching the UMI ProQuest Digital Dissertation Abstracts database. As with the present study, a large proportion, in the case of the dissertations and theses, 75%, came from the division of education, as shown in Exhibit 9.4. The humanities, social sciences, physical sciences, fine arts, and interdisciplinary areas had a much lower representation among the dissertations and theses, with 7% coming from physical sciences, 4% from humanities and 6% from social/ applied science. This collection included no studies from degree programs in the fine arts. In terms of specific departments from which the studies considered emerged, after education, leadership departments were the next largest producers of service-learning dissertations, with 9%. All other departments fell between 1-5%.

Although education was significantly represented among the author affiliations in both the dissertations and theses and the *MJCSL* and *ASLR*

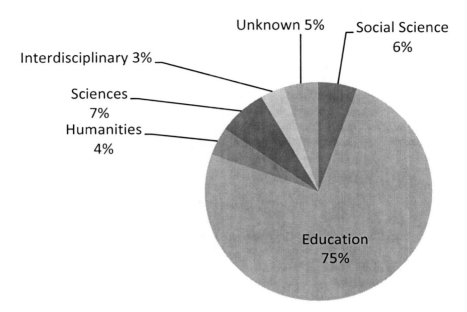

Unknown 5%   Social Science 6%

Interdisciplinary 3%

Sciences 7%

Humanities 4%

Education 75%

Exhibit 9.4.   Academic study areas of dissertation/theses.

series, the extent of that representation differed significantly. While the *MJCSL* and *ASLR* series showed more articles coming from authors with an affiliation to the social sciences (noneducation) than any other division, this was not the case with the dissertations and theses, where research stemming from education departments predominated and research from social science departments accounted for only 6% of the total. The *MJCSL* and *ASLR* population did show a large number of articles from authors affiliated with the academic division of education (24%), which was the second most common author affiliation for these articles. The dominance of the education affiliation in the dissertation and thesis authors means that there are simply fewer dissertations and theses coming from other areas and therefore a lesser degree of interdisciplinarity among these scholars.

The differences in the degree of interdisciplinarity among those writing service-learning theses and dissertations and those writing articles for *MJCSL* and *ASLR* may be attributable to several factors. That dissertations stemming from education departments were a significant majority of the results may be in part because students in these departments may find it more difficult to obtain faculty and department support for interdisciplinary research such as service-learning. A likely influence on this outcome is the fact that a number of the graduate education authors, especially those in teacher preparation tracks, are unlikely to have as much incentive to continue research and publication as authors from other fields. Therefore, some of this difference may simply represent a decrease in the number of authors with education affiliations from graduate school to professional scholarly careers. Additional factors may include the extent to which service-learning is institutionalized in noneducation departments, the high-level proficiency in multiple intellectual discourses demanded by rigorous interdisciplinary research, and the lack of institutional support promoting such research (Lau & Pasquini, 2004).

DISCUSSION

Study Limitations and Opportunities for Future Research

This study has several basic limitations emerging from its design. First, the study is limited by the selection of the initial data sets. Further, while there are likely connections between the service-learning research context and that of service-learning practice, as discussed below, this study only measures the interdisciplinarity of the service-learning research context. Moreover, citation analysis is only one means to assess the interdisciplinarity of a field, and while a measurable indicator is somewhat limited for its founding assumption that scholarly citation is a particularly meaningful behavior reflecting an evaluation of the usefulness and relevance of the sources cited as opposed to reflecting other factors.

This study also only examined the interdisciplinarity of the body of service-learning scholarship broadly as represented primarily by citationality. It did not examine interdisciplinarity at the individual scholar level (i.e., whether individual scholars are drawing from a wide range of disciplines in their research). Additionally, where the authors did look for indicators of interdisciplinarity outside of citationality, specifically, in the area of author affiliation, it was a challenge to obtain trustworthy, current, and transparent information.

As an initial inquiry in this area and given these limitations, there are clear next steps for further examination of the interdisciplinarity of the field. In addition to analyzing citationality and author affiliation within a broader and more representative set of texts, the authors hope to conduct a more detailed analysis of the disciplinary identifications of the authors considered, eventually, perhaps to include a survey of a sample of researchers regarding their experiences as interdisciplinary scholars. Tracing the publishing and citation patterns of the most prolific service-learning scholars to identify further patterns would be an additional valuable contribution to understanding the interdisciplinarity of service-learning scholarship. Perhaps the most important next step for this research, though, will be to perform an analysis of all citations for a representative sample of articles to determine not only the interdisciplinarity of the field but also of individual works and to therefore determine the extent to which the interdisciplinarity of individual scholars is consistent with that of the field as a whole.

Implications

Despite the limitations of this study, the findings do indicate that the body of service-learning research, at least as represented in the leading service-learning research series, is deeply interdisciplinary both at the level of the community of researchers and at the level of the literature on which the field draws. For several reasons it seems likely that these findings would be consistent with the world of service-learning practice. First, the evidence base has an influence on practice and one that may be increasing with the establishment of formalized, evidence-based standards, at least in the K-12 setting, so the interdisciplinarity of that evidence base may be influential. Service-learning practice also takes place in multiple practice contexts, again reflecting its interdisciplinarity. In fact, as Billig and Eyler (2003) have argued,

> Service-learning draws from multiple theories because it is centered on individuals, relationships between individuals, and relationships between individuals and structures. It is inherently multidisciplinary, attached to both academic and civic institutions, and linked to personal development in one form or another. (p. 259)

Looking through the lens of the seven elements of a field identified by Billig and Eyler, drawing from Fine—distinct identity, standard practice, knowledge base, leadership and membership, information exchange, resources, and committed stakeholders and advocates (2003, p. 254)—it is clear that the interdisciplinarity of the field presents important impediments and opportunities field leaders, practitioners, and scholars should keep in mind. For example, "distinct identity" is deeply complicated by the interdisciplinary nature of the field. As can be imagined, with colleagues coming from as wide a range of academic backgrounds and contexts as is the case in service-learning, especially when the primary common ground is a concept of such complexity and diversity, developing a sense of shared identity is not as easy as it might be for a mono-disciplinary area like mathematics. It is likewise difficult to implement a single set of "standard practice(s)" for generating consistently improved results without attention to the diverse disciplinary backgrounds, and therefore capacities and professional development needs, of the fields' scholars and practitioners. The focus of service-learning often reflects the distinct learning objectives, values, and cultures of the disciplines and the professional careers for which students are preparing. With the contexts of its practice and research divided into several distinct settings—K-12, higher education, community-based organizations and with these divisions further underscored with the funding sectors used by Learn and Serve America—the development of a sense of a single distinct identity or a single set of standard practices is still further complicated. Interdisciplinarity may similarly pose challenges for development of leadership/membership, exchange of information, and identification of stakeholders and advocates. At the same time, the interdisciplinarity of the field may provide unique opportunities for identifying resources and stakeholders/advocates as the field's diversity can allow for tapping a wider range of resources, whether financial or human, than more narrowly defined, less diverse fields. An increased awareness of the field's contours, even only those of its research base, may aid in this.

The most important implications for field-building of the interdisciplinarity of service-learning occur at the level of building the knowledge base. Organizations supporting service-learning research and the individuals pursuing this research both face unique challenges because of the field's interdisciplinarity. For the most part, the challenges for research, practice, and ultimately, field-building will be consistent with challenges in other interdisciplinary realms. The library science literature has identified a range of challenges for those conducting interdisciplinary research. These tend to fall into four primary areas:

- a need to be familiar with larger, more diffuse body/bodies of literature;
- a need to decipher different, fluctuating vocabularies;
- a need to work across, through, and between provinces of research and practice in a world structured around well-defined disciplines with traditional limits and boundaries; and
- a need to work in a professional context suspicious of or hostile to interdisciplinarity (Dilveko & Dali, 2004; Klein, 1996; Palmer & Neumann, 2002).

While interdisciplinarity does not by definition suggest the need to be proficient with all of the literature of each of the disciplines making up an interdisciplinary area, in practice, this expectation often comes to the fore. In particular, interdisciplinary scholars may be required to (e.g. in graduate school) or may themselves feel the need to "engage in both substantially more information seeking—and of a different kind—than scholars in a conventional discipline" (Bates, 1996, p. 159). This information seeking work requires a functional level of proficiency and "understanding of other fields of study to be able to seek information in them and to evaluate their applicable and relevant research" (Hernon & Schwartz, 1996, p. 97). These factors can conspire to make rigorous interdisciplinary research a daunting task.

In this same vein, the difficulty of ever evolving terminologies which plague any developing field is exacerbated in an interdisciplinary setting. In a recent survey of interdisciplinary scholars 91% experienced "difficulties in adapting to the vocabularies and culture of their nonaffiliate disciplines. This finding was consistent at all academic levels" (Spanner, 2001, p. 354). On the individual level this can lead to a stalled dialogue between colleagues or between scholars and the literature as "two scholars can be discussing the same concept by using different terminology or, even worse, using the same terminology but with different meanings" (Spanner, 2001, p. 356).

If learning the norms, literatures, and vocabularies of the different disciplines in an interdisciplinary area is challenging, the infrastructures in place to support scholarship can themselves pose impediments. This is especially clear in libraries where:

> interdisciplinary approaches call into question the familiar verbal, numerical, and spatial systems on which we rely. Classification systems function as a "hegemonic representation of human knowledge." Interdisciplinary studies and many modern subjects must be squeezed into preexisting outlays of knowledge that no longer fit the shape of current scholarly output. (Searing, 1992, p. 9)

In such a discipline-based setting, an interdisciplinary researcher "may experience difficulties in using information sources and services organized on a discipline-based model" (Hurd, 1992, p. 285). The very construction of libraries, where subjects are ordered by discipline, resource databases are not standardized, and there is "lack of fit between users and information systems" (Palmer, 1996, p. 131) appears inescapable (Kutner, 2000; Palmer, 1996).

For the interdisciplinary scholar, this "lack of fit" extends beyond models and organizational systems to the very cultures of academia themselves. The discipline-based culture that is still dominant in the academy has real consequences for the careers of aspiring and established scholars. Experts from traditional disciplines tend to view with suspicion scholars lacking a firm anchor in any single discipline. Regardless of the quality of their work, interdisciplinary scholars often experience difficulties securing research grants, going on exchange programs, publishing, gaining recognition, securing a job, or being promoted: "Researchers who identify themselves professionally with cross-disciplinary categories face the entire panoply of gate-keeping mechanisms, which by and large favor existing disciplinary categories" (Klein, 1993, p. 193).

Strategies for Scholars and Their Supporters

In a context of such clear challenges for pursuing service-learning research, it is especially important—for the individual scholar, for the institutions and individuals supporting such scholars, and for the field as a whole—to develop intentional strategies well-matched to the field's interdisciplinary context and all of its implications.

For the individual interdisciplinary scholar, and specifically, for the individual service-learning scholar, understanding the special challenges of conducting research given more widely distributed evidence sources, more conflicting terminologies, and infrastructures not designed for such research is a key step for pursuing research successfully. This understanding can allow the researcher to budget more time for the literature review, seek information in more diverse database and repositories, and look to the information retrieval expertise of librarians early enough in the research process to have positive effects. Moreover, given the diversity of the research base on which service-learning draws and given the importance of grey literature within that research base, conducting research onsite in a subject-specific interdisciplinary repository or searching in a range of article databases can bring together a broader research base.

For the individuals and organizations supporting service-learning researchers, it will be important to help service-learning scholars find what Searing called " 'information leeway' or the range of initiatives that make room for, or create the freedom to do, interdisciplinary work" (as quoted in Dilevko & Dali, 2004, p. 217). Some of this leeway will come by facilitating collaborative research and other opportunities to make connections across departmental affiliations. For example, organizations like the International Association for Research on Service-learning and Civic Engagement are invaluable for fostering interdisciplinary dialogue likely to overcome some of the challenges inherent to the field's interdisciplinary context. Dilevko and Dali (2004) have suggested that librarians can use an "objective portrait of the field's intellectual interconnections and tendencies in [our] collection development and reference work" (p. 219). Practically, it is hoped that the present study provides such an objective portrait that a range of service-learning research supporters can use to develop new strategies for organizing service-learning information in ways likely to be more meaningful to scholars and practitioners from a range of backgrounds and contexts. For example, at NSLC this work will eventually inform development of a new taxonomy and information architecture better matched to the information needs of an interdisciplinary field. Supporters of service-learning scholars may also find that identification of service-learning as an interdisciplinary field has meaning for the creation and selection of service-learning materials, the provision of training and technical assistance, and the importance of providing tools for facilitating communication between scholars.

For the field as a whole, it will be important to continue to invest in initiatives designed to bring scholars, especially early-career and established scholars, together in formal and informal conversations. As more sophisticated strategies for information organization for this interdisciplinary field are developed, it will also be important to continue to provide resources to support development of more sophisticated research and other databases with the capacity to support complex searches across multiple vocabularies. An additional strategy only brought to light with the present project is the potential value of joining forces with others in the academy pushing for recognition and support for interdisciplinary scholarship.

NOTE

1. LC class and LC subclass are the organizational categories within the Library of Congress Classification System. Within this system, all knowledge is divided into 21 classes, which are then subdivided into more specific subclasses.

REFERENCES

Bates, M. J. (1996). Learning about the information seeking of interdisciplinary scholars and students. *Library Trends, 45*(2), 155-164.

Billig, S. H., & Eyler, J. (2003). The state of service-learning and service-learning research. In S. H. Billig & J. Eyler (Eds.), *Advances in service-learning research: Vol. 3. Deconstructing service-learning: Research exploring context, participation, and impacts* (pp. 253-264). Greenwich, CT: Information Age.

Committee on Facilitating Interdisciplinary Research. (2004). *Facilitating interdisciplinary research*. Washington, DC: National Academy Press.

Dilevko, J., & Dali, K. (2004). Improving collection development and reference services for interdisciplinary fields through analysis of citation patterns: An example using tourism studies. *College & Research Libraries, 65*(3), 216-242.

Domino, S. E., Smith, Y. R., & Johnson, T. R. B. (2007). Opportunities and challenges of interdisciplinary research career development: Implementation of a women's health research training program. *Journal of Women's Health, 16*(2), 256-261.

Feller, I. (2007). Interdisciplinary: Paths taken and not taken. *Change: The Magazine of Higher Learning, 39*(6), 46-51.

Fine, M. (2001). *What does field-building mean for service-learning advocates?* Washington, DC: National Service-Learning Partnership.

Frost, S. H., & Jean, P.M. (2003). Bridging the disciplines: Interdisciplinary discourse and faculty scholarship. *The Journal of Higher Education, 74*(2), 119-149.

Grey Literature International Steering Committee. (2007). *Guidelines for the production of scientific and technical reports: how to write and distribute grey literature. Version 1.1.* Rome, Italy: Author.

Hernon, P., & Schwartz, C. (1996). Interdisciplinarity and scholarly research. *Library and Information Science Research, 18*(2), 97-98

Hickey, D., & Arlen, S. (2002). Falling through the cracks: just how much "history" is history? *Library Collections, Acquisitions, & Technical Services 26*(2), 97-106.

Hurd, J. M. (1992). Interdisciplinary research in the sciences: Implications for library organization. *College & Research Libraries, 53*(4), 283-297.

Klein, J. T. (1993). Blurring, cracking, and crossing: permeation and fracturing of discipline. In E. Messer-Davidow, D. R. Shumway, and D. J. Sylvan (Eds), *Knowledges: historical and critical studies in disciplinarity* (pp. 185-211). Charlottesville: University Press of Virginia.

Klein, J. T. (1996). Interdisciplinary needs: The current context. *Library Trends 45*(2), 134-154.

Kutner, L. A. (2000). Library instruction in an interdisciplinary environmental studies program: Challenges, opportunities, and reflections. *Issues in Science and Technology Librarianship, 28.*

Lau, L., & Pasquini, M. W. (2004). Meeting grounds: Perceiving and defining interdisciplinarity across the arts, social sciences and sciences. *Interdisciplinary Science Reviews 29*(1), 49-64.

Leatherman, C. (1996). More faculty members question value of tenure. *The Chronicle of Higher Education, 43*(9), A12-A13.

Library of Congress. (n.d.). *Library of Congress classification online.* Retrieved September 1, 2008, from http://www.loc.gov/catdir/cpso/lcco/

Palmer, C. L. (1996). Navigating among the disciplines: The library and interdisciplinary inquiry. *Library Trends 45*(2), 129-133.

Palmer, C. L., & Neumann, L. J. (2002). The information work of interdisciplinary humanities scholars: Exploration and translation. *Library Quarterly, 72*(1), 85-117.

Pfirman, S. L., Collins, J. P., Lowes, S., & Michaels, A. F. (2005).Collaborative efforts: Promoting interdisciplinary scholars. *The Chronicle of Higher Education, 51*(23), B15-B16.

Redden E. (2007, July 25). 'Institutionalizing' interdisciplinary research. *Inside HigherEd.* Retrieved August 31, 2008, from http://www.insidehighered.com/news/2007/07/25/interdis

Redden, E. (2008, November 6). Encouraging interdisciplinarity. *Inside HigherEd*. Retrieved from http://www.insidehighered.com/news/2008/11/06 /interdiscipline

Searing, S.E. (1992). How libraries cope with interdisciplinarity: The case of women's studies. *Issues in Integrative Studies, 10*, 7-25.

Smith, L., & Martin, H. J. (Eds.). (2007). *Recent dissertations on service and service-learning topics: Volume IV, 2004-2006*. Scotts Valley, CA: Learn and Serve America's National Service-Learning Clearinghouse.

Spanner, D. (2001). Border crossings: Understanding the cultural and informational dilemmas of interdisciplinary scholars. *The Journal of Academic Librarianship, 27*(5), 352-360.

W. K. Kellogg Foundation Service-Learning Consortium. (2005). *An investment prospectus: Strengthening education and democracy through service-learning*. Columbus, OH: Glenn Institute. Retrieved August 31, 2008, from http://www .glenninstitute.org/slforum/art/Final_Investment_Prospectus.pdf

White, H. D. (1996). Literature retrieval for interdisciplinary syntheses. *Library Trends, 45*(2), 239-264.

CHAPTER 10

CIVIC ENGAGEMENT AND SERVICE-LEARNING

The Challenge and Promise of Research

Lori J. Vogelgesang

ABSTRACT

This keynote address reflects upon what we have learned from service-learning and civic engagement research and summarizes current challenges. The author suggests future directions for the research work, opportunities for collaboration, and possible roles for IARSCLE.

INTRODUCTION

We come to this conference from diverse professional and personal experiences, yet I venture to say we share in common a passion for "doing good" as individuals, scholars and educators. We bring an intellectual curiosity, varying levels of experience with research, and probably multiple understandings of the terms civic and community engagement. In the course of this conference so far, I've heard of at least two partici-

Creating Our Identities in Service-Learning and Community Engagement
pp. 237–250

pants who never heard of service-learning till recent weeks. And here you are! Welcome.

I am convinced that we move forward in our work by sharing our diverse perspectives, by challenging each other, and by renewing our own commitments at gatherings such as this. To that end, I want to share some things I have learned about our common adventure, share some national work being done, explore some challenges, frame some questions and suggest some future directions for research. Then I hope you will share some thoughts and questions—some in this large session, more in conversations with each other through the conference and afterwards. I will count this as a success if I can generate some reflections and questions among you all.

I want to acknowledge the limits of my experience in this area—my work has been primarily in higher education, and primarily from a researcher and evaluator perspective. I have spent most of my time in this area looking at impacts of service-learning, and what might lead to civic engagement. I consider this opportunity to address you an honor, and believe me I do NOT come to the podium with what Jim Wright yesterday termed the 'arrogance of expertise' sometimes found at institutions like mine, but rather from a place of gratitude—I have had the great privilege over the past 12 years of working and reflecting with colleagues in community organizations, scholars of other disciplines, and faculty and staff practitioners, a number of whom are here today. This includes the opportunity to read and discuss research—precious time I know is hard to find. I hope by sharing some of the questions and thoughts milling about the research world, I can get you thinking about connections with your own work and maybe even open up some possibilities for future endeavors.

It's an exciting time to be thinking about community and civic engagement research. There has been huge growth in programs, projects and infrastructure over the past 10-15 years. In the past 5 years, I've noticed more "big" monetary donations to strengthen practice, more institutions acknowledging the importance of the work, and more scholars considering research. Still, many seem to be looking for irrefutable proof that service-learning and civic engagement are "magic bullets" if you will—something that will address all our challenges in education and in communities. We here in this room know it's a little more complicated than that.

WHAT WE KNOW

Indeed, we know a lot more than we did 15 years ago about the impact of service-learning, but the efforts have led us to many more questions. A handful of you in this room will recall the 1997 meeting in Denver, where we discussed a research agenda for service-learning. I know this wasn't the first such meeting, but it was the first for me. The Denver meeting produced a research agenda, and I want to share with you the following list of issues, summarized by Giles and Eyler (1998):

> Top issues in service-learning research include how service-learning enhances subject matter; defining expected outcomes; identifying the processes of effective service-learning; faculty involvement; effect on educational institutions; institutional policies, practices supporting/enhancing service-learning; nature of effective community partnerships; value to participating communities; impact on student's citizenship and social participation; and contribution to development of social capital.

Sound familiar?

Today, we know something about what is necessary for this work to be institutionalized. The work of Barbara Holland, Julie Hatcher, Bob Bringle, Andy Furco, and Sherril Gelmon, among others, has been very influential.

By looking at reward systems and other cultural aspects, researchers know something of the transformative potential for faculty and educational institutions. Here the work of Kerry Ann O'Meara, Jon Wergin and Larry Braskamp have shaped and contextualized the kinds of challenges that yesterday Jim Wright framed as "the 10 biggest challenges" to partnership work. Cultures are different, calendars are different, the players change.

We know from research something of the benefits and attributes of quality partnerships. Recently, we read a report in the *Michigan Journal of Community Service Learning* about a study sponsored by Campus Compact: Marie Sandy, Barbara Holland, and others conducted research that examined partnership issues from a service-provider, or community perspective (Sandy & Holland, 2006). It was a systematic study of the issues from a number of different providers, and was conducted as a collaborative experience.

We know something about the college experiences that impact prosocial and civic engagement outcomes. With Janet Eyler and Dwight Giles' seminal work reported in their book, *Where's the Learning in Service-Learning* (1999), as well as our work at the Higher Education Research Institute (HERI) at UCLA, we, among others, documented that professors/teachers helping make connections matters, and that reflection matters—and in the case of our study at HERI (Vogelgesang & Astin, 2000), discussing one's experience with other students appeared to be a more consistent predictor of learning outcomes than was writing in a journal or discussing one's experience with a professor.

Since our work is U.S. based, it was interesting to hear Dr. Naude present her work yesterday, as her work is in the South African context. She also found collective reflection (along with individual reflection) to be a more powerful predictor of learning outcomes, as compared with only individual reflection.

We know something about the role of high quality experiences, and what constitutes quality has been a cornerstone of work done by Janet Eyler, Dwight Giles, Andy Furco, Shelley Billig, and others.

We know something about the role of motivations: People respond to invitations to participate in service. Our work suggests that wanting to help others is a strong motivator, as is wanting to make a difference, and wanting to do something about an issue; it is not necessarily framed by students as wanting to change policy. This notion was reinforced by college students participating in Wingspread Conference and subsequently the Compact-Sponsored Raise Your Voice Campaign (Long, 2002; Raill & Hollander, 2006).

I want to make an argument for longitudinal research here, by highlighting several findings from our HERI study. We surveyed students across the U.S. when they entered higher education in 1994, 4 years later, and then again in 2004, 10 years after they entered college. Approximately 8,400 students participated at all three time points. Let me note here that our study includes only students who entered college as first-time, full-time freshmen.

As you can see in Exhibit 10.1, the strength of importance of social/civic outcomes such as the goal of "influencing social values" does change over time, and the gains made during the college years seem to disappear after college. By looking at the 1994 time point, you can also see the self-selection factor: Service-learning students entered college in 1994 with stronger commitment to this (and other) social values, and the differences between service-learning and other students remain fairly steady over the next 10 years (Astin et al., 2006).

In fact, the self-selection might be influenced by prior service. The work of Jim Youniss and others suggesting that motivation might be a *product* of engagement, not just a precursor—might be counterintuitive (Youniss & Yates, 2007), but in fact there is other evidence that reinforces this notion. For example, there was an attenuation effect found in a study done as part of the Diverse Democracy project (Hurtado, 2003), when researchers looked at the role of taking one diversity course as motivator for taking another, and how that strengthens the impact of the second course. Linda Sax has also identified this notion of the habit of volunteering using earlier HERI longitudinal data (Sax, 2000).

A CIRCLE working paper by Meira Levinson finds that poor, non-White youth demonstrate "lower levels of civic and political knowledge,

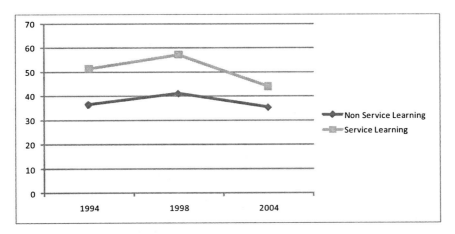

Exhibit 10.1.   Percentage of college graduates reporting that the goal: *Influencing social values is* "very important" or "essential." Drawn from Astin, Vogelgesang et. al. (2006).

skills, positive attitudes, and participation as compared to their wealthier and White counterparts" (Levinson, 2007). Furthermore, a study by Joseph Kahne and Ellen Middaugh of over 2,500 California high school students finds that access to school-based opportunities to develop civic commitments and capacities are unevenly distributed: "College-bound students have significantly more access to these opportunities than students not planning to attend college" (Kahne & Middaugh, 2008) HERI data reinforces this notion that students coming from different kinds of high schools had differential opportunities and different expectations of them around service.

We know individual faculty commitment to engaged scholarship and service matters. The work of Anthony Antonio, Chris Cress, and Lena Astin and at HERI found common dispositions among engaged faculty (Antonio, Astin, & Cress, 2000), as have we in the study I directed. This might be likened to the pretest we talk about with students; faculty who are committed to these issues go ahead and do the work, without waiting on institutional recognition.

As we have learned these things, we are reminded that there is much work to be done. I'm going to acknowledge a huge gaping hole in our work—we know very little about young adults who don't enter our higher education system, or who drop out early on. I understand some reasons this gap exists, but in the end if we are about transforming communities, this cannot continue.

WHAT ARE THE CHALLENGES?

There are any number of conceptual challenges I could dwell on, but a big one for me is defining civic engagement for assessment—how can we know if we are doing it right (or doing it more, or better) if we are not clear on what the "it" is?

Is civic engagement a means to broader goals such as addressing regional issues as we've seen in Australia, or nation-building, as we've seen in the context of South Africa? Or is it an individual outcome that we desire to see come to fruition as a result of developing skills, efficacy, and knowledge within the schools?

With civic engagement, as Rick Battistoni (2007) has remarked, there is increasing conceptual blurring as the work unfolds across multiple contexts. With service-learning there may be variations on the definition, but generally we agree on the common elements. In contrast, the net is cast ever wider when it concerns what is called civic or community engagement. It's one of those terms that risks losing credibility as leaders, practitioners, and others seem to count everything as engagement.

Let me be clear, I'm not advocating for a single definition; what I am advocating for are local articulated understandings of what are program and partnership goals, institutional goals for students, community goals for community members, etc. When UCLA says it educates students for civic engagement, to what extent do we need clarity on what that means? I have to say that if you want me to evaluate the impact of your program or partnership, there needs to be conceptual clarity around the desired outcomes. In other words, we need to know what we are measuring.

From personal experience designing the survey instrument used in the HERI study, I can attest that it's difficult to narrow down what counts, even within a focus of individual outcomes—is it unpaid work in a community setting (i.e., volunteerism)? Or is civic, by definition, limited to a public sphere? The research center CIRCLE has defined 19 measures, encompassing electoral indicators, political voice, and civic indicators (Lopez, Levine, Both, Kiesa, Kirby, & Marcelo, 2006). It's a helpful rubric. But how do we (or should we) capture the friendly helpful neighbor? Number of hours spent being friendly? Or the caring for one's extended family? It might be argued that the "civic involvement" as illustrated by membership in community organizations such as Elks Club or the Rotary Club is itself a cultural artifact that is changing with new immigrant communities and certainly, overwhelmingly, transformed by the "dot.net" generation.

Still, neighborly and community relationships are an important fabric in our civic context. What about people who devote their careers to a helping profession? The teacher who spends long hours after work correcting papers? Does it matter if they are well-paid? Would a doctor be considered less of a helping career than a social worker? What about working at a company—or starting a company—that promotes socially conscious or environmentally friendly policies? These may sound unimportant, but if we are talking about long-term, large-scale surveys, we have to address such issues.

What do we mean by civic engagement? Do we care what the end is or do we just measure engagement as activity? If describing the myriad ways that engagement might play out is not possible, do we revert to counting hours as a measure of success? This happens in places where service is required sometimes, and can render the service meaningless. We need resources that support high-quality work.

This works brings into sharp relief the reality that, at least in U.S. higher education, the public collectively sees universities as places for not only disciplinary work, but life skills training, job training, and as a source of resources, such as student volunteers and faculty consultants—a resource-rich place with somewhat unmet potential to solve any number of social issues.

In part due to increased public scrutiny, higher education institutions are being held accountable in new ways. There has also been some self-reflection work such as the Kellogg Forum, which has turned our attention to issues of engagement and partnerships. Accrediting agencies are ever-more explicit in expecting institutions to have measurable learning outcomes. This is an opportunity to shape those discussions. Work presented at this conference by Lorilee Sandman, Julie Williams, and Eleanor Abrams addresses issues with accreditation.

Faculty—even when they agree that engagement should be a goal of the institution, might not agree it's *their* role to be doing engaged scholarship. In the 2004 HERI Faculty Survey, 81% of faculty agreed that "Colleges and Universities have a responsibility to work with their surrounding communities to address local issues" but only 48% had actually used their scholarship to address local community needs, and 42% had collaborated with the local community in teaching or research (Lindholm, Szelenyi, Hurtado, & Korn, 2005).

Even if the public thinks that graduates should, by and large, have a certain set of skills if they have a degree, these skills are not necessarily mapped to particular experiences in college. At large public institutions in particular it is only recently that any attention at all has been given to a truly comprehensive, developmental pattern of experiences ... and still, we're only barely beginning to see evidence of accountability in this area. The increased attention and pressure to develop learning outcomes emerging from U.S. accrediting bodies represents a real potential for engagement work, as universities are attempting to lay out the ways in which they comprehensively attend to student learning. Still, for the most part, the entire game plan is not explicit and most institutions are relatively new to this work. Most faculty members are not trained to teach. They are not trained in course design, evaluation, and so on. The promotion and tenure systems of most disciplines and institutions are playing catch up at best to deal with cross-disciplinary work as well as community-based and engaged scholarship.

I want to return to what I call the assessment question—are we teaching to the intended outcome? Because what we teach will impact the outcome.

Shelley Billig, Sue Root, and Dan Jesse's study explores the relationships between different elements of a service-learning experience and the outcomes (Billig, Root, & Jesse, 2005). The study's findings support the importance of a quality experience, but also point out that different kinds of experiences (i.e., direct vs. indirect) lead to distinct outcomes. What is the intended outcome and how can we teach to that?

Similarly, as researchers or even evaluators, are we asking the right questions? This has methodological implications as well as political ones. If we view service-learning or community engagement as an activity we naturally go towards isolating (in quantitative analyses) the impact that it has on whatever outcome we have in mind, or conversely, what experiences can strengthen, or "cause" community or civic engagement. While this makes sense—we want to know what contributes to stronger civic engagement, this risks creating completely artificial boundaries between different aspects of learners' experiences.

Currently, we are in an environment where there is pressure to isolate experiences and ascertain causality. This suggests a randomized experimental approach. We've long known in higher education that this doesn't work so well when students cannot be randomly assigned to much of anything beyond a particular section of a course. They cannot be assigned to a major or to an institution. And in K-12 students are not randomly assigned to institutions. And institutions are not equal. Of course, when a study can assign students to different "treatments" within a course we can begin to isolate a variable, if you will, and this kind of research does inform our practice. But I'm talking about understanding something deeper here.

Illustrations from our HERI study suggest either common elements of a set of college experiences (i.e., "challenged my worldview") or a cumulative effect of multiple experiences that either "compete with" or "build upon" service-learning, depending on your perspective. I'm convinced that future research needs to not only acknowledge but to address the interconnectedness of liberal education, civic engagement, globalization, and an increasingly multicultural world. The American Association of Colleges and Universities has played a leadership role in this work and I encourage you to visit their Web site if you are not aware of their work.

Our findings that cross-racial interactions, enrolling in women's studies courses, and study abroad all seem to shape students' worldviews would suggest one might examine the elements that are common in high quality courses and examine that in the aggregate. This is congruent with what we know from college student development theory about broadening one's perspective, challenging preconceived notions, and the like.

In their work examining spirituality, or the search for meaning, among undergraduates in The Spirituality in Higher Education project at HERI, the researchers Alexander and Helen Astin are finding that the same set of experiences I just mentioned lead to positive outcomes. As some of you may well know, this work is all interconnected. We have a mounting body of evidence that these horizon-broadening, stereotype challenging, experientially powerful experiences are all relevant to what we want to accomplish. We need to connect the research dots.

What we know about high-quality service-learning is the same as what makes a high quality learning environment, period. That is, teachers, faculty members or other educators, as well as fellow students, help learners make connections (reflection), the experiential and academic components are connected, the course design is intentional, learning goals are explicit, the course and evaluations are designed to meet learning goals, and so on. All these things are converging to describe the skills, values and commitments that students need for the increasingly complex, fast-changing world they live in.

WHAT ARE THE QUESTIONS?

What might shape the next big study? What might research to examine this high quality learning look like?

Longitudinal. We have to capture the "value-added" of our endeavors. We need to understand what learners bring to the experience if we are to understand its transformative power. As you know, there is a real hunger for understanding the long-term impacts of what we do. The challenge is that researchers need to anticipate what the questions might be 10-12 years down the road. And we have to be able to anticipate we might have resources to conduct the research 10 years down the road. We didn't know in 1994 that we'd be studying service-learning at HERI, so in 1998 we included some items on our follow-up survey, but even then we had only very basic measures of quality of the experience. The rudimentary quality of measures has been a valid criticism of our work. But I think the funders were right to say they wanted this work done from a place like HERI where there would be an institutional commitment to the endeavor. If we are going to secure funding for longitudinal work on a large scale, we have to demonstrate capacity to manage that and convey an understanding that the agenda is bigger than one person.

We need to understand how this learning impacts students years down the road. There simply are not pretests for everything because what a sixth grader does is different from the activities and involvements of 12th grader, or a recent college graduate. As we consider the question engagement to what end, I'm particularly intrigued and encouraged by this notion of capturing a sense of civic identity or civic vocation and how that develops. This is a construct that can mature over time. The American Association of Colleges and Universities's publication, *Peer Review* (2008) mentions, among other strategies that hold promise: "demonstrate that programming to elevate civic agency can lead to higher quality education." It makes sense.

Cross-disciplinary. We need to work with our colleagues doing research in areas of globalization and diversity as well as looking more to other established fields for theory that can guide our work.

In partnerships and collaboratives. With limited funding, we need to use our human resources to create larger studies that examine learning across contexts.

I'm advocating for clarity on goals and outcomes at a local level, which might suggest many small evaluations, but in fact I see it as a role of this conference and this association to take that collective knowledge and find the underlying theoretical constructs, and to generate and disseminate research that informs a range of practices. This organization (IARSCLE) can be a place of multiple research collaboratives (others have also suggested this).

One reason why our work is so challenging is that in many ways we are challenging the systems as we know them. We are suggesting a new way of learning, and a central role for community issues, community partners and student voice in our work. And what we are finding—and indeed have known—is that the status quo has long gone unchallenged, and reframing how learning happens and suggesting a different role for educational institutions and new relationships is really different. If you really are very new to this work, perhaps you haven't stopped to think "well, we never really have evaluated how well the large class lecture works as a teaching method" but one is not long at these types of gatherings without having that reflection ...

A study of learning. This grand study would be a reflective experience for all participants. It would be a study of physical (brain), psychological, social, and community. It would contain public policy aspects, and draw upon studies of social movements. It would generate theory as well as test theory. At the same time we are systematically narrowing our focus—what is it about the partnership, what preconditions lend themselves to greater learning, how important is the nature of the experience ... we must also push to be broader, to understand service and engagement in the context of complex learning, developing skills for a pluralistic, technological world. How do we do research for tomorrow in today's environment?

MOVING FORWARD

Who is doing the research? Who participates in conceptualizing it? Is it primarily the faculty member and/or service provider who might have a stake in the outcomes, and is therefore seen as "less objective?" How do we "do" participatory research of impacts and gain the credibility advantages of a detached observer?

As I think about how we do this, I have five tips for emerging researchers:

1. Network: Know who is out there and what they are asking ... because there's a time lag between work and publications, and we need to talk to each other to learn what's working, what's not, who can support your work, who can you support.
2. Do good work; read the existing research, do careful and rigorous work (read the original studies).
3. Practice what you preach; reflect on your own work in systematic ways to improve research and practice.
4. Connect your work with that of others ... form partnerships!
5. Publish AND otherwise disseminate your work. This will require writing for different audiences, developing "elevator summaries" of your work (the 30 second version of your 2 year project), etc. In other words, make your work accessible.

WHAT IS HAPPENING NOW? WHAT ENCOURAGES US?

There are many new programs and initiatives, but are there resources for assessment and research? Not so much ... but a few new and ongoing resources are worth mentioning for those of us whose work in not currently immersed in the civic engagement arena:

- Spencer strategic initiative in civic learning and civic action with research grants
  http://www.spencer.org/content.cfm/civic-learning-and-civic-action
- This organization—IARSCLE; a chance to network and find support and challenges for your work: The increased number of scholars here and exciting presentations at this year's conference are encouraging.
  http://www.researchslce.org/
- The American Association of Colleges and Universities
  http://www.aacu.org
- Campus Compact Indicators of Engagement and Consulting Corps
  http://www.compact.org/initiatives/civic_engagement/
- Research Universities Collaborative
  http://www.compact.org/initiatives/research_universities/
- Service-learning Clearinghouse
  http://www.servicelearning.org
- The *Michigan Journal of Community Service Learning*
  http://www.umich.edu/~mjcsl/

Research at K-12 is exemplary and worth examining by those in higher education as well. This moment in history is not without its challenges and frightening aspects. But the increasing acceptance of engaged work is kind of exciting!

For me, research in service-learning and engagement has been a journey. Wrestling with both the conceptual and methodological aspects of what I call civic engagement have provided a window into other issues: What is the purpose of education? How do we understand knowledge (what is it and how is it transmitted or learned)? How might this work change cultures in education to transform the reward system, address institutional needs, community needs, and student learning? How do we as a community struggle with divergent views on the best path? How do we treat each other? I mean, as researchers? Are we authentically collaborative or protectively territorial?

In my current position, in addition to conducting evaluation work, I've been charged with helping university managers (those who make decisions, oversee the program, train and supervise professional and student staff) to make data—driven decisions. I see firsthand how this is a challenge for people, especially when the data don't support their working assumptions, or the data are incomplete. Although many of us really do seek knowledge for its own sake, and want to feed our intellectual curiosity about the way the world works and how people and organizations learn, in the end a good deal of it must lead to informing practice and policies. I'm very encouraged and only a little intimidated to be among so many colleagues who have done groundbreaking work, and especially among you who represent the next wave of researchers. Thank you.

REFERENCES

AAC&U. (2008). *Peer Review, 10*(2-3). Retrieved from http://www.aacu.org/peerreview/pr-spsu08/pr-spsu08_index.cfm

Antonio, A. L., Astin, H. S., & Cress, C. M. (2000). Community service in higher education: A look at the nation's faculty. *The Review of Higher Education, 73*(5), 373-398.

Astin, A. W., Vogelgesang, L. J., Misa, K., Anderson, J., Denson, N., Jayakumar, U., et al. (2006). *Understanding the effects of service-learning: A study of students and faculty.* Los Angeles: Higher Education Research Institute, UCLA.

Battistoni, R. (2007). *Active citizens or passive consumers: Choices for higher education.* Plenary address at the Missouri Campus Compact Statewide Conference, Lake Ozark, MI.

Billig, S., Root, S., & Jesse, D. (2005). *The impact of participation in service-learning on high school students' civic engagement.* CIRCLE Working Paper 33. The Center for Information and Research on Civic Learning and Engagement.

Eyler, J., & Giles, D. E. (1999). *Where's the learning in service-learning?* San Francisco: Jossey-Bass.

Giles, D. E., Jr., & Eyler, J. (1998). A service-learning research agenda for the next five years. *New Directions for Teaching and Learning, 73*, 65-72.

Hurtado, S. (2003). *Preparing college students for a diverse democracy.* Ann Arbor: Center for the Study of Higher and Postsecondary Education.

Kahne, J., & Middaugh, E. (2008). *Democracy for some: The civic opportunity gap in high school.* CIRCLE Working Paper #59. The Center for Information and Research on Civic Learning and Engagement.

Levinson, M. (2007). *The civic achievement gap.* CIRCLE Working Paper #51. The Center for Information and Research on Civic Learning and Engagement.

Lindholm, J. A., Szelenyi, K., Hurtado, S., & Korn, W. S. (2005). *The American college teacher: National norms for the 2004-2005 HERI Faculty Survey.* Los Angeles: Higher Education Research Institute.

Long, S. E. (2002). *The new student politics: The Wingspread statement on student civicengagement.* Boston: Campus Compact.

Lopez, M. H., Levine, P., Both, D., Kiesa, A., Kirby, E., & Marcelo, K. (2006). *The 2006 civic and political health of the nation: A detailed look at how youth participate in politics and communities.* The Center for Information and Research on Civic Learning and Engagement.

Naude, L. (2008, October). *Preparing students for life: The role of service-learning and critical reflection.* Paper presented at the Eighth International Research Conference on Service-learning and Community Engagement, New Orleans.

Raill, S., & Hollander, E. (2006). How campuses can create engaged citizens: The student view. *Journal of College and Character,* 7(1), 1-7.

Sandmann, L., Williams, J., & Abrams, E. (2008, October). *Higher education community engagement activated through accreditation.* Paper presented at the Eighth International Research Conference on Service-learning and Community Engagement, New Orleans.

Sandy, M., & Holland, B. A. (2006). Different worlds and common ground: Community partner perspectives on campus-community partnerships. *Michigan Journal of Community Service Learning,* 13(1), 30-43.

Sax, L. J. (2000). Citizenship development and the American college student. In T. Ehrlich (Ed.), *Civic responsibility and higher education* (pp. 3-18). Westport, CT: ACE and the Oryx Press.

Vogelgesang, L. J., & Astin, A. W. (2000). Comparing the effects of service-learning and community service. *Michigan Journal of Community Service Learning,* 7, 25-34.

Wright, J. (2008, October). *The world's third biggest lie: "Hi, I'm from the University and I'm here to help you."* Plenary address at the Eighth International Research Conference on Service-learning and Community Engagement, New Orleans.

Youniss, J., & Yates, M. (1997). *Community Service and Social Responsibility in Youth.* Chicago: University of Chicago Press.

CHAPTER 11

RESEARCH FOR WHAT?

New Directions and Strategies for Community Engaged Scholarship: International Perspectives

**Sherril Gelmon, Tim Stanton,
Cobie Rudd, and Diana Pacheco-Pinzon**

ABSTRACT

This chapter is an edited transcription of a plenary panel session during the Eighth International Research Conference. The panel was moderated by Sherril Gelmon, Portland State University, and the panelists were Tim Stanton, Stanford University, United States; Diana Pacheco-Pinzon, Universidad Marista de Mérida, Mexico; and Cobie Rudd, Edith Cowan University, Australia.

OPENING COMMENTS AND INTRODUCTIONS

Sherril Gelmon: Our theme this morning is "Research for What?" It is intended to set up not only a conversation today but also the Ninth Inter-

Creating Our Identities in Service-Learning and Community Engagement
pp. 251–263

national Research Conference next year in Ottawa, Canada. At the IARSLCE Board retreat in August 2008, John Saltmarsh (now board chair), said: "You know what we really just need to be talking about? It is answering the question—research for what?" Some Board members then started to say, "Research—why? Research for whom? Research—how?" It quickly became clear that John's question sparked a lot of discussion. So we want you to be thinking about this theme during this conversation, and also be thinking about what might be the things you would want to think about around "Research for What?" over the coming year. What you would like to present at next year's conference, and how would you move this discussion forward?

Because this is an international association, we want to ensure that we have international as well as North American perspectives. So today's panel has representation both by citizenship as well as considerable time spent in various countries including the United States, South Africa, Mexico, Australia, and Canada. If you looked at each of our passports, you would probably find stamps from many other countries as well. So we are trying to bring you a wide range of perspectives. I am going to ask each of the panelists to first introduce themselves and then we will have some facilitated dialogue.

Tim Stanton: My name is Tim Stanton and I'm a senior fellow at Stanford University's John W. Gardner Center for Youth and Communities, which is a community-based participatory research center in the School of Education. I was also recently appointed as director of a new Stanford overseas studies center in Cape Town, South Africa. I've done a lot of work in South Africa on my own, working with several South African universities as well as for Stanford. I also work in Singapore, Southeast Asia, a little bit in Australia, and I'm virtually working in Canada by instructing an online course at Queens University. In terms of disciplinary perspectives, I've never been very disciplined. Just to give you an idea, I have an undergraduate degree in English, a master's in education, and my doctorate is in something called human and organization systems. And I counted it up, I think that I've taught in six different departments and schools at Stanford, ranging from African studies to the School of Medicine to urban studies. So I am all over the map in a "disciplinary" sense.

Diana Pacheco: Hello. My name is Diana Pacheco. First of all I want to thank you for inviting me to this panel. It is a huge honor for me to be here with all of you. I am from Mexico and I work with Universidad Marista de Mérida in the Yucatán Peninsula. I've been working in higher education my whole professional life. Right now, I am the director of the service-learning program in my university. As a student, I got involved in service-learning when I was doing my masters degree at Michigan State and was working with a day care center for elders. It was a very rewarding experience and wonderful to be there with them. Since 1997 I have been involved in service-learning as a professor. My bachelor's degree is in educational psychology, and my master's and PhD are in education. I have done some research on service-learning and on student outcomes, mainly critical reflection, in the university that I work with, where all the students have to participate in the service-learning program.

Cobie Rudd: Hi everybody; I am from Australia and I live in Western Australia and work at Edith Cowan University. I'm a professor there and head of the department called the School of Nursing, Midwifery, and Postgraduate Medicine. Also, I am director of a research center that is called the Systems and Interventions Research Centre for Health, and it basically looks at where there are problems in systems and how we might devise solutions. So that includes areas like scenario-based learning, which in some ways is a new type of experiential learning. In scenario-based learning we use actors, high-fidelity mannequins and standardized patient equivalents, who are trained community members, to recreate authentic industry environments. Through our health care simulation center, we deliver this form of teaching and learning for students, alumni and health care professionals and are able to create realistic scenarios for all the settings and situations they will encounter. This simulation center affords participants a safe environment in which to learn and develop competencies and competence in clinical, communication, leadership and teamwork domains. My PhD research was in the area of diffusion of innovations applied to the medical profession's acceptance of new policy ideas and change in health care. It is a pleasure to be here.

QUESTIONS AND RESPONSES

Sherril Gelmon: In the context of the country or countries where you live, work, and spend time, what do you see as two or three of the most important areas of research that relate to service-learning and/or community engagement, or whatever terminology you are using in your country?

Tim Stanton: I come at this question primarily as a practitioner, although I've done my own research on faculty development through service-learning, the history of this field, and on graduate studies in research universities as they relate to community engagement. With this practitioner's perspective, I think about service-learning research with the assumption that it ought to contribute directly and effectively to improvement of practice. Lori Vogelgesang answered this question of the importance of research to service-learning yesterday, at least for the United States. I thought she gave a brilliant summary of the role and purpose of research on service-learning that we all should reread and think about. But when I started thinking about the question this morning, I recalled back in the year 2000 when Dwight Giles invited me to develop an article for a special issue of the *Michigan Journal* that was focused on a research agenda for service-learning. I found myself thinking then about the praxis between research and practice. I reflected on my own work, the work of my colleagues in California and across the country and even overseas who I talk to quite regularly, about how we do service-learning and in particular how we as teachers carry out our goals. And I couldn't think of a single incident where anybody said to me: "You know I changed something in the way I do service-learning because of something that I've read in the research."

We could all identify important pieces of research that interested us and made us reflect on our pedagogy, but nobody made a direct correlation between research and practice. So why was that, I wondered. I began to think that one reason is because I am talking to the wrong people, and there actually are practitioners who carefully go through the research and then plan their syllabi and their courses. But I had not met any up to this point. So, maybe there was a second reason. And that is that most service-learning people, like me, tend to be activists in our approach to our work. We kind of make it up as we go along. In that sense we are experiential learners learning our practice as we go, learning how to work with our students and our community partners so that they become our teachers, not our research subjects. So I've concluded that we practitioners are not very good students of the research.

But then when I began to look more carefully at the research and I realized that so much of it is directed at, and funded to look at, outcomes. Particularly in those early years, we needed to justify this work; we needed to make a place for service-learning in the academy. The funders needed to justify their expenditure of funds to support us. It made sense that the research was highly outcomes or impact focused. In the last few weeks, in thinking about this morning's panel, I did the same kind of semi-scientific survey of my memory that I did back in 2000 and concluded, "I still can't remember anybody who talks about research when they talk about their practice in a direct way … until yesterday." Yesterday I was at a presentation at this conference and one of the presenters talked about how she shaped her approach to her service-learning teaching based upon her research. At last I was finally seeing research directly affect practice. However, when I went through the catalogue for the conference before coming to New Orleans, I counted 42 impact or outcomes focused presentations,

out of a total of maybe 80-90 presentations—close to half. I tried to categorize the different presentations and this was the largest category by far.
Perhaps because of funding, because of our interests, or whatever reasons,
we are continuing to produce outcomes-related research, even if it is better research, and more diverse with a lot more focus on civic education
and civic leadership development. But as a teacher, I am not sure it is tell-
ing us how to do service-learning any better when we go back into the
classroom, at least in a "thick," richly detailed kind of way. There are
exceptions to this but I think it is generally still the case.

In addition to improving practice, another area that I think is highly
important but not sufficiently addressed in the U.S., or anywhere else, is
the community side of service-learning. There are very few presentations
at this conference that address the community needs and issues related to
service-learning, especially how our community partners go about playing
their roles in the pedagogy. What is their experience working with us and
what is that like?

So for the state of service-learning research in the U.S. I find myself
taking a glass half-empty rather than half-full view, though one must
acknowledge the tremendous growth and increased diversity of existing
research. The improvement in quality is really dramatic and we all should
feel really good about that.

In thinking about South Africa, I think I would say that I see a similar
pattern there. Perhaps research in South Africa is even more outcomes
focused, because South Africa has a highly centralized education system,
both within K-12 and higher education. Assessing outcomes is very
important in this context. So South African service-learning research has
been funded to a great extent to address this need. There are exceptions
to this, however, which are very strong.

Diana Pacheco: Let me first give you a little sense of what the educational
context is in my country. The Mexican history of service-learning is very
different from the United States story. Here in the U.S., service-learning
is a nationwide program, from elementary to higher education level, and
with huge resources for it: service-learning centers, foundations that support practitioners and researchers. So what is the situation in Mexico? We
have a long tradition of service, not service-learning, mainly for higher
education. For students to get their bachelors degree they are required by
the Mexican Constitution to accomplish 480 hours of service in public
institutions. But this service is not curriculum-related, there are no reflection activities and it is not necessarily community-oriented. So it is not
really service-learning. For K-12, we have nothing in the official curriculum that could somehow be close to service-learning. However, there are
some efforts, out of the official program, and a few educational institu-

tions, from elementary to higher education, have service-learning experiences. It is easier to find some examples in higher education although we have some examples in elementary and high school. We have few resources to carry out service-learning programs and research; we are starting to have service-learning centers in some higher education institutions. This is more or less the situation for service-learning in my country.

I would suggest three areas of research for my country, given the context. On one hand, we should develop research that gathers accurate information about the state and art of service-learning in Mexico. It would be very helpful if this research could also include Central America and even better if it includes Latin America. I think we need to know what kind of institutions are doing service-learning and to what extent. Which of these institutions are doing research on service-learning? What are the specific fields and is there any kind of relationship between practitioners and researchers? This could give us a baseline to compare in the future because we want more institutions working with service-learning. It could also help us to build a network of all Latin American educational institutions doing service-learning as practitioners/researchers.

The second idea is that research should be conducted to give us information on how to improve the practice and understanding of service-learning. We need to explore the parameters of service-learning and evaluate those that are most likely to lead to the outcomes that we are looking for. It is crucial to find out how to create and sustain high quality programs, and we need those programs to actually show the way to outcomes for all parties involved—professors, students, communities, and educational institutions. Research must be very perceptive and sensitive to practitioners, students, and community feedback and needs, and very attentive to the results they get and the impact they experience. In order to contribute to improve practice, the research agenda and results must be very meaningful for practitioners, community and students. This is one of the reasons why conferences like this one, where researchers and practitioners share their experiences and results, are very important.

The last focus of research that I think would be very helpful is on service-learning institutional organization, with a specific focus on better ways to get all parties to support and be involved in service-learning and community engagement.

So, how do we go from institutions where there are few opportunities to get involved in service-learning, where the relationship with the community is not clear, where students are not actively involved, to institutions where service-learning programs are part of the main institutional concern? How do we create mechanisms for service-learning where the communities and students have a voice in the program?

Cobie Rudd: From the Australian perspective, we don't use the term service-learning to the degree that you do in the U.S. We talk more about university-community engagement research instead of service-learning. We tend to use the terms "experiential learning" or "work-based learning." So service-learning is not commonly used. In fact many Australian universities tend to just use the word "engagement." My three points are like Tim's. What makes research around engagement different from other research in Australia? In terms of how it is done, that is engaged research, it would be about a focus on the process, impact and outcome. I would put emphasis on that first word: process. That's because community-engaged research really needs to be based on the community as a partner; that is, the whole concept/study design and methodology not being *on* the community, but being *with* them as partners. The differences actually are going to be quite significant compared to how research is conducted traditionally in Australia.

The second point is that this new approach to research brings some risk-taking or risk management with it, certainly in the Australian context. With the community as a partner, you are saying that the whole process—the origins, the nature of the research, the planning and implementation, methodology and evaluation—may actually have the community members leading the research. Now often the community members involved will not be researchers and may not actually have research track records. But if you actually want to have them as a partner, there is something about putting them up on that same level from the start, so that the process is one of meaningful engagement of mutual benefit and reciprocity. If the idea is from the community, there can be expectations around where they sit in the authorship line up. This has ramifications for the academics involved, given their requirements for publications and thus academic promotion.

The second point is: What is the risk associated with this? How do you actually win competitive grants when, in Australia for instance, some of the funding regimes have 40% of the assessment weighted on the caliber of the team and their research track records? How can engaged research and collaboration on grant proposals align with building track records? This is a bit of a dilemma at the moment and it is actually on the front page of the newspapers in Australia as I speak. In Australia currently, we are working out how we actually mentor, nurture, develop our community partners and even early career researchers, so they develop not only capacity but track records in research, as a parallel strategy to changing institutional responses, including funding programs.

My third point, and this is very important to me, is about the broad-reaching benefits of engaged research. I use the term "serendipitous outcomes" from engaged research. Traditionally in Australia, universities haven't always been out there doing engaged research or research around community engagement, as has been the case here. So in some respects there is a serendipitous effect for us as a result of engaging with communities as partners. Not only is it helping to break down the barriers around universities, or perceptions of them as being difficult to access and intimidating, but there is a tangible translation of benefits in a range of other areas. For instance, engaged research can also help to assist in making access to university courses easier, it can open up new potential career pathways, and identify additional issues or problems where collaborative research can help with finding solutions. So in summary, we need to consider the process of engaged research; what sort of risk assessment might be needed to ensure we aren't setting people up for failure: and being mindful of, and facilitating, the serendipitous effects of doing engaged research.

Sherril Gelmon: One of the things I hear from each of you is this interplay among many of the forces in your own country within the context that will then lead us to think about service-learning and community engagement research. One of the reasons this conference was first organized in 2001 was to provide a venue where research could be presented and discussed, and would focus on research. The subsequent drive to develop IARSLCE as a formal association was to accelerate that research capacity and presence and we continue to build on that very important foundation. But still, when we look at the major drivers, they are often focused around funding. So we can reflect upon the creation of the Corporation for National and Community Service in the United States that created funding streams, and that then supported university-based activities, many of which relate to service-learning activities and not necessarily to the research. The work in Canada has been driven in large part by the philanthropy of the McConnell Foundation, a private philanthropy that is going to put a lot of money into support programs, again to build knowledge and capacity for community service-learning. In South Africa, many of us here today have been involved as outside consultants in a multiyear project that was largely driven and funded by the Ford Foundation—funding to create the capacity of South African higher education institutions to participate in the democratic transition in that country. That was done through the creation of partnerships and educational strategies like community service-learning. In Australia there have been drivers from government policy and potential funding, with the focus on various kinds of community engagement and industry partnerships, which often lead to changing the educational system. So in many cases the strategy is about the teaching and learning approaches, and then we have to get into research.

So think about the service-learning and community engagement research in the context of where you are working. What are some of the drivers? Is it the governmental organization and their centralized education system that leads us to consider the scholarly inquiry? Is it that there are national associations that are either facilitators or barriers? Is it around accreditation? Is it funding? Is it technology?

Given those questions, I would like to ask you to each highlight one important facilitator of research and one important barrier.

Cobie Rudd: Let me start with the key facilitator for engaged research and research around community engagement. From my perspective that would be reputational factor. I don't think Australian universities can prosper unless they are seen to be relevant to their communities. I don't think they can be researching something over here that has got absolutely nothing to do the communities they serve over there. There is a drive from communities to actually want to be assisted in helping find solutions. So I think that would be the major driver and it will be earned as a result of having articulated clear directions, actions taken (doing what you say you would do), and the resultant net benefits that have partner ownership and are measurable from the outset, and on a continuing basis.

The barrier would be about how this research is counted. At the moment it is often considered "soft" research. For instance, in Australia we use academic workload points and models, which given our differences in terminology, would be related to tracking progress towards tenure. Australian academics need to actually reach a certain number of workload points per year and it's generally agreed that the split is 40% learning and teaching, 40% research, and 20% community service or enterprise. Engagement shouldn't be tacked on there but it should be integrated throughout. One of the difficulties is that research activity "points" won't always actually include the type of research that we are talking about here because it is often not funded through the nationally competitive grant schemes which carry substantial weight in Australian universities. Much of the research traditionally in this field is funded by industry. So therefore it hasn't actually been counted in terms of research track records and impact for academics, and that is increasingly becoming a big issue. The barrier would be how to change institutions so this sort of type of research does count as much as other types of nationally competitive research.

Diana Pacheco: One very important facilitator that could really encourage service-learning research as well as service-learning programs in Mexico is the government. We need both, the service-learning practice in more and more schools and, at the same time, to get funding to do research. It is very important to have the government listen to practitioners and the results of some research, because they will start to pay attention to serving-learning. We have to put that concept on the debate agenda for the government and for the education ministry.

One barrier in my country, and probably in most of Central America, that I would like to think about it more as a challenge, is that there are few institutions doing service-learning. These institutions are not necessarily connected to each other. So we don't have information about what others are doing. We don't have research networks or forums like this one where we can share our concerns, results and practices. We don't have information on who is doing what. Practitioners and researchers in most cases are working alone. In order to strengthen the field it would be very helpful to create a community of service-learning researchers and practitioners. It would empower the field to facilitate the collaborative work of practitioners, researchers, community and students.

Tim Stanton: Thinking about facilitators in the U.S., one obviously thinks about funders, this organization of IARSLCE, the *Michigan Journal*, and organizations that have been stimulators or encouragers of service-learning research. The one facilitator that I land on is the fact that I don't think any of us do this work because there is money available. Money is certainly a facilitator, but I think most of us engage in this kind of research because we have a passion for the work, for engagement. We came into this work to get away from conventional education, to bring alive learning and service for young people, to improve communities. What makes this work so compelling, and these meetings so interesting, is that everybody is here because they love the work. I think that love is a key facilitator.

I mentioned two barriers earlier—first, funders and researchers focused on outcomes and practitioners reluctant to mine research to improve practice, and second, lack of focus on the community side of service-learning. With regard to the need for more practice-focused research, I think we as practitioners need to be more aggressive consumers. We need to start demanding that our research colleagues address the questions that we have on Monday morning, when we go into the classroom; about how to be better mentors and teachers, how to help our students become better partners, how to engage and serve the folks we work with in the community. We need to consider the cogeneration of knowledge, collaboratively developed by practitioners and researchers. How might we build alliances on our campuses where the practice people, and the program people, and researchers could join together to do some collaborative research on service-learning practice? Similar research collaborations could be developed with community partners.

Another barrier that helps to sustain most service-learning research focuses on students and faculty rather than on communities. This is the fact that going into the community is just more difficult. It is easier for researchers to focus on students, because they are a captive audience—if you want them to fill out a survey, they will. Tracking down community people to get them to answer surveys or actually sit down and take time to plan a collaborative research project is very challenging and time-consuming. My challenge to all of us is that if we are really going to bring community voices and information needs into our research, we have got to express the same determination, courage and sensitivity to diverse cultural norms and demands as we ask of our service-learning students. We've got to make the effort to walk away from our campuses, into the communities, and build relationships with community partners—research relationships as well as practice ones. Then perhaps we can begin to bring community voices loudly, clearly and effectively into our dialogue.

Sherril Gelmon: So as we address "Research for What?," one of the words that Tim just mentioned was passion. When Portland State hosted this conference in 2006 in Portland, Oregon our theme was "From Passion to Objectivity," emphasizing that we all come to this work with passion. But look around the room and think of some of the areas that IARSLCE is trying to support. For example, with graduate students, "Research for What?" would hopefully result in selecting a topic that you are passionate about and you are doing the research to get a PhD or whatever the graduate degree might be, to then move forward with your career and make your contributions. We are supporting early career scholars and practitioners. "Research for What?" for them may be to get tenure and to continue to move forward, but hopefully there is that passion there. When your institutions make commitments, what is the research for? "Research for What?" is hopefully to establish a place in your community and in your society where your institution has a role. So as you are all thinking about "Research for What?" what points would you want us to raise? What would you want us to think about? What do you think we should be talking about at next year's conference to answer that big question?

Let's consider "Research for What?" in the context of public work but also in terms of the support of a civil democratic society. How would the panel respond to that?

Tim Stanton: Obviously that is the most important question that is on my mind every morning. How do I research that? I really don't know. For me I would have to bring it home: what does that question mean when I think about the students I am going to sit down with tomorrow? One of my agendas with students always is helping them to develop, and to encourage them to become stewards of a more just and democratic society that we are turning over to them. There are a zillion research questions about that. But the one I am focusing on this morning is about how I would engage students more effectively in thinking about civil society questions that relate to their experiences working, for instance, with development organizations in South Africa. If we think about our more microlevel, what-do-I-do-on-Monday questions that we want to see addressed, which we see as more addressable through a feasible research project that can get funded and completed in a limited amount of time, we will get to this big one, the capital "D" democracy question, that is indeed what we are hopefully all about.

Cobie Rudd: I think for me it is specifically about sustainability. Sustainability of the research capacity in this field, so that this isn't just some sort of a trend. To build the sustainability of these efforts in Australia will take concerted action, across many areas such as ongoing learning and professional development, and better engagement with our students and alumni. Certainly in Australia, ensuring authentic student participation is a new field and most universities are striving to portray their defining characteristics and values as something with which students can identify. The premise is that if these values have meaning to students and the engagement of students is authentic, then the value will be part of the students' ongoing life—that is, it becomes linked to their identity. Perhaps this capturing of hearts and minds will create a sustained link that reflects the institutional leadership and binds students and graduates to lifelong learning in areas important to the environments in which they live. Thus, the long-term capacity is going to need some quite radical change with a real emphasis on organizational values and culture, and meaningful involvement of our students, graduates and early career researchers.

Diana Pacheco: From my own viewpoint service-learning is an important piece of education to help students think in a better world, where they are supposed to be social change agents, where they can feel the power and the commitment to change the world around them to become a more inclusive, tolerant, respectful place for everyone. A world where there are better ways to relate to each other, where we care for each other, where we work collaboratively very hard and seriously to have a better life level for everyone, everywhere. To bring back the utopias. So what research is required to make sure that we think in that kind of way?

Sherril Gelmon: I think this question helps us to focus, given the current political environment in many of our countries. Think of the energy that there is right now anticipating the federal election next week in the United

States and whatever may happen; think about the Australian election a year ago and the huge energy that came forward in a positive way with new leadership and many positive social statements, including "The Apology" to the Aboriginal populations on the first day of Parliament; and, considering the results of the Canadian federal election a few weeks ago, what for many of our Canadian colleagues was a disappointing outcome in terms of hoping for a direction that would promote, rather than hinder, progress around the kinds of issues that make many people in this room excited and engaged. These varied political climates affect our work in higher education and all other aspects of the educational spectrum, and our challenge is to determine if we can do something to influence the socio-political environment, while also seeking to prepare our students and ourselves to work in that society, and to pursue those democratic ideals.

Time limits mean that we must bring this conversation to a close and anticipate next year. For the first time in the history of this association and this research conference, we will meet outside of the United States, in a different county—Canada. It is not that far away but it has a fundamentally different social structure in some ways from the United States, yet there are many aspects of life that are quite similar to the United States. If we look at all the countries represented here, we bring many different perspectives on how we view government, how we view education, and how we view certain social and political rights or responsibilities and privileges.

We've heard from our panelists about different perspectives on what counts as research, what drives that research, and what motivates us as teachers and researchers to engage in this research. We've also heard about various barriers, and while they were presented in the context of specific countries or contexts, most would cross geographic borders and be very similar from country to country. The major question continues to be what difference this work makes, and how we know that we make a difference—whether the research derives from the study of service-learning or other educational strategies for teaching and learning, whether it is based on methodologies such as community-based research, whether it is driven by opportunities for well-resourced industry partnerships that contribute to economic initiatives, or whether it is motivated by a community-based collaboration that seeks to address some fundamental social issue.

I hope you will think about these contexts and challenges as you prepare your proposals for submission for next year's conference in terms of "Research for What?" and in the context(s) that you represent and how you can help us to build knowledge across this community and continue to advance the research agendas. I want to thank our panel: Tim Stanton, Diana Pacheco, and Cobie Rudd. Thank you all and we will see you in Ottawa in October 2009.

CHAPTER 12

RESEARCH INFORMING PRACTICE

Developing Practice Standards and Guidelines for Improving Service-Learning and Community Engagement

Shelley H. Billig, Barbara E. Moely, and Barbara A. Holland

ABSTRACT

In K-12 service-learning, standards and indicators for quality practice have been identified on the basis of a thorough review of the research literature and standard-setting by appropriate groups of service-learning experts. This chapter summarizes the process by which the K-12 standards were developed, offering them as a model that might be followed to create guidelines for quality service-learning practice in higher education. The International Association for Research in Service-learning and Community Engagement (IARSLCE) has taken positive steps to build the research field; additional activities and roles for the organization are suggested in building the validity and quality of future research.

Creating Our Identities in Service-Learning and Community Engagement
pp. 265–282
Copyright © 2009 by Information Age Publishing
All rights of reproduction in any form reserved.

INTRODUCTION

The amount and quality of research on service-learning and community engagement (SLCE) has increased dramatically since the publication a decade ago of summaries of the research literature in higher education (Eyler & Giles, 1999) and K-12 (Billig, 2001) As evidenced in this *Advances in Service-Learning Research* book series, researchers now regularly conduct studies of multiple aspects of service-learning implementation and outcomes, and present their work at international and regional conferences. As Smith et. al. in chapter 9 of this volume point out, while there is still a considerable amount of "fugitive" literature, researchers and practitioners can relatively easily find summaries of outcomes from multiple Web sites and emerging scholars can find copies of published and unpublished works.

Accessibility, though, is only the first step in the use of research to inform practice. Helping practitioners reach awareness is important, but assisting them to become good consumers of research and providing them tools that allow them to transfer the research into practical advice for continuous improvement is better.

In this chapter, ways in which research can better inform practice are discussed, along with ways to stimulate and support high-quality research on service-learning and community engagement. An example from K-12 is provided to illustrate the ways in which the research, both in the fields of service-learning and community engagement and from the broader field of educational reform was used to guide the formation of standards and indicators for service-learning practice. Finally, a research agenda tied to next steps for K-12 and suggest what can be done in higher education to increase the utility and use of research to improve the field.

THE ROLE OF RESEARCH IN FIELD BUILDING

In the 2005 volume in this book series, Billig and Eyler analyzed the factors related to field building, and called for researchers within the field of service-learning to help members of the field understand and distill the identity of the term, define the parameters of approaches that were called service-learning, and standardize practice to the extent that the factors related to impact could be known. As explained by Billig and Eyler (2005) based on an earlier paper by Fine (1999), the seven factors related to building and sustaining an educational reform initiative included (1) the formation of a distinct identity with clear, differentiated, and recognized activities that can be described; (2) standard practice, that includes criteria for quality practice known to be linked with achievement of desired outcomes; (3) a knowledge base supported by a cumulative body of research that identifies results connected to activities and the conditions necessary to achieve desired outcomes; (4) leadership and membership that includes practitioners who are prepared and supported by organizational structures, including those that offer professional development, to advance the quality of practice and to credential practitioners; (5) information exchange for disseminating knowledge; (6) the development of resources and structures to facilitate collaboration between and among practitioners and allies; and (7) committed stakeholders and advocates who ensure continued support of key stakeholders.

The role of research in these seven factors comes into play in multiple ways. Researchers conduct rigorous and exploratory studies to formulate a distinct identity and promote standard practice through the discovery of the factors that are most strongly correlated to achievement of desired outcomes. Scholars build the knowledge base and provide some of the necessary information to exchange. The research informs the types of professional development necessary to promote quality practice and TO give advocates the evidence they need to nurture the support of key stakeholders.

Building the research network itself also requires implementation of the seven factors. In fact, these ideas comprised the theory of change implemented to promote the formation of a research network, this book series, and other strategies to build and strengthen the research in this field. For example, the International Research Conference on Service-Learning was created in 2001 to serve as a venue to help researchers begin the process of sharing research and building upon one another's work. A call for the establishment of an association appeared in the 2005 edition of this book series (Billig, 2005) and was operationalized in 2006 with the founding of the International Association of Research on Service-Learning and Community Engagement (IARSLCE; http://www.researchslce.org/). The founding of the Association was an important step toward formalizing the relationship and moving what had been a loose coalition of scholars toward an identity as members of a field of study.

As pointed out in chapter 9 of this volume, the interdisciplinarity of the Association and indeed of the field in general is a strength, with the potential for cross-fertilization of theory and methods enriching research efforts. Interdisciplinarity is also a challenge to the development of a coherent body of literature with clear lines of converging and diverging theories, frameworks and practices. IARSLCE offers a venue for improving the capacity of researchers to build on prior work and to increase the rigor of research overall. Of course, some service-learning and community engagement researchers will choose not to participate in IARSLCE so convergence and coherence of research continues to be a challenge for building the research base for service-learning and community engagement, especially in the context of higher education. The collective logic and strength of the overall body of research is an essential underpinning to the ability of practitioners to interpret research into practice.

Other organizations also play a large role in helping to develop a sense of community and a common research agenda and accumulation of knowledge across multiple studies. For example, the *Michigan Journal of Community Service Learning* (http://www.umich.edu/~mjcsl/) has been publishing research about higher education service-learning for some time, and recently expanded its focus (beginning with the 2008-2009 volume) to include not only articles about academic service-learning, but also articles about campus-community partnerships and faculty engaged scholarship. The addition of community engagement as a concept conjoined with service-learning recognized the multiple ways in which service-learning was being conceptualized and implemented internationally.

The National Service-Learning Clearinghouse http://www. servicelearning.org/ was recently expanded and has increasingly become focused on the dissemination and promotion of research summaries, fact sheets, and tools to use to increase the quality and reach of research in service-learning and community engagement. Other organizations, such as the National Youth Leadership Council (http://www.nylc.org/), Campus Compact (http://www.compact.org/) and the National Service-Learning Partnership (http://www.service-learningpartnership.org/) have featured research studies and guidance for quality practice. Conferences and publications sponsored by the American Association of Colleges and Universities (http://www.aacu.org/) provide ways of sharing information with others interested in liberal education.

The annual networking of researchers, the expanded number and reach of journals and books that publish service-learning and community engagement research, the vehicles for dissemination, and the number of studies being conducted are all signs of a growing body of knowledge. However, it is clear from the multiple listservs and inquiries received by researchers that more tools are needed to assist practitioners to interpret, assess relevance, and use the research, not only for making the case for service-learning and community engagement practice, but also for improving the quality of the practice and the impact that service-learning and community engagement has on its participants and the community being served. There is also still clearly a knowing-to-doing gap, as evidenced by too few programs and practitioners accessing, understanding, and using the research to implement quality practices.

What can be done? The field-building theory calls for the development of a knowledge base and standard practices that lead to predictable, high-impact results. In response, K-12 service-learning practitioners recently worked together to develop practice standards and indicators to nurture quality and promote the institutionalization of service-learning and community engagement in schools. These standards are presented in chapter 6 of this book and are currently being tested by multiple researchers. The next section describes the etiology of the rationale and the development of the K-12 standards and indicators and their use to date.

K-12 SERVICE-LEARNING STANDARDS AND INDICATORS FOR QUALITY PRACTICE

The strategy of developing standards and indicators as a tool to close the knowing-doing gap and to drive better practice in the K-12 arena came from multiple sources and for varied reasons. First, teachers and administrators pointed out that in the past 5-10 years, nearly all of their work had become standards-based. Each state in the U.S. required teaching to specific content standards in English/language arts, mathematics, science, and most other content areas. Many educators also had to meet cross cutting standards for mastery of technology. Some state policymakers also recognized the power of standards, and passed legislation asking schools to address additional standards in areas such as civics, social-emotional learning, and problem-solving skills. Since "teaching to the standards" was a key driver in instructional decision-making, K-12 educators strongly suggested that service-learning employ standards to be consistent with the field in order to gain increased credibility.

Second, research began to show that professional wisdom in the field about best practices was not as accurate as it needed to be. Researchers who were testing the Essential Elements (National Service-Learning Cooperative, 1999) as indicators of quality, for example, were finding that while the set of Elements as a whole predicted outcomes, specific Elements did not. In fact, one study (Billig, Root, & Jesse, 2005) suggested that several Elements had no relationships to outcomes and one of the Elements, celebration, was actually negatively correlated with outcomes. Both for political and practical reasons, the field needed to promote research-based best practices, so revision of the Elements had to occur.

Third, service-learning appeared to be at a point in its history as a field to be receptive to adopting common definitions and ideas. Perhaps due to the W. K. Kellogg Learning in Deed initiative, the National Commission on Service-Learning, or the more sophisticated dissemination properties of the Internet, service-learning became a more widely used term and practice. Dozens of articles started appearing about the benefits of service-learning, reaching both practitioners in journals targeted to administrators and teachers and the public, in the popular media such as

Parade Magazine and *Family Circle*. With greater interest in the "what" and "how" of the field, the demands to provide clearer descriptions of implementation and evidence of success emerged.

Finally, and most importantly in bringing about the effort, opinion leaders in the field advocated for creating standards to show what high-quality service-learning looks like in practice. The National Youth Leadership Council, with support from State Farm Companies Foundation, led the movement toward creating the standards. Working collaboratively with the National Service-Learning Partnership and the State Education Agency Network (SEANet), NYLC engaged a group of researchers from RMC Research to conduct the process and worked with multiple partner organizations and individuals to encourage stakeholders to participate in setting standards for high quality practice, following an established, well-documented method.

Widespread participation in the standards-setting process included educators, youth, other practitioners, and organizations in 27 states. Adoption of the standards became part of a clarion call for improvement in the field, and was promoted by nearly all prominent organizations. The standards have been subsequently embraced by the field, providing objective measures of quality for funders, researchers, evaluators, and practitioners.

In summary, leaders of the initiative responded to a real need, built in the factors needed for success by founding the process in rigorous research, facilitated the process using experts and proven processes, and prompted prominent individuals and organizations to champion the initiative. There was a sufficient state of readiness to make standards-setting possible. All in all, the process itself built in the seeds of success from the inception.

The Standards-Setting Process

The process used to create the standards was one that had been used to set standards in other areas such as reading and mathematics. The process, as facilitated by RMC Research staff members and other colleagues, was reasonably straightforward. After determining the need and groups to facilitate the process:

1. the research literature was reviewed and synthesized into a form that could be easily translated into overarching statements and substatements of factors influencing outcomes;

2. a group of service-learning experts was convened to create the initial set of standards and indicators;

3. a reactor panel process was used with large numbers of current practitioners and others in the field to tune the standards and indicators; and

4. the results from the final panel were mapped back onto the research to ensure fidelity and language was finalized for clarity and internal consistency.

Each of these phases will be detailed next.

Step One: Synthesize the Research

The K-12 service-learning research was comprehensively reviewed to determine areas of convergence in terms of which factors associated with the practice of service-learning appeared to impact academic, civic, and social/personal outcomes for participating students. More than 100 studies including published research, published and unpublished program evaluations, and unpublished reports were reviewed.

Only studies that had either quantitative research or mixed qualitative and quantitative methods were included in the summaries since the educators that specified the need for standards also specified the need for scientifically-based research or as close as one could get to it. This meant that the majority of studies that were summarized were quasi-experimental studies. In the best of all worlds, effect sizes would have been determined, but unfortunately there is little service-learning research that specifies effect sizes or even the data in a form that could be reanalyzed for effect size. Research summaries were then written and categorized in terms of similarities among the variables that appeared to have the greatest impact.

The research was compiled and synthesized, and then compared to findings in the more general K-12 education research in the same outcome areas. For that phase, more than 400 studies from the general body of recent educational research were reviewed and only the most pertinent were cited. This kind of extensive review of research literature was a significant attempt to collate and interpret multiple research studies; it would be intriguing to do a similar synthesis of research literature in higher education service-learning.

Step Two: Convene Experts

A group of key leaders in the field was then convened to sift through the research. Leaders included administrators, teachers, coordinators, researchers, policymakers, and members of professional services organizations. Their charge was to distill the research into a series of statements that reflected the overarching factor, along with all of the indicators or subfactors that appeared to be directly related to the factor. For example, in the area of meaningfulness, key ideas had to do with personal relevance, developmental appropriateness, the nature of the service activities, the ways in which specific activities engaged students, the ways in which young people could understand and interpret their experiences in light of the issues context in which the activities occurred, and the degree to which the outcomes could be attained, visible and considered valuable. Ideas like sense of belonging, trust, open expression of ideas, and bonding with adults were also initially a part of this cluster.

Leaders worked together to distill information, translate the ideas into actionable form, and align the ideas to key constructs which they then named. At the end of the two days, eight nascent standards and approximately 135 indicators were derived.

Leaders also made initial decisions about the form of the standards, such as whether they should include preschool and/or higher education, community-based organizations, and so forth. The group endorsed the reactor panel process to be used to distill the standards and indicators further and to engage in the "wordsmithing" needed to ensure that the standards and indicators were actionable and compatible with the language being used in the field.

Step Three: Conduct Reactor Panels

Reactor panels were held in 27 states. Participants were determined by hosts and generally included policymakers, state and local administrators, local organizational representatives or community partners that participated in service-learning, principals, teachers, and occasionally, students. All panels were facilitated using standardized reactor panel protocols. Groups considered each of the standard areas, along with all of the indicators, using a standardized set of questions that asked them to review and weigh the work of the two panels that had occurred immediately before theirs. The groups made decisions about revisions to the quality standards and indicators using the criteria they were given that showed what constituted a good standard and set of indicators, and they could also add or delete indicators. They then shared their work with another group in the room using a tuning protocol. Finally, the entire group reviewed the work of all of the groups in the room. The final product from each group became one of the options the next two groups considered.

As consensus was reached on multiple standards or indicators over at least five panels, the next panels that were convened were asked to concentrate on those standards or indicators that had the least amount of agreement. Later panels were also asked to make recommendations about language or format that was difficult in earlier panels. For example, early on, it became clear that some groups liked to call adults who work with youth in service-learning activities "facilitators" while others liked the term "practitioners." Still others liked "instructors" or "guides" or "mentors" or "partners." Groups simply could not agree on labels for the adults. The resolution was not to refer to the adults at all, but rather to describe service-learning.

Step Four: Check Fidelity With the Research

The standards and indicators that resulted from the last reactor panel were then reviewed in light of the research summaries to ensure that there was fidelity with results. Several of the indicators had to be slightly reworded to be consistent with the research. Language was finalized for clarity and consistency, and the original group was given a chance to review the results and offer any last reactions they had.

Dissemination and Impact

The new standards and indicators were unveiled at the National Service-Learning Conference in April 2008, a venue that attracts significant participation from the K-12 service-learning sector. The standards and indicators were presented by the National Youth Leadership Council in three forms: in an attractive booklet placed in all attendees' conference bags and available for purchase; in an online, downloadable free version; and in an article in a research booklet, *Growing to Greatness*, that explained them and their origins.

Over time, the information became widely disseminated in conferences, the National Service-Learning Clearinghouse, publications, applications for program funds, webinars, and during professional development seminars provided by experts in the field. Supplementary materials were developed, including lesson banks, assessments, training modules, and more. As of 2009, most states required them as part of their Learn and Serve subgrantee applications.

Early analysis of the results of standards implementation is promising. As a group, studies have shown that the standards strongly predict academic, civic, and social-emotional outcomes for student participants (see, e.g., Billig, 2008; Brodersen & Billig, 2008; Meyer, 2008; and this volume, chapter 6). Each specific standard with its associated indicators has also been tested, with nearly all of the standards also strongly predicting outcomes.

More research is needed to validate each of the standards and indicators as a predictor of specific outcomes, and to understand how they are being operationalized in various contexts. The specific tools, dissemination practices, support mechanisms, and role of accountability structures and school or community contexts also bear investigation to determine which strategies are most effective. Nonetheless, this example shows that the knowing-to-doing gap can be successfully bridged given the right process, the right tools, and the right modes of dissemination.

IMPLICATIONS FOR HIGHER EDUCATION

While the culture of higher education does not support the same strategies for promoting standard practice as those being used in K-12, there are strong implications from the K-12 standards and indicators and its underlying research and standards-setting process that can promote higher quality service-learning and community engagement practices in higher education. For example, a comprehensive of service-learning in higher education would provide a lens on areas of convergence in research across different disciplines and institutional types. In this way, researchers that examine service-learning and community engagement in higher education could develop a set of guidelines or principles for best practice, rather than specific standards. The analysis would be especially valuable if it focused on linking such guidelines or principles of practice to particular types of learning objectives and/or outcomes desired regarding participant learning and development, impact on institutional culture and values, or impact on community partnerships and community capacity.

There will be a number of benefits from such an effort. Principles or guidelines could help promote greater consistency and high quality in service-learning course offerings, nurture stronger impacts for both students and the recipients of service, and provide some regularity in what "service-learning" means in higher education. The principles or guidelines could also serve to prompt the formation of a framework for evaluation of faculty members' service-learning efforts, yielding more data on what works best under which contexts, contributing to inclusion and evaluation as part of teaching performance and promotion/tenure. The analysis of existing research literature itself would provide an invaluable overview of approaches, findings, and unanswered questions within current research areas.

A process similar to that used in developing the K-12 standards and indicators could be implemented, wherein summaries of research from both the service-learning/community engagement field and the larger field of educational reform could be developed; convenings of leaders could be held to distill the research into a set of principles or guidelines; and reactor panels could be held at various campuses across the United States using a structured process. International comparisons could be made and/or internationally cross-cultural sharing could be focused so that practice could be improved globally. The IARSLCE could play an instrumental role in implementing these strategies.

In addition, other dissemination strategies are needed. In more established fields, textbook writers serve a "translation" function, working from original research reports to summary chapters that students find easier to process in order to reach a level of general understanding. Because there is no agreement that service-learning and community engagement are a discipline or field of study that can be taught (as opposed to a method for research and teaching practices), there are few textbooks available for sharing information at this time. Review articles (Stukas, Clary, & Snyder, 1999), Wingspread reports, or special journal issues (Howard, Gelmon, & Giles, 2000) appear from time to time, but they may not be well-publicized, have small circulation, may be too narrow or detailed, or may not be readily available to busy practitioners. A collaboratively-generated document synthesizing extant research on effective service-learning in higher education, and the implications of this knowledge for practice, as well as a description of important research questions that have not been adequately addressed, would be of great value to the service-learning community, both for practitioners and for current and future researchers.

Implications for Topics for Researchers to Study

As the field develops, researchers need to develop broader research questions that go beyond program evaluation to address processes in the individual and causal factors from the immediate and larger environment that influence outcomes. Some research has addressed questions of how students from different backgrounds and with differing preferences react to service-learning experiences. Dunlap, Scoggin, Green, and Davi (2007) and Simons et al. (chapter 8 in this volume) have published important findings on how students with various racial and ethnic backgrounds react to multicultural service experiences. Morton's (1995) paradigms of service are important in understanding the impact of service-learning experiences on students (Bringle, Hatcher, & McIntosh, 2006; Moely, Furco, & Reed, 2008). Students' past community involvement, their cultural competence and social attitudes, and other related variables may all be important in determining their reactions to varied kinds of service. This is an area in which rigorous qualitative research can be particularly useful in describing change over time and the impact of service-learning experiences and suggest important hypotheses that can then be tested by rigorous quantitative research.

Service-learning activities may have effects on children and young adults' cognitive development, health, and social competencies in ways that have not yet been well researched. Studies of youth and adult development, as described by Vogelgesang in chapter 10 of this volume are early important attempts to determine the long-term impact of community-based experiences and program effects, as well as possible "sleeper effects" in which delayed effects appear at some later point in time (Brim & Kagan, 1980). In such longitudinal studies, it may be worthwhile to control for cohort (generational) differences that reflect the influences of the social/political climate at times when data are collected, so that these can be separated from the impacts of earlier experiences.

Rather investigating outcomes for just one group of participants in a service-learning or community engagement intervention, there is value in research focusing on all of the participants in the endeavor, as Driscoll, Holland, Gelmon, and Kerrigan (1996) suggested. The role of partnerships between higher education and community partners is especially significant to the sustainability and quality of service-learning in higher education contexts (Sandy & Holland, 2006). Harwood and Radoff (chapter 7 in this volume) and Simons et al. (chapter 8 in this volume), have addressed more than one component, looking at both college students and the recipients of students' service. For any community engagement endeavor, the expectations, preferences, and evaluations of faculty members, community partners, students, and the direct recipients of the service or program all contribute to an understanding of the experience.

Conville and his colleagues at the University of Southern Mississippi (2008) have been identifying dimensions on which the views all participants in such an endeavor can be indexed. Studies of partnerships (e.g., Janke in chapter 4, Phillips & Ward in chapter 5 of this volume) could be extended to include students and community service recipients. Such approaches allow a better sense of the ways in which working relationships develop and change over time and the ways in which variables interact with each other, serving as mediators or moderators of outcomes.

As the work proceeds, researchers also need to be mindful of the implications for policy and be active in providing a voice to influence public policy at local and national levels. Current proposals to expand national service programs in the United States have given lighter attention to the value of service-learning in part because the evidence base for service-learning's impacts remains diffuse at best. The IARSLCE can play a potentially powerful role in moving the field to a place where scholarly products are producing convergent findings, establishing links between practices and outcomes, influencing policy, shaping practice on a large scale and providing information that will make it possible for schools and postsecondary institutions to make informed decisions about the relevance, quality, apparent benefit, and probable sustainability of adopting service-learning or community engagement programs and practices with the goal of enhancing particular learning and developmental outcomes for students.

Research Quality

Practitioners can also be helped when researchers conduct more and better research. While there has been a great increase in research activity in service-learning and community engagement in recent years and much work that conforms to principles of excellent methodology and design, there are still some needs in the field for improving the quality of the research being conducted. Those needs seem to be most acute in the areas of measurement, design, and sampling.

Researchers should employ measurement tools that are appropriate for the questions they ask, rather than relying on tools that were developed by others, possibly for different purposes. While there is value being aware of work previously done to create measurement tools, as described in the summary of research scales by Bringle, Phillips, and Hudson (2004), for example, it may be more appropriate for a new project to create measures that directly tap the constructs of interest, or to modify existing measures dramatically to meet the needs of the project. Doing so may involve time in item development, pilot testing, creation of coding procedures, and statistical analyses, but will be worthwhile in yielding findings higher in validity for the questions addressed. As always, though, studies of validity and reliability must accompany the creation of any new measures.

This volume includes a number of chapters that focus on content analysis of oral or written records of research participants' views (e.g, Harwood & Radoff in chapter 7, Janke in chapter 4, McGuire et al. in chapter 3, Phillips & Ward in chapter 5 of this volume), or of written documents (Jetson & Jeremiah in chapter 2, Saltmarsh et al. in chapter 1). These techniques make it possible to describe the rich variety of patterns that individuals or individual records contain. There is particular value on combining the qualitative approach with quantitative measures, to allow for statistical inferences about group differences or change over time. Simons and colleagues in this volume have made good use of multiple methods to gain an understanding of college students' reactions to a service-learning experience emphasizing cultural factors.

Efforts to develop measures that have validity for the populations assessed can involve individuals from those populations as consultants as measures are being developed. A survey of campus-community partnerships might invite several community partners to take part in the development of measure or at the least, to take part in pilot work aimed at improving measures. Similarly, students can contribute valuable insights to the creation of measures for assessing student characteristics, processes, and outcomes.

Researchers should be aware of the potential for response biases to influence responses, especially in quantitative research involving rating scales or agree-disagree options. Use of relatively brief survey forms that include some qualitative responses along with occasional reverse-scored items will maintain participants' attention. Social desirability scales can be useful in some instances to assess participants' tendency to represent themselves in an unusually positive manner.

In addition, researchers must find a way to address the challenge of obtaining and maintaining an adequate sample. This challenge appears to be particularly acute in the published research in higher education where many studies address impacts on single classrooms of students or one service-learning project.

Faculty, students, and community partners participate voluntarily in our research and sometimes refuse requests to participate. This becomes especially problematic when evaluating the outcome of an intervention or when studying groups over a period of time. In addition to their efforts to obtain high levels of participation, researchers should report data that will offer information on the extent to which sample bias is operating. This might involve addressing the generalizability of the sample to the larger population in terms of demographic characteristics or other measures, or, in longitudinal studies, the differences on pretest measures of those continuing and not continuing to participate. As always, researchers must report group equivalence when they are comparing participants and nonparticipants and adjust for the equivalence statistically as needed.

Suggestions for IARSLCE Initiatives

The IARSLCE has taken many positive steps to address these issues. Multiple sessions provided during the conference feature experts helping emerging scholars both by giving examples of high quality research but also by giving feedback on the studies being conducted by those who are at the beginning of their research careers. Presessions frequently feature ideas for research for those seeking topics for their theses or dissertations. Mentors are available and matched in advance, and affinity groups have been formed. However, as with any developing professional association, more can be done.

The IARSLCE can promote a focus on increasing the quality of research, providing a more rigorous approach to measuring the impacts and outcomes of service-learning and community engagement by accepting only well-designed and implemented studies for certain types of presentations such as single-topic sessions. The IARSLCE could promote or execute a series of products that translate research into practical suggestions, standards, guidelines, or principles for improving practice and closing the knowing-doing gap. Further, the Association can encourage more communication among scholars, practitioners, and policymakers to promote advocacy for the field. As a start, each of the following strategies could be implemented as a means of building the field:

Affinity Groups

At several conferences, affinity groups have had an opportunity to convene, but there rarely is follow-through. In the future, more such opportunities could be made available to people coming to the conference, with topics to be determined on the basis of proposals submitted for conference presentation and with planned strategic webinars throughout the year to share research and suggest additions to a research agenda.

Master Lectures

Presentations at the IARSLCE conferences could be made by scholars giving an overview and critical evaluation of work going on in popular areas of research. These lecturers could offer a broad view of past research, including but not restricted to their own work, along with suggestions for next steps in research.

Public Policy Forums

Panel discussions on the implications of SLCE research for public policy could be organized at IARSLCE conferences. These panels could include representatives of the research field, local and national political figures, and representatives of governmental agencies and foundations that have supported SLCE research and programs.

Mentoring Relationships

Ongoing relationships between established and emerging scholars could be arranged by IARSLCE, capitalizing on the successful but short-lived relationships formed during the conference. Perhaps the IARSLCE could solicit volunteers from among established researchers, whom newer researchers could contact in order to have a manuscript reviewed prior to submission for publication, or to get feedback on a research or programmatic idea, a grant application, or a dissertation prospectus.

Building Support for SLCE in Traditional Academic Disciplines

There are advantages to interdisciplinarity, in terms of possible creative breakthroughs, cross-fertilization of theories and research methods, but faculty involved in these efforts still must deal with their home disciplines in terms of encouragement and support of their research and rewards for their work, including promotion and tenure. Further, faculty members' decisions about where to present and publish research—disciplinary sources or SLCE outlets—may lead to high quality research being presented or published in sources that are not typically accessed by members of SLCE.

The IARSLCE must set a strong standard for rigorous research and seek to raise the value of its conference and publications as prestigious venues for presentation and publication. A hallmark of success will be an increase in the percentage of researchers who are not advocates or practitioners of SLCE, but scholars interested in SLCE as an intervention or methodology that can impact a number of different potential outcomes for students, institutions, and communities. A partnership with Campus Compact and other academic associations or disciplinary groups would also help improve research quality and build support from faculty and campus administrations by showing that SLCE work produces progress toward goals that are valued in the disciplines and on the campus generally, including the acquisition of knowledge, enrichment of student learning and satisfaction, procurement of external funding, and other needs identified by the field.

SUMMARY

Research in the field of service-learning and community engagement has come a long way, both in terms of the amount being conducted and its quality. Service-learning and community engagement are no longer considered to be the "fad of the day," both at the K-12 and higher education levels. The growth of the field can in part be attributed to research showing tangible benefits, along with illuminating varieties of practice, issues surrounding sustainability and institutionalization, and generally what is needed for support, including roles of leadership, professional development, and research.

In K-12, additional steps have been taken to discover the specific components of service-learning that are most closely related to impacts on participating youth. The research has been compiled, and standards and indicators for quality practice have been identified using a traditional standards-setting approach.

This chapter suggests ways in which higher education can adopt some of the same processes for developing guidelines for quality practice and the ways in which the research itself can be improved so that the results are more valid and reliable. The many roles that the IARSLCE can play in this process have also been suggested.

The passion that both researchers and practitioners have for this field can thus be leveraged so that the advantages of service-learning and community engagement can be made clear, even for those less passionate. As active contributors to field-building, researchers play a critical role in closing the knowing-doing gap, Using both qualitative and quantitative approaches, researchers can illuminate what practitioners need to do to produce the strongest academic, civic, and social-emotional outcomes for the field. Receptivity across the United States and indeed the world is high, for both research and practice. Researchers should heed to clarion call, both for more and better research and for greater dissemination to affect policy, practice, and further research.

REFERENCES

Billig, S. H. (2000, May). Research on K-12 school-based service-learning: The evidence builds. *Phi Delta Kappan, 81*(9), 658-664.

Billig, S. H. (2005) The International Service-learning Research Association: A call to action. In S. Root, J. Callahan, & S. H. Billig (Eds.), *Improving service-learning practice: Research on models to enhance impacts* (pp. 215-224). Greenwich, CT: Information Age.

Billig, S. H. & Eyler, J. (2005). The state of service-learning and service-learning research. In S. H. Billig & J. Eyler (Eds.). *Deconstructing service-learning: Research exploring context, participation, and impacts* (pp. 253-264). Greenwich, CT: Information Age.

Billig, S. H., Root, S., & Jesse, D. (2005). The relationship between quality indicators of service-learning and student outcomes: Testing professional wisdom. In S. Root, J. Callahan, & S. H. Billig (Eds.), *Advances in service-learning research: Improving service-learning practice: Research on models to enhance impacts* (pp. 97-115). Greenwich, CT: Information Age.

Brim, O. G., & Kagan, J. (Eds.) (1980). *Constancy and change in human development.* Cambridge, MA: Harvard University Press.

Bringle, R. G., Hatcher, J. A., & McIntosh, R. E. (2006). Analyzing Morton's typology of service paradigms and integrity. *Michigan Journal of Community Service Learning, 13*(1), 5-15.

Bringle, R. G., Phillips, M. A., & Hudson, M. (2004). *The measure of service learning: Research scales to assess student experiences.* Washington, DC: American Psychological Association.

Brodersen, M., & Billig, S. H. (2008). *Evaluation of the School District of Philadelphia Partnerships in Character Education Program.* Denver, CO: RMC Research Corporation.

Conville, R., & Kinnell, A. (2008, October). *Structural elements of service-leaning: Common ground for faculty, students and community partners.* Paper presented at the Eighth International Research Conference on Service-learning and Community Engagement, New Orleans.

Driscoll, A., Holland, B., Gelmon, S., & Kerrigan, S. (1996). An assessment model for service-learning: Comprehensive case studies of impact on faculty, students, community, and institution. *Michigan Journal of Community Service Learning*, *3*, 66-71.

Dunlap, M., Scoggin, J., Green, P., & Davi, A. (2007). White students' experiences of privilege and socioeconomic disparities: Toward a theoretical model. *Michigan Journal of Community Service-Learning*, *13*(2), 19-30.

Eyler, J., & Giles, D. E., Jr. (1999). *Where's the learning in service-learning?* San Francisco: Jossey-Bass.

Fine, M. (1999). *Field building for service-learning.* Paper written for the Learning In Deed initiative. Author.

Howard, J. P. F., Gelmon, S. B., & Giles, D. E., Jr. (Eds.). (2000). Strategic directions for service-learning research. *Michigan Journal of Community Service-Learning*, Special Issue, Fall, 2000.

International Association for Research on Service Learning and Community Engagement. (n.d.). Retrieved http://www.researchslce.org/index.html

Michigan Journal of Community Service-Learning (n.d.). Retrieved from http://www.umich.edu/~mjcsl/index.html

Meyer, S. (2008). *Evaluation of the Michigan Learn and Serve Program.* Denver, CO: RMC Research Corporation.

Moely, B. E., Furco, A., & Reed, J. (2008). Charity and social change: The impact of individual preferences on service-learning outcomes. *Michigan Journal of Community Service Learning*, *15*(1), 37-48.

Morton, K. (1995). The irony of service: Charity, project, and social change in service-learning. *Michigan Journal of Community Service Learning*, *2*, 19-32.

National Service-Learning Cooperative (1999). *Essential elements of service-learning.* St. Paul, MN: National Youth Leadership Council.

Sandy, M., & Holland, B. A. (2006, Fall). Different worlds and common ground: Community partner perspectives on campus-community relationships. *Michigan Journal of Community Service Learning*, *13*(1).

Stukas, A. A., Jr., Clary, E. G., & Snyder, M. (1999). Service-learning: Who benefits and why. *Social Policy Report, Society for Research in Child Development*, *13*(4).

ABOUT THE AUTHORS

Enrica J. Ardemagni is an associate professor of Spanish at Indiana University–Purdue University Indianapolis and has been teaching service-learning courses for several years. She has been involved in the Engaged Departments Initiative, was a Boyer Scholar and a 2008-2009 faculty fellow in the Center for Service and Learning.
E-mail: eardema@iupui.edu

Martina Bailey is a federal work study community service worker, who has been working with the National Service-Learning Clearinghouse since 2008. She attends the University of California at Santa Cruz.
E-mail: martinab@etr.org

Shelley H. Billig is vice president of RMC Research Corporation in Denver, CO. She serves as principal investigator of multiple studies in service-learning and educational reform and evaluator of multiple interventions designed to impact academic and socioemotional learning and civic engagement.
E-mail: billig@rmcdenver.com

Nancy Hirschinger-Blank is as associate professor of criminal justice in the Social Science Division of the College of Arts and Sciences at Widener University in Chester, PA. Her research focuses on service-learning and student development.
E-mail: nbblank@mail.widener.edu

Creating Our Identities in Service-Learning and Community Engagement
pp. 283–288
Copyright © 2009 by Information Age Publishing
All rights of reproduction in any form reserved.

Suzanne M. Buglione is a doctoral candidate at the University of Massachusetts, Boston, in the Leadership in Higher Education Program. She teaches at Worcester State College in health sciences, education and sociology and is principal and lead consultant at CommunityBuild, Individual, Organizational and Community Development.
E-mail: CmUnityBuild@aol.com

Jason Burrage is the resource specialist for the National Service-Learning Clearinghouse. His research interests include comparative philosophy and psychoanalysis.
E-mail: jasonb@etr.org

Patti H. Clayton is founding director of the Center for Excellence in Curricular Engagement in the Office of the Provost at North Carolina State University. She serves as a senior scholar with the Center for Service and Learning at Indiana University–Purdue University Indianapolis, consults widely, and leads a multifaceted interinstitutional scholarship agenda.
E-mail: phclayton@mindspring.com

Sherril Gelmon is a professor of public health and chair, Division of Public Administration, Mark O. Hatfield School of Government, Portland State University.
E-mail: gelmons@pdx.edu

Dwight E. Giles, Jr. is a professor of higher education administration and senior associate at the New England Resource Center for Higher Education in the Graduate College of Education at the University of Massachusetts, Boston. His research interests include scholarship of engagement, community-campus partnerships, community-based research, and linking service-learning practice with research and scholarship.
E-mail: dwight.giles@umb.edu

Angela M. Harwood is a professor of secondary education at Western Washington University, where she also facilitates a faculty fellows program for the Center for Service-Learning. She has been integrating service-learning in her courses for more than 10 years and focuses specifically on middle school teacher education.
E-mail: Angela.Harwood@wwu.edu

Barbara Holland is pro vice chancellor of engagement at the University of Western Sydney in Australia. She also continues her affiliations with Learn and Serve America's National Service-learning Clearinghouse and with Indiana University–Purdue University Indianapolis as a senior

scholar in their Center for Service and Learning. She is executive editor of *Metropolitan Universities* journal and coeditor of the *Australasian Journal of Community Engagement*.
E-mail: B.Holland@uws.edu.au

Emily M. Janke is an assistant director for service-learning in the Office of Leadership and Service-learning at the University of North Carolina at Greensboro. Her research interests include the role of communication and identity in faculty-community partnerships, preparation of future faculty for public scholarship, and organizational adaptation and change.
E-mail: emilymjanke@gmail.com

Rohan Jeremiah is an instructor at St. Georges University in Grenada and a doctoral candidate in applied anthropology at the University of South Florida.
E-mail: rjeremiah@sgu.edu

Judith A. Jetson is director of the Collaborative for Children, Families and Communities at the University of South Florida, where she builds connections between researchers and community leaders.
E-mail: judi@judijetson.com

Kathy Lay is an assistant professor at the Indiana University School of Social Work and is interested in transformative pedagogical approaches as they relate to teaching theory and practice in social work. She is a Boyer Scholar and a member of FACET which recognizes excellence in teaching.
E-mail: kalay@iupui.edu

Heather J. Martin is the librarian of Learn and Serve America's National Service-Learning Clearinghouse. Her research interests include bibliometrics and the role service-learning plays in library and information science education.
E-mail: heatherm@etr.org

Lisa McGuire is an associate professor at the Indiana University School of Social Work and has long been a proponent of reflective writing to integrate life experience with academic content in classroom and community-based learning. She was a Boyer Scholar and teaches service-learning courses in the undergraduate and graduate social work programs.
E-mail: lmcguir@iupui.edu

Barbara E. Moely is professor emerita in psychology and research affiliate of the Center for Public Service at Tulane University in New Orleans. Her research is concerned with factors affecting service-learning outcomes for college students and the development of campus-community partnerships.
E-mail: moely@tulane.edu

KerryAnn O'Meara is an associate professor of higher Education at the University of Maryland, Department of Education Leadership, Higher Education, and International Education. Her research explores faculty professional growth, especially in community engagement and teaching, faculty reward systems roles.
E-mail: komeara@umd.edu

Diana Pacheco-Pinzon is a professor of educational psychology, School of Psychology, and director of service-learning, Universidad Marista de Mérida, Mérida, Mexico
E-mail: pachecodiana@gmail.com

Jason T. Phillips is an instructor at the Naval Academy Prep School in Newport, RI. He is currently working on international educational partnerships between the United States and Afghanistan. This chapter is based on the research completed for his doctoral dissertation, which led to the award of an EdD from the Johnson & Wales University in 2007.
E-mail: jasontphillips1@aol.com

Sara A. Radoff is a program coordinator at Western Washington University's Center for Service-Learning where she directs youth outreach initiatives. She served as facilitator for the mentoring program and will attend graduate school at the University of British Columbia starting fall 2009.
E-mail: Sara.Radoff@wwu.edu

Sarah Ragland is a federal work study community service worker, who has been working with the National Service-Learning Clearinghouse since 2008. She attends the University of California at Santa Cruz.
E-mail: sarahr@etr.org

Cobie Rudd is chair in mental health nursing and head of school, School of Nursing, Midwifery and Postgraduate Medicine, Edith Cowan University, Perth, Australia
E-mail: cobie.rudd@ecu.edu.au

Brittany Russell is an undergraduate student at Widener University, majoring in psychology.
E-mail: bmrussell@mail.widener.edu

John Saltmarsh is director of the New England Resource Center for Higher Education in the Graduate College of Education at the University of Massachusetts, Boston, where he teaches in the Higher Education Administration doctoral program. His research interests include democratic engagement in higher education, civic engagement through teaching and learning, institutional culture, and institutional change.
E-mail: john.saltmarsh@umb.edu

Lorilee R. Sandmann is an associate professor in the Department of Lifelong Education, Administration, and Policy at the University of Georgia. Her research focuses on major institutional change processes to promote higher education community engagement and on criteria and processes to define and evaluate faculty engaged scholarship.
E-mail: sandmann@uga.edu

Lori Simons is an associate professor of psychology in the Social Science Division of the College of Arts and Sciences at Widener University. Her research focuses on cultural-based service-learning and student development.
E-mail: lnsimons@mail.widener.edu

Liberty Smith is program manager of Learn and Serve America's National Service-Learning Clearinghouse. Her research and teaching interests include the information transfer cycle in service-learning and other interdisciplinary fields and the interaction between personal relationships, political engagement, and artistic and intellectual collaborations in U.S. and Latin American women's and queer culture.
E-mail: libertys@etr.org

Megan E. Standridge is a National Service-Learning Clearinghouse's Library intern. She is currently pursuing her MLIS in library and information science at San Jose State University.
E-mail: megans@etr.org

Tim Stanton is director, Bing Overseas Studies Program in Cape Town, South Africa, and visiting senior fellow, John W. Gardner Center for Youth and Their Communities, Stanford University.
E-mail: tstanton@stanford.edu

David Strong is a lecturer in the Department of Sociology at Indiana University–Purdue University Indianapolis. He is a former Boyer Scholar and coordinates the Sociology Department's service learning efforts.
E-mail: dastrong@iupui.edu

Lori J. Vogelgesang has been conducting research on service-learning and civic engagement for about 12 years, including two national longitudinal studies (of college students and college graduates), while at the UCLA Higher Education Research Institute.
E-mail: lvogelgesang@orl.ucla.edu

Cynthia V. L. Ward is a professor in the doctoral program in higher education leadership at Johnson & Wales University, where she served as the major advisor for Jason Phillips' doctoral dissertation.
E-mail: cward@jwu.edu

Elaine Ward is a doctoral candidate at the University of Massachusetts, Boston, in the Leadership in Higher Education Program. She is student services coordinator in the College of Public and Community Service.
E-mail: Elaine.Ward@umb.edu

Elizabeth Williams is an undergraduate student at Widener University, majoring in psychology.
E-mail: lizzy510@aol.com

Kimyette Willis is an undergraduate student at Widener University, majoring in psychology.
E-mail: kmwillis@mail.widener.edu

Patricia Wittberg is an associate professor of sociology at Indiana University–Purdue University Indianapolis, where she teaches upper-level undergraduates in coursework on urban sociology and the faith community, often in an online format. She has integrated service-learning components into many courses.
E-mail: pwittber@iupui.edu

LaVergne, TN USA
09 November 2009
163361LV00006BB/6/P